Advance Praise for *The Thin Blue Lie*

"*The Thin Blue Lie* is the newest truth teller in this explosive nonfiction read exposing police corruption. Bad guys on all sides of justice are exposed in this real life story of an FBI whistleblower."

—Joaquín "Jack" Garcia, FBI agent (retired) and
New York Times bestselling author of *Making Jack Falcone:
An Undercover FBI Agent Takes Down a Mafia Family*

"Behind the Oz-like curtains of justice, there exist a few good guys unafraid to tell the whole truth, regardless of the consequences. Greg Dillon is one of those guys. Read this book."

—Norm Pattis, lawyer, author of *Taking Back the
Courts, Juries and Justice*, and *In the Trenches*

"I trust every good cop and FBI agent who reads this book with an open mind will recognize the trials and tribulations Greg Dillon experienced on his journey to reveal the truth. Greg's exposure of administrative bureaucracy which allowed this to happen is proof positive that good triumphs over evil."

—Alan A. Malinchak, FBI Unit Chief (retired)
and CEO of Éclat Transitions LLC

THE THIN BLUE LIE

AN HONEST COP vs THE FBI

GREG DILLON

BOMBARDIER
BOOKS

A BOMBARDIER BOOKS BOOK
An Imprint of Post Hill Press
ISBN: 978-1-64293-685-8
ISBN (eBook): 978-1-64293-686-5

The Thin Blue Lie:
An Honest Cop vs the FBI
© 2022 by Greg Dillon
All Rights Reserved

Cover Design by Tiffani Shea
Cover Image: © Can Stock Photo / pklick360

Post Hill Press
New York • Nashville
posthillpress.com

Published in the United States of America
1 2 3 4 5 6 7 8 9 10

Dedicated to my father
Bernard A. Dillon
(8/13/25–2/28/20)

"…There is a lot of debate about what whistleblowers are, and what they are not. I believe whistleblowers are patriots and heroes. A lot of them don't ever intend to blow the whistle. They don't ignore the law, or set out to make a lot of money or become famous. The vast majority will never be publicly known….Whistleblowers are harassed, fired, and blacklisted. Their careers, relationships, and health can all suffer as a result. However, their retaliators often go unpunished…."

—US Senator Chuck Grassley, Chairman,
Senate Judiciary Committee at a Whistleblower
Appreciation Day Luncheon, July 27, 2017

PROLOGUE: LETTER TO A WHISTLEBLOWER

I never wanted to be anything but a policeman. I was a court officer in my teens, a patrol officer at twenty, an FBI agent at thirty, and eventually an investigator for the Connecticut Chief State's Attorney's Office. I loved my work, and I was an honest cop. I caught a lot of bad guys along the way, and I like to think that I did some good in this world.

Police work is largely—especially at the advanced levels—all about paperwork: every official action must be documented, evidence must be tagged, statements taken, and papers meticulously prepared for presentation to the court where they must be attested to under oath. For every four hours of investigation, you'll spend an equal number of hours documenting your efforts. Anything you say under oath had better be accurate and truthful. All a police officer has is his or her word and reputation; therefore, he or she must always tell the truth or else the whole justice system implodes.

Being a good cop is not all it takes to have a successful career in law enforcement. There is also the critical science of office politics (which is never taught at any police academy). Superiors must be managed as carefully as subordinates, sometimes more so. Bosses need to look good to *their* superiors, and if you make them look bad, you will suffer. Punishment can take many forms: being reassigned, harassed, ignored, transferred, passed over for promotion, and so on. Careful etiquette must be maintained when working with other agencies. There is a lot of pressure inside the thin blue line to be a regular guy; you go along to get along. The worst thing that can happen to an honest cop is when being a good cop butts up against the pressure of being a team player.

The sad reality is one must constantly navigate the constantly changing tides and currents of department politics. There is no escaping it. It was not something I was prepared for, and apparently I never got good at it either. During the course of your career, there are certain personality types you will regularly deal with. Everyone usually falls—at least in part—into one of these categories, often more than one. Over time, people may start as one character, then meld into another. Age, experience, and circumstances may move an individual through several of these personality types during the course of his or her career. Here are some of the more common types you will likely encounter:

The Poser:

The person who tries to portray an image and pretends to be someone they are not, and can be quite comical when taken to an extreme. One will usually see through this character over time. This is often the loudmouth who tries to come off as a tough guy, or the dimwit who tries to come across as an intellectual. This will often create friction once coworkers see through the charade.

The Cowboy:

A close cousin of the Poser, this is the person who epitomizes the adage "the ends justify the means." They believe whatever action they take is for the greater good, so no corner is too big to cut when necessary.

Oftentimes this person leads a charmed life and is looked upon favorably by the management, as they are the big-play makers, the person who can get things done, the "go-to" guy (it is almost always a male). They eventually crash and burn, at which point the Cowboy is abandoned and everyone agrees—after the fact—that it was only a matter of time.

The Boy Scout:

Almost always an idealist and an optimist, but naive and not a realist. Has a false sense that everyone plays fair and should think and act like they do, and is surprised and disappointed when others don't. They are usually well suited for internal affairs (an assignment also attractive to the Careerist and the Specialist), as they eventually become comfortable in the role of the outsider. Will almost always clash with the Cowboy, as they are at opposite ends of the ethical spectrum.

The Job-Jumper:

This is the professional "dabbler," the one who looks at their career as a checker board, constantly plotting moves and jumps. This person usually does so for one of two reasons: they are easily bored, or because the grass is always greener. As soon as they get to their new assignment, they are planning their next move. This is not to be confused with the next person...

The Careerist:

This person moves around as often as the Job-Jumper, but their moves are made solely to advance their career and have little to do with whether they like their work or are any good at it. While the Job-Jumper plays checkers, the Careerist plays chess. As they constantly look to polish their résumé, they try to anticipate what role or assignment will put them in the best position to move up the career ladder. These are the ones with their ears to the ground, have keen survival instincts, and maintain an extensive network of contacts.

The Specialist:

Almost the polar opposite of the Careerist, this person finds their niche and becomes a barnacle in the system. Oftentimes they are considered an expert in their field, finding something they enjoy and/or are good at. This person can be a valuable asset to a department but is often resistant to any type of change. May sometimes be confused with the next one…

The Time Killer:

This is the person who has decided they have found a "gig"—a cushy assignment that no one else really wants—and are content to ride out their remaining time there. We see this oftentimes in "non-police" police jobs, like scheduling, evidence rooms, dispatch, training, asset forfeiture, crime prevention, media spokesperson, and the like. Sometimes they are on "light duty" due to physical restrictions, typically marking time until retirement.

The Worker Bee:

The person who shows up every day, keeps their head down, and does their job. They are the grinders, the ones who seldom complain and will do what is asked of them. They tend to be the backbone of the organization, the ones who are easy to overlook but are actually essential to the success of the department.

The Pretender:

Can oftentimes be confused with the Worker Bee, but this breed just *pretends* to work rather than actually work. Considered passive-aggressive, they are well known for bad attitudes and being very familiar with union rules and grievance procedures. This allows them to keep their jobs without necessarily *doing* their jobs. Often leads the pack in overtime and private duty assignments.

The Nepotist:

As the definition does not limit itself to family members—but also includes friends—this is pervasive in every company and organization, and does not exclude law enforcement agencies. While it is easily identified among familial members, it becomes murky when applied to cronies and the well-connected. This is a morale killer within agencies, creating hard feelings and pervasive mistrust of the promotional process within the rank-and-file. I have witnessed countless examples of this in every department and agency I have ever worked, as I'm sure anyone reading this can attest. In my last employment, every single time there was a promotional interview, I could predict with 100 percent accuracy who was going to receive the position.

Like others, I probably transitioned through various categories during my career, but the predominant one was likely the Boy Scout. I chose to be an honest cop. I blew the whistle on colleagues who were telling lies under my name and the names of my subordinates. As a result, I saw my career blighted, my reputation tarnished.

Everything you read here is true to the best of my recollection and research. When I wrote this book, I was aided by my handwritten notes that were taken contemporaneously with the conversation. Dialogue and conversations are based upon newspaper articles, memos, personal notes, depositions, and court transcripts. If I come across as bitter at times during this account, it is because I still am. If you are like me, you may believe your honesty will be fairly received, only to learn *you* are now the problem. It did not go the way I expected. Not by a long shot.

Mine is a cautionary tale for anyone who is considering confronting authority because of concerns about wrongdoing, unethical behavior, illegal activity, or corruption. Think long and hard about what you are prepared to do, and make sure you are doing the right thing for the right reason. If you are discovered doing the *wrong* thing for the *right* reason, you will be scapegoated; if you do the *right* thing for the *wrong* reason, you will be vilified for ulterior motives.

The role of a whistleblower is not for the faint of heart or spirit. If you decide to embark on that path, your career and your life will never be the same. Regardless of the outcome, prepare yourself for the reality there will be no winner; one side is just going to lose worse than the other.

Document, corroborate, and have irrefutable proof. When possible, have witnesses. But don't be surprised if people have poor—or worse—"evolving" memories that differ from yours. I witnessed career prosecutors take the witness stand and perjure themselves in an effort to protect themselves and their cohorts.

You will be damned regardless of your choices. For example, when I discovered the first falsified affidavit, I dithered in deciding what to do and opted for a "wait and see" approach; for this, I was criticized for not immediately reporting the matter. Of course, had I called someone out on it as soon as it happened, I would have been rebuked for overreacting and being a "Boy Scout." Likewise, when I began to suffer symptoms of depression, I did not seek professional help. Had I done so, I would have been deemed unpromotable and not credible due to my instability. By not seeking professional help, the toll it took on me was minimized in court by the defense, that I had not suffered enough to be considered worthy of compassion or compensation.

At the start of my career, I enjoyed an unimpeachable reputation and spotless work record. I was the previously described "Boy Scout." After I blew the whistle, my work habits were questioned, my time and attendance scrutinized, my personal life analyzed, all in hopes of putting me on the defensive and silencing my voice. Fortunately, I had no skeletons in my closet. If you have any, rest assured they will be found, dragged out, and put on public display.

I am sometimes asked if I could have handled things differently. Being the person I am, I don't see how I could. In life you play the hand you are dealt and make decisions based upon the facts you have available. I refused to compromise my conduct or countenance the unethical behavior of others. Yes, there were negative consequences, not only for me but for others—both good guys and bad guys. When I look back, I don't regret my actions, but I do lament the consequences of the *reactions* to my actions. While sometimes brutally blunt, what is written is heartfelt and accurate. And that is the beauty of the truth: it was true thirty years ago, is still true, and will be thirty years from now.

Despite my tumultuous career, I have never regretted my decision to become a police officer and still believe there is no nobler profession. The majority of people I met in law enforcement were honorable and decent; most of them I trusted with my life. I have nothing but respect for my brother and sister officers who risk their lives daily to keep our communities safe and our country secure.

CHAPTER 1

I sat on the floor and thumbed through the well-worn sheaf of FBI "Most Wanted" flyers. Staring back at me out of the black and white mug shots were fugitives from various states, wanted for a variety of crimes. The identical offense of Unlawful Flight To Avoid Prosecution was printed in extra-bold font across the top. I would stare at the faces, my lips sounding out the words as I read the physical descriptions. Scars, marks, tattoos. Dyed hair, prescription glasses, false or missing teeth. Gunshot scars, missing fingers, medical conditions. Habits, addictions, weapons. The more bizarre, the more fascinating I found it. What the brief narrative lacked in detail, I made up for with my imagination. When there was mention of a former address, I would adjust my goose-neck lamp and aim it at my map of the United States, just to see if it was anywhere near my house.

I got the wanted flyers from my father, who worked at the post office. Sometimes I would borrow my grandfather's magnifying glass to more closely examine the menacing faces. I scrutinized the black inked fingerprints, not quite sure what I was looking for but certain that the images were included for a reason. I would run a black marker over one of my fingertips and quickly roll it onto a white index card while the pungent ink was still moist. I would study my print, comparing it to the fugitive's, to see if we had anything in common.

One fugitive had a blank square where his pinky finger should have been; all it said was "AMP," which I learned in a footnote meant his little finger had been "amputated at the first joint." Now that was something to ponder. Had he been teasing a dog or got it caught in a window when trying to steal a cooling pie? Maybe it got blasted off in a shootout. For sure it would make him that much easier to spot if I ran across him. It turned out my dad was only bringing home the flyers of fugitives who had been apprehended or were verifiably dead, which mathematically lowered my chance of a successful identification from one in a million to none in a million.

Nevertheless, I always felt I was destined to be a "G-Man," a government man, which was old-time slang for an agent. FBI. Federal Bureau of Investigation. Fidelity, Bravery, Integrity. Once I had decided upon my career path, it was only a matter of waiting until I was old enough to become one.

I remember my dad rushing home one day with a large RadioShack radio that he claimed would let us listen in on police calls. Fascinated, I watched him turn the dials until we were listening to the New Haven Police Department radio dispatches. Eventually, he was able to obtain a copy of the radio signal codes. Whenever he was home, the scanner would be on in the background, allowing us to eavesdrop on all the radio transmissions. This first wet my whistle for police work.

As I got older, I started watching some police TV shows, first *Adam-12*, then later *Kojak*. While I was always entertained by the wisecracking, lollipop-chewing detective Kojak (played by Telly Savalas), I always identified with the straitlaced, clean cut *Adam-12* police officers (Martin Milner and Kent McCord). Years later in high school, I became fascinated with the movie *Serpico*, whose eponymous lead character was portrayed by Al Pacino. I even bought and devoured the hardcover book authored by Peter Maas. Little did I realize the significance of this in 1973.

New Haven in the 1960s was like most East Coast cities. Our neighborhood was primarily Irish, Italian, and Jewish, tough but lily-white. As time went on, though, what we called the "colored" neighborhoods expanded, melding into the white neighborhoods. Those who could afford to retreated to the suburbs. When I was born in 1956, my family lived in a multiunit, three-story apartment building. When everyone began moving, so did we, sort of. We relocated but only one block south, to the third-floor converted attic of my grandfather's house. I lived in that cramped, dormered, sweltering attic apartment until I was twenty-four.

I was a scrawny kid—a "skinny balink" as my Italian aunts put it. I was small and afraid of bullies. I've always hated bullies. I did whatever I could to avoid the last resort: having to fight them. You knew you would lose and it would hurt. It was considered a rite of passage. I was small, so I made it a habit to avoid the known bullies whenever possible. I tried to blend in, get along, and keep a low profile. But even the best chameleon eventually becomes a meal.

One September afternoon after school, my friends and I were taking a shortcut through a parking lot that involved squeezing through a small gap in an old wood plank fence. I was the last one in the queue and in no particular hurry to crawl through. Once I did, I locked eyes with two African American teens who were sitting on the hood of a parked car next to the fence. They were strangers, as no black families were yet living in the area, with robust Afros and actual muscles. I immediately had a bad feeling, confirmed by the expressions of my classmates who quickened their pace. I was too slow.

"Get over here!" one of them said.

"Who, me?" I croaked. I looked plaintively at my buddies, Dave, Bobby, and Ronnie. They had slowed down to watch, but they were not coming back to help me.

"Give me your money."

I turned my pockets inside out to show them they had chosen the kid whose dad worked in the post office. The bigger one grabbed my shirt in his left hand and cuffed me across the head with his right. The second blow was a glancing one, and if there was a third, I wasn't there for it, as I spun on my PF Flyers and took off after my friends. On Dave's front porch, I shouted at them through tears, demanding to know why they had left me. The three, equally ashamed, looked away and told me I was stupid to stand there and should have run right from the start.

I didn't know who to be angrier with: the toughs for hitting a scared twelve-year-old, my friends for leaving me to fend for myself, or me for not having the sense to run when I had the chance.

It was Sam K. who showed me the way. Most of my neighborhood friends commuted to Notre Dame High School in West Haven, trying to avoid the stress and turmoil of the chaotic inner-city public school system. As such, we were on the bus a lot. Sam was a year behind me. While not quite a genius, he was bookish by nature and wore those black plastic-framed glasses that never seemed to have been in fashion.

This made him a ready target for John S., a notorious bully and troublemaker from East Haven. John was an imbecile in class, but on the bus he was a Mensa-level ball-breaker. He would sit behind Sam and flick his ears, muss his hair, poke him in the back, daring him to complain. Of course, no one would think of standing up for Sam, as this would be an invitation to become John's next target. We would pretend not to notice and collectively hope the bus got all green lights to speed up our journey.

Notre Dame had a dress code: jackets, ties, and dress shoes. To protect our shoes from inclement weather, some of us wore galoshes. It was a glum, rainy afternoon, and John was trying to pluck Sam's Totes off his shoes, scanning the crowd to make sure everyone was watching. He did not see what I could—that Sam was unbuckling his belt and removing it from his pants, methodically wrapping it around his fist, leaving about six inches of leather and the large Western-style buckle loose.

Suddenly, crying and yelling at the same time, he stood and turned in the aisle and began flailing away at John, yelling about not being able to take it any longer. Sam hit him again and again, the belt buckle whistling down on the cowering John, who covered his greasy mop of hair with his hands and offered no resistance.

We were stunned. No one tried to stop it, not even the driver. After a minute or less, Sam tired of his efforts and slumped in his seat, spent, ignoring his tormentor directly behind him. We held our breath to see how the final act would play out, but there was none. The show was over. John—all eyes fixed on him—backed off. To my amazement, he now shined up to Sam and told him he was only joking around, didn't mean to get him mad, and said he liked him and was just playing. Then he looked around sheepishly, trying to laugh it off like it was no big deal.

But it was a big deal, and it made a lasting impression on me. I learned that the biggest fear of every bully is *real* confrontation. I hated bullies and would never again back down from one. What Sam taught me that day was the sooner I could shift the odds in my favor, the easier life would be, especially in light of my chosen career. I needed to get big and strong, which I did through exercise and weight lifting. Then came training in martial arts. Soon I reached the point where confrontation was not something to avoid at all costs, but an opportunity to take a stand and make things right.

This was a turning point in life. My dislike of bullies became personal but at a cost. It served me well in my chosen profession but later became a path to career suicide. I prepared myself for the expected criminal bullies but never anticipated that the bullies entrenched in law enforcement bureaucracies would eventually lead to my downfall.

My first week as a Special Deputy Sheriff at age eighteen.
Photo taken in the hallway of our attic apartment.

CHAPTER 2

I n those days it was very rare to go to college to become a police officer. Luckily for me, one of the only three accredited four-year criminal justice programs in the entire country at that time was just down the street from my high school. I received a scholarship to the University of New Haven and commuted there while I lived at home with my parents, who were so proud when I graduated magna cum laude with a bachelor of science in criminal justice, law enforcement administration in 1978.

While attending college, I was able to land a part-time job as a special deputy sheriff. In Connecticut, the sheriffs (now called judicial marshals) oversee courtroom security and prisoner transportation, and my assignment was at the state courthouse in downtown New Haven. It was a patronage job: my mom's sister's husband was a good friend of Henry Healey, chief deputy sheriff from 1958 until 1972, then high sheriff until his death in 1996. It was a quasi-law enforcement agency with little oversight or accountability. There was no academy, no formal training, no operations manual, no union—one simply served at the pleasure of the high sheriff. The work force consisted primarily of relatives or close associates of the high sheriff along with "the chosen ones" of political heavyweights.

While the nepotism and cronyism were blatant and obvious within the sheriff's department, they were more nuanced at higher levels. I witnessed the many versions of this throughout my law enforcement career at the local, state, and federal agencies. It happened during the hiring process, it happened during the promotional process, and it happened during the disciplinary process. It is universal, pervasive, and unfair—and inevitable. It is natural for people to want to see the persons they like do well, and these "rabbis"—as they are often called—will move mountains to see their favorites jump the line or be spared the rod.

I was notified to report for my first day of work at the courthouse wearing a white short-sleeve dress shirt and black slacks, black shoes, black belt, and black clip-on tie (so prisoners could not try to strangle us or pull us through the cell bars with our own ties). After I completed some paperwork, I was told to purchase a badge and some shoulder patches from the high sheriff's secretary. And that was it. No academy, no orientation, just on-the-job training from day one.

Here I was, age eighteen, escorting murderers, rapists, robbers, pedophiles, and other assorted miscreants back and forth between their basement cells and the various courtrooms as the defendants attended their arraignments, proceedings, trial, conviction, sentencing, and appeals. Hepatitis? Tuberculosis? Blood-borne pathogens? We didn't even wear gloves, never mind a mask. I was a college student on Mondays, Wednesdays, and Fridays, and a special deputy sheriff on Tuesdays and Thursdays—and five days a week during summer vacation. I was living large, being paid twenty-five dollars per *day*—pre-taxes.

But it was quite an education, getting paid to sit behind the defendant's chair and watch a trial. I studied the witnesses, cops, criminals, and victims, making up my own mind about their credibility. Alibi witnesses, character witnesses, hostile witnesses, expert witnesses all came under my scrutiny. I was particularly interested in the sentencings. Would the convicted be apologetic, stoic, defiant? Would he continue to insist on his innocence? I made friends with the clerks, prosecutors, and judges; our long acquaintances were occasionally helpful as my own career later progressed. Again, nepotism at play.

Each state's attorney had a small staff of inspectors, who were often former Connecticut state troopers or retired city detectives. These men (no women at the time) were hired to assist in preparing cases for trial: finding witnesses, serving subpoenas, tracking evidence, taking statements, and writing reports. This looked like a great job: the pay was good, the hours regular, the work fairly safe. You got all the good police perks, such as state arrest powers, state police radios in an unmarked take-home car, authority to carry a firearm, and a twenty-year hazardous duty state pension. I made a mental note.

Having set my sights on a career in law enforcement at an early age, I had taken my preparation seriously. Though not a naturally gifted student, I made up for what I might have lacked in intelligence with effort and hard work. I hit the gym hard, because a professional police officer must also be an athlete. I went from a 160-pound college freshman to a 200-pound senior. I also began studying Tae Kwon Do at a local dojang. I enjoyed the mental and physical discipline of the art, along with the confidence it gave me. Once I obtained my brown belt—and the commensurate wrecked hands—I began looking for a martial art that did not emphasize punching and was more suited to police work. I discovered an Aikido school in New Haven and trained there until eventually earning my black belt after several years.

While I was working as a special deputy sheriff, my former high school and college classmate, Tim Buckley, had been accepted as a supernumerary police officer in his hometown of Branford, a shoreline town with a disproportionate number of liquor stores, bars, discos, pubs, taverns, and nightclubs.[1] To bolster the number of officers on its aging

---

[1] Supernumerary, from the Latin *super numerum,* meaning "beyond the number"; the word designated a part-time police officer used to supplement the

force—especially on weekend nights and holidays—Branford held a hiring drive. I figured the more police entrance exams I took, the better I would get at taking them, so I applied. The hiring process consisted of a written exam, physical agility test, medical screening, oral interviews before the police commission, and finally an acceptance letter. A dozen other young guys and I began taking evening classes in the basement of the police station; we were going to be weekend muscle.

The pay was even worse than at the sheriff's department. The night classes were on our own time, as were the mandatory one hundred hours of unpaid "ride-along" time. We had to buy our own uniforms and revolvers, but at least this time they threw in the shoulder patches and badge. After graduation, I worked full-time as a special deputy sheriff in court, and weekends as a supernumerary officer, or "super," in Branford until I was hired as a "regular" in 1981.

The courthouse was educational, but being a police officer was exhilarating.

One hot Friday night in August, I went into the station for a "ride-along." My field training officer—commonly referred to as an FTO—that night was a laid-back, mellow sort, content to cruise around aimlessly killing time until the end of his shift at midnight. Finally a call came in; multiple residents were reporting a dark, oversized pickup truck driving over sidewalks and across flowerbeds, knocking down mailboxes and tearing up lawns.

We came around a corner, and at the far end of a long straightaway, we spotted the reflectors of a large vehicle driving without lights. My partner hit the gas and called in our location. We lost the pickup for a minute, then spotted it again, and began a lights-and-siren pursuit. We were gaining on the truck when we realized we were both barreling down a long straightaway that ended at a "T" intersection. Rather than turning left or right, the driver locked up his brakes in a cloud of acrid blue smoke, jumped a high curb, and drove up the steep side of a meadowed hill that led to a shopping plaza on Route One. Our car would never even make

ranks.

it over the berm, never mind climb the hill. As my partner radioed in the driver's strategy, I leapt out of the car and began to chase the truck. My FTO was yelling at me to get back in the car, but I was committed. The chase was on.

The oversized tires were tearing up huge patches of tall grass, and I was catching the brunt of it: first tire smoke and thick dust, and then as I got closer, clods of two-foot-long grass. As the incline grew steeper, I was on my hands and feet, grabbing fistfuls of grass and pumping my legs in an attempt to gain ground. The truck began to slow as it got closer to the top; the tires were spinning on the matted-down hay, the rear end swinging wide, first one way, then the other. I veered over to the driver's side as I began to close.

At first, I was concerned the driver might spot me in his side view mirror. As I got closer, I was more afraid that the struggling truck would either swing out sideways and hit me, or the driver would abandon his plan and unintentionally back over me. Just as the truck was inching close to the crest, I was able to pull myself alongside the pickup, groping through the blinding smoke and choking dust to feel for a handhold. I realized just then that the driver had his window open, so I reached in and grabbed for his long hair.

I'm sure he never expected a hand to reach through his window at that point in the chase, and it caught him by surprise. I grabbed a second handful and yanked his head through the window, yelling at him to put the truck in park and turn it off. Fortunately he did. I was happy to make the pinch but enjoyed more the fact that the story made the rounds in the station house, bringing me some temporary recognition.

Six of us were eventually hired as full-time patrolmen. Sixteen weeks at the municipal police academy and Officer Gregory Dillon was dispatched to a complaint of a street robbery—unusual in our town—right on the main drag of Route One.

It was January 31, 1982. The tearful victim, barely a teenager, had been relieved of his large "boom box" by a pair of older kids. The robbers drove past him, parked, returned on foot, and forcibly relieved him of his portable stereo system. The victim provided a decent description of the young men and their car, noting a loud muffler and a temporary license plate in the back window. Since it was the weekend, the detective division was off. I took the victim's statement, put out a broadcast, then sent a teletype to surrounding departments.

I didn't leave it there. Even though the nearby pool hall/pinball joint was just outside my usual sector, I made it a point to cruise the parking lot there every night. The victim had been in there just before the robbery, and it wasn't far from the intersection where he'd been ambushed. I figured that is where they first noticed him and his boom box.

Several weeks later, I saw a junker with a temporary plate in the back window parked in the pool hall lot. I notified the dispatcher I would be out of service on a surveillance, then parked across the street in a darkened used car lot and waited. When a trio of young males came out, entered it and started it up, I could hear the defective muffler from across the street. I requested backup and stopped the car. Soon the street was full of flashing lights. The driver resembled the description, but now I had to scramble. I raced back to the station to telephone the victim—who fortunately was at home—picked him up, then drove him back to the scene where he made a positive ID. Upon arrest, the driver soon confessed and named his accomplice. Both were arrested for robbery, conspiracy to commit robbery, larceny, and conspiracy to commit larceny.

Soon after—much to my surprise—the driver was sentenced to prison, despite being a teen himself. I was gratified to receive the appreciation of the victim and his parents, and their gratitude translated into an article in the local newspaper and my second medal of commendation. That medal only fueled my ambition to aggressively investigate whatever crime came my way. This was one of the advantages of working in a town and not a city. I got to investigate crimes as a uniformed officer that would have been kicked upstairs to the detectives in a larger department like New Haven.

I enjoyed most aspects of patrol work, except for motor vehicle accidents and domestic violence calls. Somebody, if not everybody, was either injured, angry, or upset, and the documentation was time-consuming. I wanted to get back on patrol and find my own work, even if it was only scoping out bar parking lots for drug deals, fights, or drunks trying to navigate their way home.

From day one I was intolerant of big mouths, bullies, or those who disrespected the law. The jerk handcuffed in the back seat threatening to do all kinds of bodily harm if only he wasn't restrained always changed his tune down at the station. I would lock up my gun belt and begin the processing: mugshots and five sets of fingerprint cards, reminding my guest he was not handcuffed, and so we were now both unarmed and evenly matched. Few took me up on the offer. They knew, and they knew that I knew, that without an audience of friends and civilian witnesses, they were blustery cowards, as almost all bullies are. That theory would be repeatedly tested and proven over the course of my career.

Our department in Branford was relatively small at the time, about forty officers and twenty "supers." The chief and his number two (who later succeeded him) were retired, high-ranking veterans of the New Haven Police Department, and their policies and procedures elevated our standards beyond that of a suburban department. But it was still a small department in a small town, blending the familiarity of a large, dysfunctional family with the impersonality of a bureaucracy. You'd get a medal of commendation and a congratulatory letter from the police commission, but it would be crammed into your mail slot along with the usual assortment of paperwork. Not much pomp and circumstance, but I was proud of the added medals displayed above my badge.

Night time is crime time, and that was the shift the young guys worked. We had a great group; there was a synergistic energy when we would leave roll call and head out for the night. A few of us with high monthly activity and a reputation for being proactive would occasionally get to dress down and roam in an unmarked car. I don't know how "undercover" it was driving around in a four-door gold Plymouth Gran Fury with blackwall tires, but we made it work.

By 1984 I had already applied to the FBI, as well as my coworkers Tom Fregeau and Tim Buckley. We went through a protracted battery of tests. Tommy was the first one selected and was leaving for the FBI Academy in Quantico, Virginia, that summer. Tommy and I were often partnered, sometimes in uniform and sometimes in plain clothes. He was more cerebral, the only guy on the job with a law degree. He was "deliberate," which some detractors viewed as "indecisive." I was more street savvy, more physically imposing at 225 pounds, and perhaps a bit more "spontaneous," which some detractors viewed as "impulsive." The combination worked; we were always busy, worked well together, and shared a lot of laughs and a lot of arrests.

It was the end of the summer of 1985. Tommy was already at the FBI Academy, and I was working solo in plain clothes, driving the unmarked Fury. It was quieter than usual and was starting to feel like autumn. One of our new patrol officers radioed he was attempting to stop a motorcycle for motor vehicle violations. No one likes chasing motorcycles. Bikes are fast and nimble, and there is an increased likelihood of a violent ending. The officer soon called off the chase, but he'd gotten a good look at the guy's bike and black leather jacket.

Minutes later, another car radioed to confirm the description, reporting the bike was now ignoring his attempts to stop him. Other patrol cars spotted the same biker at different intersections. At one point during the on again/off again chase, the motorcyclist drove down a one-way street the wrong way, then blasted through an empty parking lot to elude. Brazenly, he would wait at an intersection until an officer caught up, give "the one-finger salute," then take off, only to repeat the taunt at the next corner.

I don't have anything against motorcycle enthusiasts, but I have never cared for "outlaw" bikers or their asshole second cousins, the outlaw wannabes.[2] In an attempt to distinguish themselves from the public, they tend to fall into one of two categories: the black-leather clad, obese, tattooed

---

[2]   They are labeled "outlaw" because the American Motorcyclist Association (AMA) does not formally recognize these groups. The more recognizable groups are the biggest gangs such as the Hell's Angels, the Mongols, the Pagans, the Outlaws, and the Bandidos.

nitwit, or the black-leather clad, emaciated, tattooed nitwit. While the Harley is the gold standard, it is also slower and cumbersome. This was a young guy on a fast Japanese bike. As my gold Plymouth had "wig-wag" headlights, a dashboard strobe, and a siren, I joined the chase.

Eventually our daredevil sped down Route One and cut down a long side street that fed into the town center. My strategy was to parallel the chase, not content to simply play the caboose on this runaway train. A patrol car had the same idea as we merged at an intersection: the marked unit pulled into the right lane, and I squeezed in just to his left. Seconds later, the bike crested the hill and sped toward us, his single headlamp leading the blue strobes behind him. Even though I had left several feet of space between my car and the parked cars to my left, the flashing lights must have ruined his night vision. In disbelief, I watched him accelerate toward my car, then slam his machine, along with his left leg, into the Gran Fury's grill. He continued on without his '82 Kawasaki about another twenty feet, eventually coming to rest sitting upright in the road, trying to figure out what happened to his leg.

My car had been struck so hard my door wouldn't open, so I slid across the bench seat and got out the passenger side. As I approached, he sat upright in the street with several beer cans fizzing in angry circles on the ground around him, steam rising from his mangled thigh. I was on my portable shouting for medical while he wailed and moaned. I told him to quit looking at it, and he eventually fell back on the pavement, staring up into the night sky. His wailing went on until it was mercifully drowned out by the Fire and Rescue sirens.

By the time the ambulance arrived, I was starting to feel the effects of the impact. They immediately laid me on a backboard with a cervical collar, while Evel Knievel and his leg were put on a stretcher. We were loaded into the same ambulance for the race to the Yale New Haven ER. It was awkward to say the least, made worse by the fact that the two attendants were giving me more attention than the soon-to-be amputee. Apparently they had been listening to the police scanner at the firehouse, and they told him, "You got just what you deserved...."

I was released from the hospital at dawn with a foam cervical collar and a prescription for muscle relaxers and painkillers. When I got home,

I sat on the edge of my bed and cried. I had seen dead and maimed bodies before but none as a result of my actions. I went back and forth over it, how I should not have crowded his traffic lane, it was only a traffic violation, but he instigated and encouraged the pursuit.

Then the telephone rang; it was the New Haven FBI Office. "Good news, Greg! Someone who was supposed to start the new agents class had to drop out, so we can get you into the next class—in two weeks!" I was stunned. "Can I get back to you?" was not what the special agent was expecting to hear.

"Greg, this is a fantastic opportunity! Who knows if there will even be another New Agents' class this year?" I told him I just needed a few minutes, as I had had a very long, difficult night and needed to sort out my thoughts. After a close friend from work urged me to go for it, I called back and accepted.

My last week of work as a Branford
police officer at age twenty-eight.

CHAPTER 3

The FBI Academy in Quantico, Virginia, occupies 547 acres of a one hundred-square-mile property established by the United States Marine Corps in 1917. It is forty miles south of Washington, DC—and 350 miles from Branford, Connecticut. I drove down with my former partner, Tommy Fregeau, who had begun classes just four weeks earlier.

My anxiety grew as we got closer to Virginia. While I had completed the sixteen-week Connecticut municipal police academy just four years earlier—graduating first in my class—this would be different. At the state-run municipal police training academy in Meriden, I had been in a commuter class, due to the proximity of Branford to Meriden, plus a shortage of dorms. Now I would be living out-of-state, 24/7, from August until December (except for the times I would be able to fly home over a couple of three-day weekends). And instead of being in a mixed class of high school and college graduates, I would now be in a class of competitive, ambitious college grads composed of lawyers, accountants, scientists, ex-military studs, and top cops. I knew I needed to bring my "A" game.

Each new agents' class is given a numerical designation, determined by the calendar year and the sequence of one's class during that year. As mine was the twelfth class of 1985, I was a member of "class 85-12." In the course of the seven-hour drive, I peppered my former partner with questions. Tommy explained how new agents roomed in groups of four, assigned by gender and alphabetically. Living with roommates was going to be a first for me. Tommy drove me around the complex pointing out the various firearms ranges, obstacle courses, and running trails.

Then we checked in and went to see my room. It looked like a college dorm room furnished by the Holiday Inn: single beds, small matching desks, and a single open-faced wardrobe divided in half. At the back of the room, a door opened into the shared bathroom, which led into an identically furnished room. I was the first to arrive, and I quickly unpacked and organized my things, then went out for a run hoping to dispel my anxiousness.

I came back and jumped in the common shower. As I didn't yet know how we were supposed to handle laundry, I opted to hand-wash my running shorts, socks, T-shirt, and jockstrap, which I hung on a hook in the bathroom.

Meeting my roommates gave me my first indication the FBI might not be the all-star team I was expecting. My roomie Dave was a non-descript guy from Florida who introduced himself as a former assistant high school football coach and driving instructor. Unless he was being overly modest, that was it. I had been under the impression my new agents class would be a mix of overachievers, the best of the best from across the country. My opinion evolved further when our two suite mates popped in through our bathroom door, introducing themselves as Mark from New York and Leo from "The Citadel," as if it were a city and not a military college.

Mark, short and stocky, with thinning brown hair and a fighter's nose, had been a professional boxer and an FBI clerk in the Albany Division, a good way to get a leg up into the new agent selection process. Leo was from the Citadel, big and tall, with wavy blond hair, a weak chin, a weaker moustache, and attitude to spare. He walked through our room uninvited as if conducting an official inspection. He picked up a pencil off my desk, examined it, and asked, "Whose desk is this?" I raised my hand like a student, acknowledged it was mine, and he stated to no one in particular: "Looks like we have a geek here." Dave and I looked at each other in confusion. Leo announced that as all of the pencils were sharpened and lined up together, it was "the sure sign of a geek," as if he had solved his first crime. Returning the pencil—out of place, of course—he strode out of the room.

Within minutes, Leo was back with my jockstrap at the end of another pencil, demanding to know whose jock it was. I sheepishly raised my hand again. In dramatic flair, he dropped it onto my bed, announcing he had first sprayed it with Lysol as a precaution. The antiseptic smell filling the room confirmed this. He then returned to his room.

Immediately Mark came in and apologized for his roommate's behavior. I grilled Mark, quietly asking him if he thought this could be some type of early test, meaning was Leo a plant that was being used to assess our reactions? Mark said he didn't think so, as he had never heard of something like this being done, plus Leo had two suitcases full of clothes, which he had already unpacked. That was enough for me. I knew I had to do something, something that would send a message, and that I had to do it right away. I asked Mark what color his toothbrush was and with a puzzled look he replied "red."

As soon as he left I picked up my jockstrap and headed for the bathroom to scrub away at it in the sink with Leo's blue toothbrush. When I was finished, I went in and flipped the toothbrush onto the end of his bed. "Thanks for letting me use your toothbrush to scrub the Lysol out of my jock."

In seconds, Leo was back in our room. "That better be a joke—you better not be serious!"

"Let's just say if I were you, I'd buy a new toothbrush."

"I'm telling you right now…" and with that I jumped off my bed and squared off.

"If you think you are going to break my balls over the next four months, you are wrong. You touch my shit one more time, and I will throw your ass right through that fucking window, do you understand me?"

Leo returned to his room. There was no further drama that night or for the remaining 110 days.

New Agent Class 85-12 assembled in one large stadium seating–style classroom, everyone discreetly evaluating their new classmates as potential competitors or possible hookups.

Quantico was a hybrid of a college campus, a police academy, and a corporate team-building retreat. I had three advantages: fitness, firearms proficiency, and a solid legal background. As these three areas made up the bulk of the curriculum, I did well and enjoyed my time there. Some of my peers found themselves in the remedial fitness classes, or on academic probation, or having to return time and again to requalify on the range. The most entertaining classes were held outdoors or in the gym, while the most tedious were those designed to teach us the hundreds of forms utilized by the Bureau, and the various ways to classify and disseminate them.

It was a steep yet dull learning curve, but you had to know this stuff. The record of your actions in conducting a search, obtaining a confession, or making an arrest must stand up to legal scrutiny and not be subject to impeachment in a court of law. That said, there is a tendency to take these things too far, and it is a common complaint of the crime-fighting types in the Bureau that they are drowning in redundant paperwork. Later as an FBI agent, I often felt I was spending more time documenting what I did than actually doing what I did.

A theme that was delicately touched upon in several classes was the notion of *never* embarrassing the Bureau. A senior instructor—who was a captivating speaker and always held our collective attention—likened the organization to "a family, but without a mother." He explained while there was a strong bond within the agency, the administration could be quite unforgiving and the discipline harsh, especially if the conduct in question cast "our" agency in a bad light.

I misunderstood this warning; I got the part that you should never do—or fail to do—anything that would cause embarrassment to the Bureau. What I missed in the warning was what the Bureau was prepared to do to anyone who called attention to something that embarrassed the Bureau. The FBI had their own strictly enforced code of "omertà."[3]

After classes, most of us would adjourn to the Boardroom bar, where we would mingle with instructors or field agents who came through Quantico for specialized training. The veterans regaled us with tales of the more unusual antics or escapades of colleagues and the consequence of discipline that followed. Agents losing their "creds" (identification credentials), their firearm, or even their car.

It was clear the Bureau had little tolerance for embarrassing behavior and would make quick examples of those who erred. A recurring theme was how agents entrusted with a take-home car would get "dinged" for the unauthorized use of same, resulting in "thirty days on the beach," which sounded benign, until I learned it meant a thirty-day suspension without pay. Each story began differently but ended the same. Some hapless agent would be somewhere *not* on official business and would get into a fender bender or worse; sometimes the agent would wriggle out of it by sneaking the government car off to a repair shop, personally paying for the body work, then not reporting the accident, thereby dodging a disciplinary suspension. Oftentimes, however, an agent was less fortunate and learned how unforgiving FBIHQ could be for this violation. Losing a twelfth of your annual salary is a heavy hit, and there was no shortage of such stories.

As graduation neared, we anxiously awaited our first-office assignments. At that time, the Bureau made a point of inconveniencing and disrupting the lives of their graduating agents, although I understand

---

3   "Omertà"; the Mafia code of silence that prizes noncooperation in the face of questioning by authorities or outsiders.

this changed drastically around 1990. When we first started the academy, we were asked to provide a "wish list" of three offices, with the understanding that nobody got an overseas posting, their "OO," or any of the top twelve big city offices in the Bureau.[4] Most people requested divisions relatively near home, unless they had hopes of living in a different part of the country.

Based upon my research and conversations with the New Haven applicant coordinator, I learned the Bureau was constantly struggling to keep the New York office supplied with personnel. Due to the exorbitant cost of living in The Big Apple, and the fact that the New York Division was the largest office in the FBI (the second largest being the Washington Field Office), there was always turnover. Agents being transferred there often resigned rather than move. Due to the fact living in NY on an agent's salary was nearly impossible—especially if one had a family—it was not unheard of to learn that some agents were carpooling in from Pennsylvania! My game plan was to graduate from Quantico, then be assigned to a small office somewhere in the continental US for a few years, then be transferred to the New York office. This would put me within a ninety-minute drive to family and friends in Connecticut. That was the plan anyway.

It was said that FBIHQ kept a chimpanzee who threw darts at a map, and based upon the way we were scattered across the country, this theory actually made the most sense. Classmates from the East Coast ended up out west, those from the north were sent down south, and so on. The day of disappointment was a sadistic ritual that veterans turned out to watch with a schadenfreude I thought unseemly. As your name was called alphabetically, you had to leave your seat, walk to the podium at the front of the classroom, state your Office of Origin, and only then open your envelope and announce your posting. Some of the women fought back tears as they returned to their seats, and I am sure more than a few of the guys felt the same.

---

4   "OO" stood for Office of Origin; this was the office you had lived closest to and applied through.

I got Alexandria, Virginia, and breathed a sigh of relief. As I had taken up with a young lady I had met one weekend while barhopping with some classmates around Prince William County, I was happy. She had graduated from Georgetown, had a place in Alexandria, and worked at National Geographic in DC. I was relieved knowing I now knew *one* person in the area; that softened the blow.

My classmate Charlie Price got New Haven. It was not lost on either of us that I had applied from New Haven and got Alexandria, and Charlie had applied from Alexandria and got New Haven. Why make two new agents happy, when you can make the same two new agents miserable? Our classmate Byron, a married schoolteacher from Chicago, received orders for Minneapolis, or as he loudly rephrased it outside the classroom, "Minnie-mutha-fuckin'-apolis, Minnie-mutha-fuckin'-sota! What the fuck do they need a black man up there for anyway?" I thought the instructors would reprimand him for his outburst, but not one instructor even made eye contact; they just quick-walked away. That evening there were longer-than-usual lines for the pair of telephone booths on the first floor. Even with the wood and glass doors closed, there was no mistaking the tone of the calls.

Receiving my FBI credentials at age twenty-nine from Assistant Director James D. McKenzie at graduation ceremony in Quantico, VA.

CHAPTER 4

T he Alexandria Division was a small office by Bureau standards: sixty or so agents, plus clerical staff and civilian technical employees. The office took up most of 300 North Lee Street in Old Town, Alexandria, an affluent burg eight miles across the Potomac River from the nation's capital.

The largest squad in the Alexandria field office was the applicant squad. Here every new agent was assigned to conduct employment background checks and security clearances on a variety of federal employees: federal magistrates, judges, and their staff; federal appointees, congressmen, and their staff; US attorneys, assistant US attorneys, FBI applicants, DEA applicants, and so on. Many of these people lived in the suburbs around DC, as did their references, associates, and neighbors who needed to be interviewed. It was tedious work and had nothing to do with catching criminals. Thankfully I managed to get out of it after only six (very long) months.

Since I was one of the few agents with a police background, I was transferred to the Criminal Reactive Squad, primarily working bank robberies. It was said the boss was a nightmare, but I wasn't deterred. I was there to catch bad guys. My partner, Dennis Condon Jr., and I got along famously from day one, two Irish Catholic kids from New England. A former federal probation officer from Framingham, Massachusetts, Dennis was already married with two boys, and like many others I encountered in the course of my career, he came from a law enforcement family. His father was a retired legendary agent in the Boston office, and his brother and sister were both Massachusetts State Police troopers.

The upside to being assigned to a smaller office was the exposure to a wide variety of work, both within and outside your assigned squad. We sometimes assisted the FCI squad by conducting "moving" and "stationary" surveillances of foreign nationals.[5] In October 1986, we were tasked to execute search warrants with the White Collar Crime squad for Lyndon LaRouche's headquarters in Leesburg, Virginia. Wikipedia describes LaRouche—who died in 2019—as an "American political activist, convicted fraudster, cult leader, and founder of the LaRouche movement, whose main organization was the National Caucus of Labor Committees." While fronting as a political movement, LaRouche and his inner circle grew wealthy by defrauding their supporters of millions of dollars by borrowing money they knew they could never repay. He was convicted on multiple counts of mail fraud, conspiracy to commit mail fraud, and conspiring to defraud the IRS. LaRouche was given a fifteen-year prison sentence in 1988 but was paroled after only five years. Thirteen of his associates received federal prison sentences ranging from one month to seventy-seven years.

The work was nonstop. I inherited the caseload of my predecessor, which meant every open, cold case he had been "working" became my case, in addition to every other new bank robbery that occurred in Northern Virginia. My workday would routinely begin at 7:30 a.m., which meant waking up before 6 a.m. Between the dictation and paperwork, I seldom left the office before 6 p.m. Throw in an occasional

---

5   Post 9-11, the Foreign Counter Intelligence squad was expanded into the new Counter Intelligence Division.

weekend or nighttime Lorton Reformatory murder, and there was hardly any downtime.[6] The burnout rate on the squad was high, as was the turnover.

Bank robberies were common in those days, not just in our area, but in most major cities. In fact, in 1981, one-third of all robberies occurred in the six largest US cities.[7] Today there is much greater bank security, both physical and electronic. But back in the low-tech 1980s, security was minimal and banks a tempting target. In many cases, all a robber had to do was put on a ball cap and sunglasses, stroll up to the teller with a paper bag, and demand that he or she fill it with cash. Typically the take was minimal—a few thousand dollars at most. Nor were they committed by high-tech super criminals like you see in the movies, but rather by low-level recidivists who were often none too bright. Bank robberies were so common in our region, some office agents admitted they would only conduct their bank business at drive-through teller windows.

By the end of my first year, Dennis and I were responding to an average of a bank job a day. And we saw all manner of robberies: note jobs, counter-vaulters, take-overs, hoax bombs, even an occasional drive-through window robbery. The robberies were committed by individuals, pairs, and occasionally trios. Some fled on foot, others in cars, motorcycles, and even bicycles. Although some days were uneventful and gave us a chance to catch up on dictation, on other days we would race from crime scene to crime scene. On those days, I would dictate interviews and memos into a small, hand-held cassette recorder while Dennis drove, so as not to get buried in paperwork at day's end.

---

6   This sprawling, derelict prison was opened in 1916 and mercifully closed in 2011. It was located In Fairfax County, Virginia, twenty-five miles away from the District of Columbia, but used to house DC prisoners. Because it was technically a federal prison, any serious crimes committed there were under the jurisdiction of our office.

7   *1983 DOJ Report: Robbery in the United States: An Analysis of Recent Trends and Patterns.*

Armed robbery of the Central Fidelity Bank in Chantilly, VA, by career bank robbers Richard Allen Gordon (in zippered jacket) and Francis Browne Hall (in hoodie). This was their seventh and most profitable robbery and both would be dead within the hour.

Once, we responded to *five* bank robberies in one day—although the same pair committed two of them. Unhappy with the meager take from the first bank, the masked duo immediately committed a more profitable one in a nearby town. This pair of robbers—convicted murderers who met in federal prison—began robbing banks in October 1986. Richard Allen Gordon, forty-three, and Francis Browne Hall Jr., thirty-six, eventually committed a half-dozen brazen, take-over bank robberies. On December 3, 1987, the duo returned to the Central Fidelity Bank near Dulles Airport in Chantilly—the same bank they had robbed eleven months earlier. After taking over the bank and gaining access to the vault, they fled with over $100,000 in cash stuffed into a pair of pillowcases.

A responding Fairfax County police officer spotted the getaway car, followed it to a dead end road, and blocked the street with his patrol car while calling for backup. The cornered career criminals, armed with a

Ruger Mini-14 .223-caliber semiauto rifle, a handgun, and 194 rounds of ammunition, opened fire on the outgunned officer, who bravely returned fire with his sidearm. Ditching their stolen Ford Escort, they then got into Hall's mother's car, which they had left in the church parking lot as their "switch" car. Dennis and I were covering a lead not far from the scene and responded with lights and siren. Just before we arrived, each man shot himself through the mouth with the .38-caliber Ruger revolver. When we arrived, paramedics were providing first aid to both men, who were soon pronounced dead at the scene. Number seven was not their lucky number.

Besides bank robberies, we would also be assigned more traditional felonies that became federal crimes simply because they were committed on federal land. This was more common than one would think, due to the number of federal properties scattered throughout Northern Virginia. In the '80s, security at some of the military bases was rather lax, and civilians had access to some of the roads and trails outside the bases, even though they were technically on federal land.

One hot summer night, two Iranian taxi drivers—who competed for fares at National Airport (now known as Ronald Reagan Washington National Airport)—decided to settle an ongoing feud by mutual combat. Their chosen field of battle was an unlit dirt road located on Fort Belvoir in Fairfax County, Virginia. As with most scuffles, it soon ended up on the ground. It was not meant to be a fair fight. The victim later told me while he was on top, trying to pin his opponent to the ground to prove he had won, the other driver was able to punch him several times in the head and neck. What he didn't realize was, due to the lack of light and the heat of the moment, his opponent was actually *stabbing* him. While getting stitched up, he told me he had felt warm liquid running down his face and neck and thought it was his sweat due to the heat, exertion, and the darkness. Only when he began to taste the blood did he realize he was bleeding heavily from his scalp and neck. As soon as he got off his opponent, the armed combatant drove off; then the stabbing victim did the same. He was able to stop a patrolling military police vehicle, where he received lifesaving first aid until an ambulance arrived.

Dennis and I soon identified the other taxi driver and went straight to his apartment, which he shared with another Iranian student. Since the attack, our suspect had already returned home, cleaned up, then fled. We requested, and received, written permission from the roommate to search the common areas of the apartment; in our rush to secure the scene, we did not have a search warrant. I located and seized bloody clothing in the shared kitchen trash can and bloody paper towels in the shared bathroom.[8] The cooperative roommate volunteered the fact he was aware of the ongoing dispute and was in fact with his roommate the previous week when he purchased a very dangerous bladed instrument at the nearby Springfield Mall. He then produced the empty box. It was an uncommon type of knife, known as a "push" dagger (also called a spear point knife or a "knuckle" knife). It is small and held in one's fist, with a short, wide, double-edged blade that comes to a point and protrudes from between the fingers of one's fist. Due to its design, it is easily concealed and even easier to maintain a grip on, even during a struggle. Any blows struck while wielding this weapon are bound to draw blood, and lots of it.

The suspect soon turned himself in after contacting his roommate and learning of our visit. He pleaded not guilty, gambled on a trial, and was convicted of and sentenced for attempted murder.

Supervisory Special Agent (SSA) Ray Connolly lived up to his billing as a brutal boss. Every ninety days he would meet with each one of us for the dreaded "file review," in which he would note in each open file every perceived deficiency. There was no pleasing the guy; any accomplishment or success you mentioned during a file review was met with this snappy retort: "But what have you done for me lately?" If an agent complained that he was arriving early and staying late each day to keep up with the overwhelming number of cases, his standard reply was always the same: "That's what weekends are for."

---

8   Because we had written permission to search the common areas, we did not
     need a search warrant; we purposely did not search any area that was used
     exclusively by the assailant. After recovering the knife box with a picture of the
     knife on the front, bloody clothing, and bloody paper towels, we had sufficient
     physical evidence for arrest and prosecution.

It became apparent to me, over the years, that there were good bosses and bad bosses. The good bosses showed an interest in their subordinates, recognized accomplishments, praised in public and criticized in private, and tried to make things easier instead of harder. The bad bosses just cared about numbers and stats, hoping to impress the higher-ups in an attempt to set up their next promotion. It reminded me of the tales of the old Pony Express, where a mail carrier would ride their mount almost to the point of death, then jump on a fresh horse and repeat the process until arriving at their final destination. During the short time I was there, I saw good agents come and go, unable to bear the burden of a never-satisfied supervisor.

There was a veteran agent on our squad who defined the category of "The Careerist." This is the person who seldom works cases; rather, they want to be *involved* in cases. This way, if the investigation is successful, they get their participation trophy. If it goes sideways, they distance themselves and move on to something more promising. Later in my career—when I was working major cases that involved entire squads being assigned to a high-profile matter—I would refer to these people as "professional caddies." They were always there to suggest a club or opine on which way the green broke but would never step up to actually swing at the ball. These were the people who never authored an arrest warrant or applied for a search warrant but were eager to be included in the arrest or the search—especially if press cameras might be present.

To Connolly's dismay, several months after joining his squad, I informed him I planned on trying out for the office SWAT team. When I mentioned it to him, his disapproving expression said it all. "Why do you want to do that? Aren't you busy enough?" He didn't get it. I had been on the Branford Police Department Special Response Team and enjoyed it. I now had law enforcement experience, was in top shape, and a crack shot. It was a natural fit, something exciting to do with similar-type agents. The head of the Alexandria team was a former original member of the vaunted Hostage Rescue Team, headquartered at Quantico. As I had aspirations of one day applying to HRT, this was a natural stepping-stone in the process. As our team was small and lived in the shadow of the larger Washington Field Office SWAT team (which lived in the shadow of the even larger HRT), I wanted in. The team was often called upon to effect the arrest of the most dangerous fugitives our office had located, plus sometimes used to augment a larger-scale operation in the region.

You might think it would be beneficial to have a SWAT team member as part of your criminal squad. Having this asset made Connolly's life easier when drawing up operational plans for arrests and high-risk search warrants. But his thinking was that the two-days-a-month mandatory training, plus the random call-out, negatively impacted his squad's productivity. Ray—too blinded by his quest for his coveted "stats"—failed to see that the office was required to have a fully manned, competent SWAT team. To retaliate for this marginal drain on my time, every month during my two mandatory training days, Connolly would assign me additional cases. But, stubbornly, I enjoyed the SWAT training and occasional call-outs too much to give it up.

In 1987, a rumor started that the Alexandria Division was going to be absorbed by the colossal Washington Field Office, or WFO. It made sense logistically, as many of our cases overlapped the administrative border of the Potomac River, generating all sorts of extraneous paperwork. It was not unusual to spend an hour putting together a package of documents, requesting an individual be interviewed or a lead followed up, then wait weeks for it to be addressed, just because the person or place was in WDC. It was maddening, when it would have been so much easier to simply drive over the 14th Street bridge and handle it in a few hours.

WFO had approximately six hundred agents supported by a huge clerical and technical staff all crammed into a crumbling behemoth of a building. This drab concrete fortress was inconveniently located beside the odoriferous Anacostia River in a nasty corner of Southwest DC appropriately named Buzzard Point. On the bright side, it offered plenty of free garage parking.

The criminal work was going to be divided between Buzzard Point and the newly constructed Tysons Corner office, located in a fashionable area of Fairfax County, Virginia. SSA Connolly called a meeting and announced he would be supervising the Tysons Corner criminal squad while a supervisor named Witzgall would be in charge at Buzzard Point. This was not news, as the rumor mill had been in full effect for several weeks, and the word was Witzgall was a solid boss. After Connolly explained that violent crimes and "88s" would be handled in DC and property crimes in Virginia, it was a no-brainer; Dennis and I, even though we both lived in Virginia, opted to work in the Washington office, and so we remained working "91s" together.[9]

There was no way to get to Buzzard Point that did not involve a drive through a rough section of DC, replete with vacant buildings, abandoned cars, and weed-choked lots strewn with scrap metal and junked appliances. On the morning commute, it was not unusual to see the torched shell of a stolen car smoldering on a sidewalk within blocks of the Washington Field Office.

DC, Dennis and I soon discovered, was not like Virginia. Here the robbers would routinely hurdle the counter and rummage through all the teller's drawers in an attempt to get the most money in the shortest amount of time, witnesses and cameras be damned. Because of that, almost every bank in the District had begun to install bullet-resistant glass at the teller counters.

These men were athletes. During our first week, an agent showed us bank surveillance photos of a counter-vaulter defeating a six-foot barrier, grabbing the top lip, and hauling himself up and over the bullet-resistant shield into the teller area. This created quite a stir among the tellers, who were only too happy to electronically "buzz" the robber back into the lobby after he finished making his withdrawal. The guy had already robbed the same bank once before; after that, the bank raised the barrier several more feet.

---

9   "88" was the FBI file designation prefix code for a fugitive case and "91" for a bank robbery.

In the late 1980s, when crack was king, the homicide rate for DC was through the roof. At the FBI, informal office pools were held on Fridays on how many murders would occur over the weekend. To put it in perspective, the number of murders in 2012 was eighty-eight; the year I left it was a jaw-dropping 483.[10] As then-Mayor Marion Barry famously put it: "Outside of the killings, Washington has one of the lowest crime rates in the country." When driving through the "non-tourist" areas, you kept your head on a swivel, car windows cracked open to listen for gunshots. Leaving the building at night, we would sometimes hear gunfire nearby, then plot our path to the highway accordingly.

Our squad was tasked to investigate any violent federal crime, such as kidnapping or bank robbery, in addition to any murder, attempted murder, or sexual assault committed on federal property. Since there is a great deal of federal property in Washington and Northern Virginia—military installations, federal parks, museums and monuments, the airports, and the headquarters of various federal agencies—we had more than enough work to keep us busy.

---

[10]   According to the *Baltimore Sun*, Washington, DC, led the nation in most homicides per capita in cities with populations over one hundred thousand.

Running a firearms "combat course" at Bill Scott
Raceway in Jefferson County, West Virginia. One
of our assigned SWAT weapons was the HK MP-5,
which we had to qualify with every month.

The SWAT team also got to be a lot more interesting after "The Merge." I went from the dozen-man Alexandria Division team (one team leader, three sniper/observers, and eight assaulters) to the WMFO forty-man team with a team leader, an assistant team leader, an EMT, two sniper/observer teams, and three assault teams. It was like moving up to the majors. We now had matching uniforms and top-end equipment. All assaulters were issued their own HK 9mm MP5 submachine guns, Remington 870 12-gauge shotguns, and AR-15 .233 semiauto rifles. We were outfitted with camo fatigues, black fatigues, and olive-gray Nomex flame-retardant jumpsuits, balaclavas, and gloves, in addition to winter gear, rappelling rigs, Kevlar helmets, ballistic vests with hardened ceramic plates, ruggedized radios with custom-molded earpieces, goggles, knee and elbow pads, flash bang grenades, semiautomatic pistols, and other military gizmos and gadgets.

We trained at Quantico two days every month and for one full week twice a year. The Marine Corps has a one-thousand-yard sniper range and a range designed for the 40mm tear gas grenade launcher, and our academy had an Olympic pool, several obstacle or "O" courses, a gas house, a helicopter, and a live-fire house. Like Disneyland for cops. We practiced for all types of scenarios: hostage rescue or deliberate assault of houses, buses, aircraft, subway cars, and motel rooms.

Specialized teams today are the norm, and practically every agency, department, and correctional facility has one. They are called different things: Specialized Weapons and Tactics teams (SWAT), Special Response Teams (SRT), Community Emergency Response Teams (CERT), but they are all pretty much the same cat: highly motivated and specially trained groups of alpha males who are willing to put themselves in harm's way. Men (it is almost an exclusively male roster with rare exception) who are willing to save a life by taking a life. These are the guys who show up when the cops call 911; when "the excrement has hit the oscillating blades"; when there are no other options; when violence or the threat of violence can only be negated and overcome by superior violence.

Not to say that every SWAT assignment was a fugitive arrest or a hostage situation. Oftentimes we were tasked with providing protection to an important government witness who was either testifying before a congressional body or cooperating in a federal prosecution. Once, we were essentially living in the government-rented home of an ex-Panamanian general who was providing key testimony against Manuel Noriega (who died in 2017). For this assignment, small teams took eight-hour shifts around the clock, living with the general and his family in an isolated two-story home on a cul-de-sac in a Virginia suburb. On the days of his testimony, an additional team would arrive to whisk him to and from the Capitol while the rest of us guarded his family.

At the other end of the spectrum, we were also tasked to babysit Vincent "the Fish" Cafaro, a top lieutenant in the notorious New York Genovese crime family. The DOJ put him up in a DC hotel, where he had a luxury suite including a kitchen. Oddly, while my teammates shunned the bespectacled middle-aged man, I was intrigued by him, and we spent most of my time there talking while my teammates watched TV. Having lived in New York his whole life, he was quite familiar with my nearby hometown of New Haven, and he was surprised I knew the names of many of the "players" there. We gossiped about restaurants, gangsters, and mob hangouts. One night when I arrived for my shift, he surprised me with a tray of homemade (hotel made?) lasagna. After we finished dinner, I asked him if he wanted me to give the leftovers to the guys in the other room. His response? "Fuck 'em, I'd rather throw it out. They got the warmth of an open grave." After his testimony against "the Teflon Don" John Gotti, Cafaro entered the Witness Protection Program; his son Tommy had taken out a contract on his life.

The "Red Line Bandit" committing his fourth bank robbery at the Perpetual Savings Bank on Connecticut Avenue in Washington, DC. Back then, bank surveillance photos were taken in B&W film by 35mm cameras, and the images were often too grainy to be of much help.

CHAPTER 5

I n the classic Hollywood bank robbery scene, the bandits rush in, fire a shot into the ceiling or pistol whip the security guard, while masked, gloved men rifle the cash drawers as several more go rushing into the vault. The leader stands at the center, periodically calling out elapsed time from his stop watch.

Our typical bank robbery was not the work of a well-oiled criminal machine but that of a lone subject using a handwritten note to rob a single teller while other customers went about their business.

On a tropically hot July morning in 1989, just after 10 o'clock, a lone black male entered the National Bank of Washington wearing a blue windbreaker with a hood over his head. This drew the branch manager's attention, as the temperature was already north of 90°F. The manager watched as the youth scanned the area where the privately hired police officer was usually stationed; the overtime job went unfilled that day, leaving the bank temporarily vulnerable. So suspicious was his behavior, the manager followed the hooded youngster out of the bank, in hopes of jotting down a license plate. But instead of getting into a car, he casually sauntered down Georgia Avenue.

Two hours later, the same customer returned, still wearing the hooded jacket. Head down, he walked to the lobby station and wrote out a savings withdrawal slip. He then took his place in the lunchtime crowd line and waited for the next available teller. When it was his turn, he slid his slip across the counter, stating, "I need you to do something for me." The note was less subtle: "This is a stick up. I have a gun. Give me all the money."

As soon as the victim teller promptly handed over $2,694, he darted out of the bank, again catching the attention of the manager. She dialed 911, and that was how she and I met. After conducting a neighborhood canvass, an alert agent found the suspect's windbreaker in a subway station trash can less than two blocks away. That was all we had, for now.

Eleven days later, the same unknown subject would pull an identical robbery on the Maryland end of Georgia Avenue, relieving a Citibank branch of $1,425. Because it was the Baltimore Division's "91," we only found this out later. Perhaps disenchanted with the meager haul in Maryland, the "unsub" concentrated all his subsequent efforts on Washington, DC, which meant every time he struck, the case would automatically be assigned to me.[11] He was now "my guy," and once he went on a streak, I would feel the heat.

On Monday, July 24, I started my work week responding to the American Security Bank on Connecticut Avenue. This time, my "unsub" made out his demand note at the lobby table, conspicuously wearing a white T-shirt wrapped around his head while he waited in the customer line. Oddly, this behavior did not trigger any suspicions of the bank staff or customers. He handed the teller a less generic, more ominous demand note: "I have a gun I will kill you. Give me all the money I'm not joking. Thank you." (as written).

Receiving less than he expected, he demanded more, but just then a customer walked in and he panicked, scooped up the money, and left. Although he couldn't help looking up at the security camera as he exited

---

[11]   Unknown subject. The FBI's term for a person's whose identity is unknown.

the bank, the 35mm footage was so grainy and unfocused, it was of little value. His take was only a paltry $988. I expected we would be dispatched to another robbery very soon.

That Friday afternoon at the Perpetual Savings Bank on Connecticut Avenue, he struck again. He now wore a loose burgundy turban and a black Batman T-shirt with the trademarked yellow logo on the front and back. Again, he presented a similarly worded note and jogged off with just over a grand for another clean getaway. However, during our post-robbery neighborhood canvass, a sharp-eyed agent spotted a dark red long-sleeved polo shirt atop a trash container inside the nearby Metro stop: our robber's headgear. This confirmed that our robber was utilizing the Metro to get to and from his targets. The media now dubbed him "the Red Line Bandit."

I had nothing at this point but several handwritten demand notes and two recovered shirts. DNA testing was still in its infancy, and our fingerprint section was having no luck with the notes. The surveillance photos so far were of marginal quality. I had no investigative leads. But my guy was on a roll and didn't look like he was about to walk away from a hot table.

Sure enough, he went right back to work on Monday, waiting until lunchtime to visit another American Security Bank on Calvert Street. Wearing a white nylon "Georgetown" athletic jacket, a white tee, olive drab green shorts, and a pair of black low-cut Reeboks, our "unsub" was observed writing something in the vestibule at the ATM. He next entered the bank and presented his written demand. The teller read his note, then promptly passed over all the currency in her drawer, which only totaled $975. He was unimpressed. "Is that all?" When the teller told him it was, he walked out and took his business elsewhere.

Turning left out of the bank, he walked west and took a right onto Connecticut Avenue. He strode into the Washington Federal Savings Bank and relieved a teller of $2,029. After half a dozen robberies in a month's time, I began to get pressure from upstairs.

The Baltimore Division eventually sent us an interagency communication known as an airtel about their Maryland robbery.[12] Recognizing the same "MO" (*modus operandi*, or "method of operation") and description, I notified Baltimore that our guy was now good for six "91s" in the District. The robber was adept at changing his appearance: he was either bringing baseball caps and tops with him to put on once he left the bank or wearing more than one layer of clothing and discarding his outer layer when he got to the Metro stop. I tacked up a Metro station map next to my desk and began push-pinning each robbery while calendar-charting their dates, days, and times. I also began cataloging each item of clothing worn (but not discarded), along with a collage of the photocopied notes and surveillance photographs. I was tired of simply responding to robberies; I was now looking for a way to get a jump on the next one.

The following Monday at lunchtime, the bandit was back for his eighth job, this one at the Sovran Bank on Wisconsin Avenue, and his biggest score to date: $5,197. To speed up the process, I drove to FBIHQ and asked the photo section to use the best surveillance stills for a "wanted" flyer, which I then distributed to every bank along Connecticut Avenue. I met with each bank manager and asked that they instruct their tellers to activate their alarm before the subject actually made his demand if they even *thought* he was in the bank. This would start the film cameras rolling before the robbery took place and give DC patrol cars a head start to the scene.

I approached my boss, SSA Dana, and requested permission to set up an "ad hoc" task force from various agencies. I wanted to assemble plainclothes personnel from the Washington Metropolitan Police Department, the Metro Transit Police, and our office agents, in addition to Baltimore FBI agents and their Montgomery County Police Department counterparts. My plan was to target select Metro stations and try to intercept our robber, either before or immediately after his next robbery.

He was intrigued but skeptical. Truthfully, I had reservations about the plan myself. Trying to profile and identify a young, slim, dark-skinned

---

[12] An airtel was a written communication (no longer in use) used for routine matters that did not carry the urgency of a teletype.

African American male in Washington, DC, could be a needle-in-a-haystack exercise. When pressed to explain how we would be able to identify the subject, I was forced to admit we would be "winging it." We only had a partial thumbprint that our lab had been able to retrieve from a demand note. I hoped we would be able to identify viable suspects, ask for their cooperation, take their photograph, then take inked impressions of their thumbs. Realistically, this would be a long shot; secretly I was hoping we might get lucky, make contact with our guy, and that his nervousness and lack of cooperation would flag him.

SSA Dana was not persuaded. No doubt, he was mulling the possible fallout from complaints of racial profiling and civil rights/privacy issues. My "plan B" pitch was that if the Red Line Bandit committed another robbery and headed for a Metro station, we would be in an excellent position to catch him *before* he changed clothes. He mulled it over for several long seconds, gazing upwards, then finally made a command decision in true FBI management fashion: he would think about it and get back to me.

At lunchtime on Monday, August 14, I cruised the Connecticut Avenue corridor in bumper-to-bumper traffic. Over the FBI car radio came the broadcast: "91 live."[13] The Red Line Bandit had visited DuPont Circle and walked off with $1,229 from a Perpetual Savings Bank. I had already driven past the bank that day and previously had provided flyers to the manager. I pounded the steering wheel in frustration, turned on my car's blue strobes and siren, and nudged my way through downtown gridlock to the bank. Arriving first, I put out a detailed description, noting some differences in his appearance.

My mood was improved by the return of my partner, Dennis, from his annual Cape Cod vacation with family, and improved more with SSA Dana's decision to proceed. "Denny" began gathering Polaroid cameras, fingerprint kits, and updated copies of the Bandit's expanding clothing portfolio. I called up the FBI's Baltimore Division, the Metro Transit plainclothes division, and the DC Metropolitan Police Department's

---

[13] Bank robbery in progress.

"ROPE" Unit, requesting their assistance in a coordinated effort to blanket Metro stations in the NW corridor the following Monday.[14] I was playing the odds: out of the eight robberies to date, five had been on a Monday, including the last four.

The briefing took place in the Metropolitan Police Department auditorium, and I was nervous. I was thirty-two years old, younger than most of the law enforcement personnel assembled before me. I brought everyone up to speed, explained what we hoped to accomplish, and made sure a cross-section of personnel was assigned to each selected Metro station.

The Red Line Bandit had never used the same Metro station twice. As every bank but one had been along the Red Line in the NW quadrant of the District, I assigned our groups accordingly. Because I wanted one WDC MPD officer, one FBI agent, and one Metro Transit officer in each group, we were only able to cover nine of the seventeen stations. I would stay mobile and respond to any station that thought they had a promising suspect. Over the next few hours, I was called to different locations but was disappointed each time. I requested everyone hold tight until 3 p.m., at which time a decision would be made.

The good news? The Red Line Bandit hit the Perpetual Savings Bank at exactly 2:12 p.m. The bad news? He changed his MO and now chose the NE quadrant of the District to rob his ninth bank.

I was hanging out at one of the stations along Connecticut Avenue with a young plainclothes Transit detective when the call came. We all realized our guy had struck again but nowhere near where I expected. I ordered everyone to remain in place, hoping our guy might be spotted leaving one of the surveilled Metro stations. The description went out: "Black male, young, thin build, wearing a black Boston Celtics

---

[14] The "Repeat Offenders Project"—referred to as the ROPE unit—was an elite plainclothes unit that targeted career criminals, both those wanted on active warrants and those determined to be actively committing street crimes.

baseball cap, gray Georgetown short sleeve sweatshirt, blue jeans, and black Reebok sneakers."

My FD-430 later described the robbery in standard FBI-speak:[15]

> Unsub entered captioned bank and stood in customer line. Upon being called to victim teller's window, unsub presented a demand note (attached) written on the front of victim bank's withdrawal slip. Unsub was given currency ($4,788), which he then placed in a red plastic "Up Against the Wall" bag which had a white drawstring at the top. Witnesses advised this bag appeared to contain clothing. Unsub then ducked under one teller-line rope, jumped over another, then ran from bank. Witnesses stated unsub ran out of the bank, ran around the rear of the bank, and was last seen on foot heading toward the Fort Totten Metro Station.

The young Transit detective informed me we weren't far from the bank, so I invited him along for the ride. As we sped to the location with lights and siren, he got on his portable radio, ordering the train at the Fort Totten station stopped until our arrival. He cautioned me the train would not wait long, as it had to keep within a tight schedule. At each intersection, I would slow just enough to confirm we could pass through safely, me looking left while my temporary partner watched right, calling, "Clear!" in a desperate attempt to shave seconds off our response time. After zooming through one intersection, we heard behind us car horns and the screech of brakes, cut short by the metallic crunch of a collision. He glanced back, proclaimed it "minor," and we charged ahead.

Skidding to a stop in the fire lane, we leapt from my car and sprinted up the stairs to the elevated platform. My companion flashed his badge to the conductor, who was waiting for us, then opened his door. Guns drawn but tucked in close to our beltlines, scanning, we shuffled our

---

[15] An FD-430 was an FBI form used to succinctly document any bank or federal credit union robbery, larceny, or burglary.

way through each car, shoulders touching. Most passengers looked at us wide-eyed in fear. Like a mantra, we kept repeating: "Everything is fine, just remain seated." Car by car we went, until we got to the end. Skunked again.

Back on the platform, deliberating what to do next, we heard radio chatter that a suspect was in custody nearby. We ran back down the same stairs and spotted several patrol cars down the street. Jogging over to them, we saw a black man wearing a black Boston Celtics cap, sitting on the curb, hands cuffed behind his back. I immediately knew the prisoner was far too old to be our guy. I introduced myself as FBI and informed him he fit the description of a bank robbery suspect. The apparently homeless man admitted he had just found the cap behind the station; he pointed out the hat was so new, it still had the licensing tags attached. He said he found the hat and some clothes in a plastic bag on a bench, and volunteered to show us where.

Sure enough, there was a red plastic "Up Against the Wall" bag, sitting on a neatly folded pair of blue jeans. I asked the uniforms to kindly uncuff our guest, and then I bagged and tagged the cap, bag, and jeans before heading back to the office. There I went right to the yellow pages and found three locations for the store, which specialized in "urban" clothing and accessories. The most promising store was right near the Judiciary Square Metro station.

As soon as the store opened the next day, Dennis and I located the manager and showed him the surveillance photos. Surprisingly he said the suspect looked familiar and had been in several times. After I mentioned a cash reward for information leading to his arrest, he recalled that one of his female clerks had waited on him. The girl was not as certain as the manager, but volunteered that he was a free spender, picking out the nicest items without glancing at the price, one time tipping her a fifty-dollar bill. I handed out my business cards and reminded them there was a substantial reward that could be collected anonymously.

The following Monday, August 28, the ad hoc task force again set up at various Metro stations along the Red Line. Again, a few temporary detentions, but no one fit the bill. By 3:30 p.m., the surveillance was shut down. I still held my breath, but there were no robberies the rest of the day. I felt certain there would be one the following day and trolled Connecticut Avenue for hours, but nothing. The following Monday the banks would close for Labor Day, so I asked if we could saturate the Red Line for Tuesday. Request denied. Between scheduled vacations, ongoing assignments, and the sporadic nature of the Red Line Bandit, I couldn't argue the point. I had no clue what schedule my nemesis was now following. I was more worried my guy might never reappear; with a homicide rate averaging more than one a day, there was a distinct chance the serial robber might have been murdered, wounded, or (less likely) arrested for a different crime.

On Monday, September 11, the Red Line Bandit resurfaced—again in the NE—and for the first time would fail to rob a bank. Finally he had chosen a teller with common sense who recognized that she was protected by bullet-resistant glass. She read his demand note, looked at the youth to see if he was in fact armed, and did not comply. The flabbergasted robber rustled his plastic bag, but the teller decided it contained only clothing. He next tapped on the glass with his finger while telling the woman, "Miss, Miss, I'm not joking—Miss, Miss, this is not a joke."

To her credit, she replied, "I'm taking care of it," then calmly walked away. This is where her common sense left her. Incomprehensibly, she failed to activate her alarm or alert others. Worse, after returning to find he had left, she simply waited on the next customer. Only after her manager happened by did she decide to mention the incident.

The next day, agents from the Baltimore FBI office called to say they were responding to a robbery in Chevy Chase and suspected it was the Red Line Bandit: "Dark blue baseball cap, dark tank top, navy blue shorts with gray sweatpants-style shorts beneath, black Reeboks (no socks), and a thick, gold herringbone neck chain." I already knew that he would quickly change his clothes, board the Friendship Heights train, and saunter off a few stops later to blend into pedestrian traffic.

Then my pager went off—with a 911 added to the end of the number; I immediately called back. The manager at the "Up Against the Wall" store breathlessly told me he thought the Red Line Bandit had just left his place after dropping $300 on various items. I asked our dispatch center to alert the Metro and Transit police at Judiciary Square to swarm the area, but it was already too late. He was in the wind once again.

En route to "Up Against the Wall," we learned from the Baltimore office that the Bandit's take that day had been over $7,000—his largest haul so far. When we arrived, the manager apologized and informed us he was unaware that our "person of interest" had been inside his store. He had been working in his back office and only spotted our suspect leaving.

When we debriefed the cashier, she noted that the customer paid for his clothing with "banded money," twenty-dollar bills still bundled with the paper denomination strap. Our subject had bought an ornate black leather belt but also wanted it in brown, so while he waited, she telephoned the Springfield, Virginia, store; the clerk said they would have it delivered to the DC store. The cashier told us he did not want to leave a name and phone number, but said he would return the next day to pick up his order.

The following day, we checked out a bland surveillance van from the motor pool and eventually found an ideal parking spot close to the front of the store. Dennis and I, along with a first-office agent fresh from the academy, settled in for the wait. Nothing happened. We returned. At the end of day two, I told the manager we would not be able to come back. He agreed to discreetly call 911 if our guy returned.

A few days later, while we were out covering leads on other cases, I asked Dennis to swing by the store again. The manager ushered us into his office and closed the door. He told us that he had overheard his cashier confide to a coworker that she had seen the robber in her neighborhood over the weekend. She was sure it was him, as he was wearing all the clothes he had purchased during his last shopping spree.

I nonchalantly wandered around the store until I ended up by the cashier. I made some small talk with her, mentioning the reward had been increased. After first scanning the store, she whispered she thought she had seen the robber over the weekend at the intersection of 14th Street and Ogden. Not only did she recognize the clothing he was wearing, but he also gave her an "up nod" when they made eye contact.

Dennis and I were on 14th Street two days later. The community was almost exclusively African American, and we stuck out like two golf balls on fresh asphalt. After driving the area to get a lay of the land, we parked near the firehouse on 14th and Newton. The firemen took a look at our photos, but no one recognized our subject. Undeterred, we went to every chicken shack, music store, barber shop, nail salon, rib joint, tattoo parlor, and beeper business in the "hood." No one thought the person in the photos looked the least bit familiar.

Eventually, we began approaching people randomly on the street. Not a single person showed the slightest sign of recognition. It was hot and muggy, and we were sweating our asses off; then, to make things worse, it began to rain. Dennis suggested we make our way back to the firehouse and wait out the downpour.

As we stood under the awning, bouncing ideas and theories back and forth, Dennis noticed a pair of black males a block away, walking toward us. One had on a white "Georgetown" jacket, while the other was wearing a black ball cap and a white "Guess" jacket and blue jeans. Both appeared to be late teens or early twenties. "What do you think?"

"Hard to say," Dennis replied, squinting. "They need to get a little bit closer."

Before any decision could be made, the pair unexpectedly turned down Newton, a residential side street. Dennis jogged to the end of the intersection as I bolted into the firehouse and quickly explained we needed some volunteers to help with an arrest. The lone fireman on duty said that everyone else was out on a call, which meant he couldn't leave the building.

"I need you to call 911 and tell the police we need assistance; two white FBI agents are going to try to arrest two black guys on Newton Street."

I ran from the firehouse and back to the street to join Dennis, then we both started jogging down the block. Just then, the pair appeared from between parked cars and started to diagonally cross the street. Guns drawn and pointed down-range, we stepped out into the middle of the street, about ten feet behind them.

"FBI!"

They jumped simultaneously and turned around, wide-eyed.

"Both of you, get down on the ground right now!" They looked at us, then at each other, then back at us. I knew this was that critical moment when a suspect decided what action he would take: surrender, fight, or flee. Advancing, making direct eye contact, pistol extended in both hands, I barked: "Get on the ground right now, or I WILL shoot you!"

Those were the magic words, as they lowered themselves slowly to their knees. Noticing the hesitation of my prime suspect, I commanded him to get facedown in the street, training my pistol directly at his face. To my relief, he complied, albeit reluctantly. Dennis stood guard while I made my approach. As I came up from my guy's rear, the suspect turned his head to my side, and I was finally able to get a clear, close look at his face.

Bingo! As soon as our eyes met, I knew we had finally nabbed the Red Line Bandit. I began beaming even while I was cuffing him behind his back. I couldn't help it.

"Dennis, your cuffs."

With one hand aiming his weapon and eyes fixed on our suspects, Dennis adroitly handed me his handcuffs. At this point, we could all hear the sirens converging on 14th Street. I handcuffed the second suspect and began my pat-down while they remained prone. Confident that neither was armed, I joined Dennis. Both men now began to get mouthy, claiming we were making a big mistake and they had done nothing wrong. Then the cursing started. I was so elated, all I could do was point at my prize and gloat: "I got you! I got you! And you know it!"

As we were escorting our prisoners up Newton Street, a detective car pulled up. I asked him to cancel the 911, thanked him for the response, and continued back to the firehouse.

Our suspect identified himself as Dean Jones—which turned out was not his real name—and his companion as his cousin. While we waited for our fellow agents to arrive, I brought the cousin into a private room to see if he was involved. Belligerent, he claimed he knew nothing of any bank robberies and that this was all a huge mistake on our part. I relieved him of his jacket, and he stormed off.

Back at the office, "Dean Jones" was quickly identified as Oral Dean General. Within hours, a search was conducted of his girlfriend's apartment, where a "NY Yankees" ball cap described in one robbery was located and the black "Batman" T-shirt from another was found, in addition to his black Reebok tennis shoes and several purchases from "Up Against the Wall." Meanwhile, at a search of his father's home, the olive-drab cargo shorts were discovered. When shown surveillance photos from several of the robberies, his heartbroken father confirmed the pictures were indeed of his son. Within weeks, several tellers also identified him during a live lineup.

On September 21, the *Washington Times* reported that a twenty-year-old man had been arrested as a suspect in a series of bank robberies. If convicted, an FBI spokesperson explained, he would face a maximum of twenty years in prison. What the spokesperson failed to mention was that General was facing a twenty-year sentence for *each* of the robberies or attempted robberies he had committed. Therefore, his exposure was actually 220 years.

Years later, I learned just how lenient our court system could be. Despite two prior felony drug arrests, Oral Dean General walked away from prison after serving less than three and a half years. Perhaps the judge took into account that on every demand note in which he wrote, "I have a gun. I will kill you," he was polite enough to add, "Thank you."

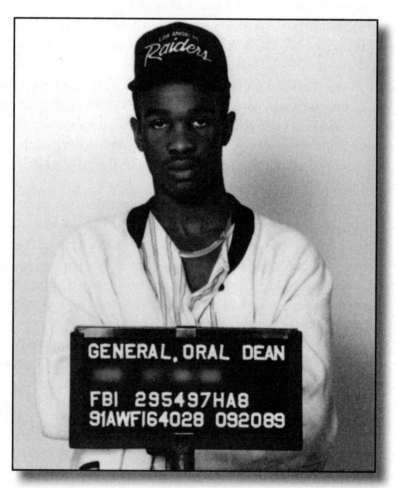

Mug shot of the "Red Line Bandit" taken the day of his arrest. Note that General is wearing the Raiders ball cap, the white Guess jacket, and the herringbone gold chain described in several of the robberies.

CHAPTER 6

Despite my frantic work schedule, I was still homesick. My mother had been diagnosed with cancer when I was fifteen. She bravely battled the disease for several years, first conceding a kidney, then undergoing a total hysterectomy, until finally embarking on a painful and prolonged series of ultimately unsuccessful chemo and radiation treatments. Twelve days after I turned twenty-four, she died on our living room couch, surrounded by her extended family. I was her only child. My dad later remarried and was still living in Connecticut, as did every aunt, uncle, cousin, and friend of mine.

I had made it clear when applying to the FBI that I wanted to work close to my home state. The six hundred-mile round-trip drive from Virginia was too long for weekend trips, and I was using all my vacation time to attend weddings, funerals, and major holidays. I also realized that when the Alexandria Division, my first office assignment, was absorbed by the Washington Field Office, my hope of a New York transfer was dashed. The merge essentially *became* my transfer, even though I remained in the same area. Although I was seeing someone from the office, I was still single and felt that if I was going to make a move, now was the time. As I was approaching the start of my fifth year, I needed some answers.

One day I asked my supervisor when I could reasonably expect to be transferred to New Haven, my designated OP (Office of Preference). He made a phone call to HQ, and when he hung up I could tell it wasn't good news. "Ten to fifteen years."

Because the NY field office was massive, and the city a prohibitively expensive place to reside, many agents opted to live in Connecticut so they could raise their children outside the city and have them attend a Connecticut school. They bought homes in Connecticut, commuted to the city, and put their name on the "wish list" for New Haven. When they finally had enough seniority, moved up the OP list, and got their ticket punched, they didn't have to move their family; they just changed their commute to either Bridgeport, New Haven, or Hartford, as New Haven had offices in all three cities.

The look on my face gave it away. "You're going to leave, aren't you?"

I nodded but said, "Yeah, but not today." Later that same day, I began making calls to apply for an inspector's position at the Chief State's Attorney's Office in Connecticut.

Competition was fierce, because while anyone with seven years of law enforcement experience (three as a dedicated investigator) could apply, more than one hundred applications were received for each opening. Luckily, some of the prosecutors and inspectors whom I had met while working as a courtroom sheriff remembered me and were now in a position to help. One week after my capture of the Red Line Bandit, I drove up to Connecticut for an interview at the Office of the Chief State's Attorney. A New Haven courthouse inspector I knew while I was in college was now one of four chief inspectors at the Chief State's Attorney's Office. We were happy to see one another when I arrived for my interview, and I knew it would not hurt my chances of obtaining a job offer.

While I had the advantage of an FBI background, I felt my age could work against me. Some of my competitors had more years of service than I was years old. Moreover, the open position was in the Economic Crime Bureau, and I had no background in either accounting or white collar crime.

Two months later, I received an early Christmas present: the offer of an inspector's position with the Office of the Chief State's Attorney. I immediately began my resignation process with the Federal Bureau of Investigation.

While I was sorry to be leaving an organization I had worked so hard to join, I was excited about returning home to family and friends. Many times over the last three years I had thought about what would happen if I was wounded while responding to a bank robbery or during a SWAT op. Who would be at my bedside at the hospital? My partner Dennis? My girlfriend? This fact troubled me and made me think hard about where I wanted to live while engaged in dangerous work. While anxious, I was buoyed by finally returning to my home state; now I would no longer miss out on the birthday parties, baptisms, anniversary celebrations, graduations, and holidays. While I had always enjoyed these rituals growing up, I did not realize how much I cherished them until I was living far from home.

On January 26, 1990, I was sworn in as an inspector by
Connecticut Chief State's Attorney John "Jack" Kelly.

On January 26, 1990, I was officially sworn in as an inspector, assigned to the Economic Crime Bureau. Located at the time in the blue collar town of Wallingford, the Office of the Chief State's Attorney occupied a three-story brick building on the grounds of the former Wallace Silversmiths Factory, built in 1856. My boss, John "Jack" Kelly, oversaw the twelve state's attorney's offices that covered the state by county.[16] I had first met

---

16   New Britain, which was formerly covered by the Hartford State's Attorney's Office, was added in 1998, bringing the total to thirteen state's attorney's offices.

Mr. Kelly when he was a young prosecutor in the New Haven courthouse. Always affable, he was now forty-three years old, with eighteen years of prosecutorial experience under his belt. He enjoyed a favorable reputation within the law enforcement community and was never afraid to try a case before a jury and slug it out with any high-priced defense attorney.

Along with the Economic Crime Bureau, the Chief State's Attorney's Office at that time also housed the Organized Crime Bureau, the Statewide Prosecution Bureau, and the Medicaid Fraud Control Unit.

I was now assigned to the Economic Crime Bureau, staffed by a supervisory assistant state's attorney, two prosecutors, a supervisory inspector, three other inspectors, a forensic accountant, and a secretary. After a quick tour of the building and introductions to the staff, I began working cases under the tutelage of Supervisory Inspector Mike DiLullo. I came clean as a newbie right away, expressing some concern about my lack of experience with financial crimes and confessing that I sometimes had trouble balancing my own checkbook. He assured me that every economic crime case—no matter how complex it appeared—was just a straight-out larceny and that all one had to do was "follow the money."

Mike DiLullo was a patient and knowledgeable boss who helped me navigate the complex world of economic crime. He answered to a chief inspector, of which there were four at the time, each with different oversight and responsibilities. All the chief inspectors were former Connecticut state troopers, but over time that would change, and eventually all the chief inspectors would hail from local Connecticut police departments.

Eventually I was exposed to a wide variety of financial crimes: Ponzi schemes, investment frauds, advance-fee loan schemes, embezzlements, defalcations, forgeries, check-kiting scams, misappropriation of funds, criminal impersonation, identity theft, and so on. Financial planners, attorneys, brokers, real estate agents, and bookkeepers often succumbed to the temptation of money entrusted to their control and care. Some initially stole with the intent of paying the money back; others believed they were too clever and would never get caught.

While some of the crimes I investigated were simply crimes of opportunity, others defied logic. Some of the perpetrators were well-respected, successful professionals who appeared to have their lives in order. But due to some vice (gambling, exorbitant spending habits, greed), they could not resist stealing money, which is the simplest way to define economic crime.

I investigated a financial planner who was employed by a large insurance company in Hartford, known at one time as "the insurance capital of the world." The guy had a number of Hartford public school teachers as clients and had convinced several of them to put some of their earnings into an investment scheme by utilizing forged variable annuity contracts. Enticed by inflated interest returns, four teachers provided $126,000 over the course of several months.

The insurance agent was a degenerate gambler. I located a convenience store owner whose business was near the suspect's rural home. When shown his photo, the owner said this individual would routinely purchase hundreds of instant scratch-off lottery tickets at a time, then park his car by the dumpster, furiously scratching away at the tickets and tossing the losers in the trash. He would then return and cash his "winners." Amazingly, he would repeat the vicious cycle until he either ran out of tickets or money. He would do this several times a week—sometimes twice a day—all in an insane attempt to repay the defrauded teachers, who were squawking about their missing money. Due to the amount of money involved and his lack of any criminal record, the mathematically challenged investor was ordered by the court to make full restitution to the victims and given a suspended sentence with probation to guarantee his compliance.

In July 1992, I was assigned an interesting case, where instead of investigating a cunning business professional, I was instead investigating a professional con man. At the start of 1992, advertisements began appearing in small neighborhood newspapers in the poorer sections of Hartford for unsecured personal loans and first, second, and third mortgages by contacting Financial Agent John Mills at Webber Financial. Interested parties would call a telephone number, which was answered by a professional-sounding woman, who would then take a message. "John Mills" would then call back the interested party and agree to come to their home, where the new client was asked to fill out a very basic loan application, provide a copy of their W-2 or pay stub, then pay $250 either in cash or by personal check. Mr. Mills explained that within three to ten business days they would have their loan. Instead, what each client received was a letter from Webber Financial explaining, "The lending institution that we have been dealing with has filed for bankruptcy… which means we are temporarily out of business."

However, there were several problems: there was no Webber Financial; the woman answering the phone was employed at an answering service; and John Mills was actually Paul A. Scavitto. The fifty-five-year-old con man also answered to Howard Williams, Paul Moore, Fred Blocker, Paul Scott, and other aliases, and had previously founded other shell companies including Northeast Mortgage & Loan Company, American Financial Consultants, Anderson Corporation, and GEM, Inc., while plying his advance-fee loan scams, first in Massachusetts, then in Connecticut.

When Scavitto first came to the attention of Massachusetts authorities, instead of prosecuting the case as a criminal matter, the Bay State naively opted to sue him on behalf of 112 victims. Scavitto was ordered to pay back $27,625, of which he simply paid a portion, then promptly moved to the tony town of Glastonbury, Connecticut, and restarted his con.

After executing search warrants for telephone records at the answering service and Scavitto's home telephone, I had estimated he had been in contact with over three hundred potential victims. As most victims had since moved, declined to be interviewed, changed telephone numbers, or did not fall for the scam, I was only able to take sworn statements from twenty victims.

Upon arresting Scavitto at his trendy condo, I had him taken to the Glastonbury Police Department to be processed. Wanting my own Polaroids for the file, I ordered him to first face me, then turn for his profile picture. After that, I told him to face me again for another set of pictures, this time without his hat. Momentarily confused, he looked at me. I then deadpanned, "The rug. Take it off." He glared at me, then removed his obvious hairpiece.

Scavitto was charged with larceny in the second degree and criminal impersonation.[17]

*John M. Bailey Jr. in his natural environment,
holding court with the press.*

The chief state's attorney in Connecticut is appointed for a five-year term by the Criminal Justice Commission, which is made up of six lawyers

---

[17]   Ten years later, my office would arrest Scavitto again on ten counts of second degree larceny, but with a twist: he took out ads in local newspapers and offered a discount to seniors who needed their furniture repaired or reupholstered. Once again, he collected thousands of dollars and failed to deliver.

appointed by the governor. In 1991, Jack Kelly's term expired and he was replaced by Richard Palmer, a former federal prosecutor.

Although I had little direct contact with Palmer, he was impressive: knowledgeable, personable, and charismatic. He was popular with everybody in the office, from the secretaries who had a crush on him (he was single and had Hollywood "leading man" looks) to the prosecutors and inspectors who worked for him.

Naturally I was flattered—and relieved—when I was temporarily transferred from the Economic Crime Bureau to a new, exciting assignment. In early 1993, Chief State's Attorney Palmer assigned me to a hand-picked team of detectives assembled to investigate allegations of corruption within the Connecticut State Police and the Hartford Police Department.

State Police Detective Ramon Valentin and Hartford Police Officer Jose Morales were both assigned to a state-run narcotics task force. Morales was called "Little Joe" to distinguish him from a senior Hartford officer with the same first and last name. Valentin was nicknamed "Smoke" for his habit of disappearing from the office "like smoke." The two became partners, then friends, then criminal co-conspirators. Their enterprise involved shaking down or outright robbing drug dealers, primarily those who trafficked in heroin. They were quite successful, and the booming heroin trade in Hartford became their personal ATM for the next two years.

Valentin, though married at the time, was romantically involved with the daughter of a well-known Hartford Mafia soldier named Louis Failla. She conspired with the two budding entrepreneurs to steal dealers' drugs and money; she then sold the drugs to another dealer, and all three split the proceeds. Valentin simultaneously took up with another woman, who introduced him to the on-again/off-again girlfriend of a heroin dealer, who began providing Valentin and Morales with information. The two began by burglarizing the dealer's home and stealing his drugs and money. Emboldened by the easy scores, they targeted this poor sap repeatedly until the guy began driving forty miles from Hartford to New Haven just to deposit his cash in a safe he installed in the home of relatives.

Always privy to the dealer's plans because of his informant/girlfriend, Valentin and Morales simply drove to New Haven in their undercover car. Conspicuously wearing their ballistic vests and department badges on neck-chains, they demanded entrance to the home. Carrying their portable police radios and waving papers they claimed were a search warrant, they walked directly to the closet where the safe was kept, lugged the safe to their state car, and drove off. Later they threw the safe—minus its $38,000—off a bridge into the Connecticut River, which the CSP Dive Team would later recover.

Desperate to find a way to avoid the vexing rip-offs, the dealer bought a new Corvette, rented a storage unit, and began keeping his money and product inside the car. Not to be outmaneuvered, Valentin and Morales ambushed the "street pharmacist" in his motel room, beat him up, tied him up, and took his jewelry and keys. They then used his keys to steal his leased Cadillac from the motel parking lot, unlocked his storage unit, then stole his red 'Vette—and the $48,000 he had stashed in it. Incredible as it seems, Valentin flagrantly drove the leased Caddy for several weeks, while Morales tooled back and forth to work in the stolen Stingray.

While Valentin might have thought cheating on his mistress was a good way to expand his circle of informants, it apparently did not sit well with his paramour. In a pique, she promptly blabbed to someone what Valentin and Morales had been up to, who in turn parlayed the intel, which eventually triggered our investigation. Although Louie Failla's daughter and Valentin soon reconciled, the damage had been done, and the wheels of justice were set in motion. When pressed, the scorned mistress realistically evaluated her options and provided riveting testimony, even producing photos of Valentin flashing bundles of stolen currency in their expensive Newport hotel room during a Rhode Island weekend getaway.

While Connecticut has the statutory authority to convene a grand jury, this prosecutorial tool is very seldom used. However, on March 29,

1993, an unusual one-man "grand juror" was convened, eventually hearing testimony from seventy-two witnesses and examining 185 exhibits over the course of eight months. I was brought in to help coordinate the interviews of witnesses, including the traumatized heroin dealer who had since moved back to Puerto Rico to avoid being victimized by the pair of rogue cops. Teams of Hartford detectives and state police investigators conducted interviews, took statements, and executed search and seizure warrants across the state in an effort to identify victims and witnesses as well as secure physical evidence that would be used to prosecute a half dozen police officers. My role was to act as liaison with the prosecutors who would be filing charges and trying those responsible.

Ultimately, Morales, Valentin, and six other defendants—including two New Britain police officers—were arrested for kidnapping, robbery, burglary, drug sales, larceny, witness tampering, and perjury. As the grand juror investigation was winding down in Hartford, things starting winding up in Rocky Hill.

While I was occupied with "Smoke" and "Little Joe," Chief State's Attorney Palmer was nominated to the Connecticut Supreme Court. The state's attorney of the Hartford judicial district, Jack Bailey, forty-eight, was making moves.

John Michael Bailey Jr. was ambitious and politically connected— the brother of US Rep. Barbara B. Kennelly and the son of the late Democratic State and National Committee Chairman John M. Bailey. Jack, upon graduating from law school in 1971, spent four undistinguished years in private practice before being hired in 1975 as an assistant state's attorney, assigned to a small courthouse in East Hartford. One year earlier, Bailey had run for the Democratic nomination for the Second Congressional District seat but lost to Chris Dodd. Remarkably, in 1978, Democrat Governor Ella Grasso nominated Bailey for a judgeship despite his young age, but he was rejected when the Connecticut Bar Association withheld its endorsement due to his lack of experience as an attorney. He was an unsuccessful candidate for the chief state's attorney job on two more occasions, until finally Governor Lowell Weicker submitted his name to the Criminal Justice Commission.

Lynne Tuohy's story in the *Hartford Courant*, dated May 12, 1993, offered the following analysis:

> This is clearly a banner year for Bailey, who is president-elect of the 11,000-member Connecticut Bar Association. And for the Bailey family — long a powerful political force in Connecticut — it represents yet another prominent position in government service to bear the Bailey name.... It is ironic that Bailey's political savvy, owing in large part to his political roots, finally secured for him the job he has applied for three times in the past eight years. Bailey often has had to fight off the notion he is "too political" to be a viable candidate for a job that is supposed to be apolitical, and can involve the investigation of political corruption.... Next week, Bailey's staff will nearly quadruple to 371 employees. He will oversee a budget of $20 million and set policy for the division that prosecutes all criminal cases and oftimes conducts complex criminal investigations.

If John M. Bailey Sr. was "Vito Corleone," then his daughter, US Congresswoman Barbara Bailey Kennelly was "Michael," and John Bailey Jr. was "Fredo." Jack Bailey's career aspirations far outweighed his qualifications. While recognized as a political heavyweight, he was known to be a legal bantamweight. Plea bargains were his specialty, as defense attorneys were now indebted to him, and Bailey would not need to test his hand at actually trying a case.

He confided to coworkers that his dream job was to someday be the director of the FBI, which would later cloud his decision-making skills during a critical time in his career—and mine. He enjoyed playing the role of the Hollywood-portrayed high-powered attorney: sunlamp tan in the winter, custom-tailored suits, stylish ties, and his trademark

White Owl cigar clamped firmly between his capped teeth in true FDR fashion. He was an unabashed fan of law enforcement, and eventually would customize his state car with so many electronic accessories, he was indistinguishable from a first responder.

One of the first problems Bailey needed to fix as the chief state's attorney was the long-running issue of bail bondsmen, fugitives, and the state's collection of forfeited bonds. The way it worked, a person would be arrested, and if the charges were serious enough or the person was considered a flight risk, bond would be set by the court. The defendant then had three options: stew in jail, pay a bondsman, or put up cash or property to be returned upon resolution of the case. As most people who find themselves at the wrong end of the law are usually not flush with cash (big drug dealers being the rare exception), they end up using a bondsman.

It was—and is—much like the insurance business. Bail bondsmen play the odds, hoping most of their clients show up for court. If not, the bondsmen are on the hook for the entire amount. Meanwhile a warrant is issued, and the bondsman is responsible for delivering the fugitive to the authorities—either themselves or by hiring bounty hunters—or, as they preferred to be called, "bail enforcement agents" or "recovery agents."

If the fugitive still avoided capture, the bondsman had to pony up. That was when things got crazy, as every judge had their own way of addressing this. The way it was supposed to work was the bondsman had six months to bring in their client. If unsuccessful, they could pay half the outstanding bond or roll the dice and get a thirty-day extension. If they could not produce the body after thirty days, they had to make good on the entire nut.

When I was a deputy sheriff, I would often see a bondsman ask the judge for an extension, claiming that his "people" were hot on the heels of the absconder and just needed "a little more time." Whether or not this was the case, the more time that passed, the better the odds the fugitive would be recaptured—oftentimes by simply being arrested for a new crime.

Even if the fugitive got away clean, the bondsman's relationship with either the judge or the prosecutor went a long way toward resolving the debt. I witnessed many compromises when the bondsman would detail how much work, time, and money had been spent in an attempt to locate the fugitive, and the court would then reduce—or even forgive—repayment. These dramas were played out daily in every courthouse across the state and took up precious time of prosecutors and judges.

Bailey's own prosecutorial career had never been much to speak of. But he turned out to be a consummate bureaucratic tactician. Thus as one of his first acts, he proposed to the legislature a new unit for his office, essentially a clearinghouse: one centralized bureau designed to track and collect forfeited bonds. The bondsmen were initially unhappy with the change and challenged the proposal through their well-financed lobbyists, angered by the fact that they believed police departments were not aggressively seeking those who failed to appear in court. They were mollified when a provision was added to establish a dedicated squad of inspectors who would be tasked to find these fugitives.

To pay for this new efficiency, a percentage of all forfeited bonds would be returned to the Chief State's Attorney's Office for the purpose of maintaining a bond forfeiture unit of prosecutors *and* a fugitive squad of inspectors. This turned out to be a major cash cow for Bailey, while bolstering his public image through the press.

Bailey sat for an interview with C. Bryson Hull, a young reporter from the *Herald Press* of New Britain in early 1997:

> "Collecting bonds was one of the worst jobs a State's Attorney could have," says Bailey. A six-month wait for the money, combined with the tedium and inconsistency of negotiating with every bondsman, convinced Bailey to develop the Bond Forfeiture Unit for the sole purpose of collecting the bonds of fugitives. Thus far, Bailey says the unit has returned $1.5 million to the state's coffers.

And since the bonds were providing new funds, Bailey decided to reinvest them into financing the recapture of the running accused. The operating budget of the fugitive squad is funded entirely by the ceded bond dollars.

"We use the bad guys' money to go after them," says Bailey, whose office keeps one-third of the forfeited funds.

The article was telling: Bailey had big plans for his agency and was adept at playing politics to make things happen to his advantage. But it also revealed that he was intent on honing his public image as a crime fighter and would capitalize on the successes of his office to make this happen. This would have dire consequences for both of us in the future.

Everyone was satisfied with this arrangement, the bill passed, and I applied for the brand-new Fugitive Squad.

CHAPTER 7

A t first I was a squad of one. Not one of the other fifty inspectors showed interest. Most of them were retirees and quite comfortable working indoors on a daytime schedule. I applied, interviewed, and was accepted by default.

I was next summoned to Bailey's palatial office to be officially told I had gotten the position: the first member of the newly formed Fugitive Squad.

One could not help but notice the various awards, plaques, and pictures that festooned the walls of his corner office. Almost all the framed photographs were of Bailey and some high-profile politician shaking hands, some older photos in black and white, the newer ones in color. He noticed me studying a vertically arranged fantail of a dozen navy-blue Flair marker pens on his desk. He asked me if I knew that years ago, J. Edgar Hoover ordered the agents in his FBI Lab to create a signature blend of blue and black ink. Bailey explained Director Hoover exclusively used this unique ink when signing documents, so there was no doubt his signature was authentic. It was apparent Mr. Bailey held Director Hoover in very high regard. After congratulating me on the new assignment and some small talk about my prior experience in the FBI, he concluded by telling me he planned on adding more inspectors as the Bond Forfeiture Unit collected more money. That was welcome news, as I didn't relish the idea of undertaking dangerous work all by myself.

While in the FBI, I had been involved in several fugitive investigations, but primarily my time was divided between bank robberies, violent crimes, and SWAT. Now I would be devoted to just fugitives, which was a perfect fit for me, as I could now utilize all my skill sets. I loved fugitive investigations and everything about them. Any investigator worth his or her salt was tested by these cases. Best of all, the subjects were already wanted felons. Step one in a criminal case is to determine if a crime was in fact committed; step two is to determine who committed the crime; step three is to find and arrest them; and step four is to prove it. In fugitive investigations, steps one and two, and maybe even step four (if they absconded before sentencing while on bond), are already done; your job is step three: finding and arresting the culprit who does not want to be found.

Fugitives from justice are willing to go to extreme lengths to avoid detection, and each case was unique. A moneyed professional would try to elude authorities in a much different way than a foreign-born "undocumented person" or a local drug dealer who only knew one "hood." The best fugitive hunters have perceptive interview skills, an aptitude for research, legal acumen, street instincts, the patience of Job, and the luck of the Irish.

There was no shortage of work. One recent study suggests that at any given time, there are approximately three million active criminal warrants outstanding across the country. Police and sheriff's departments are overwhelmed and can barely keep up entering the wanted persons into the National Criminal Information Center (NCIC) database. Currently, Connecticut has approximately forty thousand active arrest warrants, meaning these are unserved, outstanding warrants. Translation: at any given time, there are about forty thousand Connecticut residents actively eluding authorities while they live their lives as wanted subjects. This does not make for a particularly safe society. The number is likely far higher, as oftentimes I found that unless a department considered the fugitive dangerous, or believed they had left the area, they simply held the warrant "in-house" and did not bother entering the information into the NCIC. While a few departments actually had a "warrant squad," most did not, with resources always stretched thin. They assumed the fugitive would eventually be rearrested on a new charge, then they would simply serve the warrant once the absconder was back in custody.

My first assignment on the Fugitive Squad was to learn how each of the state's twelve judicial districts handled FTA (failure to appear) cases. After several weeks of phone calls and visits, I learned two things: (1) no two of the state's attorney's offices handled failure to appear cases in exactly the same way, and (2) all of them resented my interest.

Because my office administratively oversaw the other twelve state's attorney's offices, there was built-in suspicion. Anytime I attempted to determine how the judicial districts handled outstanding warrants, the first question always asked was "why?" It was a sore subject apparently, as no one seemed exactly sure how the problem should be addressed or fixed. The state's attorney's office staffs did not want to be bothered dealing with this nagging issue, but at the same time they resented any "outside" help.

The relationship between the Office of the Chief State's Attorney (OCSA) and the dozen state's attorney's offices could be testy. There has historically been resentment due to the fact the main office administratively oversees the other offices, with budget, staffing, and vehicles doled out by OCSA personnel. As every courthouse across the state has always been typically overwhelmed with too many cases and too few employees, there is always pushback. Add to this the fact the state's attorneys and their staff perceived the OCSA as top-heavy and bloated.

When I was first hired, there were four bureaus: Statewide Prosecution, Economic Crime, Medicaid Fraud, and Organized Crime. When Jack Bailey arrived, he envisioned an organization more like his vaunted FBI, so he expanded the size and scope of his office, eventually creating the Bond Collection Unit, the Fugitive Squad, the Gang & Continuing Criminal

Activity Bureau, the Witness Protection Unit, the Asset Forfeiture Unit, the Workers' Compensation Fraud Control Bureau, the Welfare Fraud Control Bureau, and the Elder Abuse Unit. This did not particularly sit well with the other state's attorneys, who saw the budget pie being cut into smaller and smaller slices while Bailey's office grew.

I soon discovered a bountiful buffet of unserved warrants at my disposal. While local police officers and the state police were limited to their own warrants, I was able to draw from all the state's attorney's offices across the state, as well as all the state probation warrants. Most probation offices were relieved to see someone take over the search, as it was one less chore for them to manage.

Because so little attention was devoted to this issue, I was initially able to locate many of these fugitives safely from behind my computer just by searching the NCIC database. These were the easiest apprehensions: some were already locked up under an alias or were incarcerated out of state; then it was simply a matter of telephone calls, faxes, and computer entries. However, after I had worked my way through the low-hanging fruit, the work would become more challenging—and more dangerous.

With this new assignment came a new boss: Chief Inspector Dave Best, who had come along with Bailey from the Hartford State's Attorney's Office and needed something to do. Dave and I hit it off well from the start. He was a big "gear and gadget" guy, always thumbing through a police equipment catalog or gun magazine. He had big plans for the new squad and rightly predicted we would soon be able to hire and equip several inspectors with the monies brought in by the two prosecutors tasked with collecting forfeited bonds. Dave was usually insightful when it came to office politics but only to a point; his crystal ball would later fail him during some critical times. While Dave and I became friendlier as time went on, our relationship would later be tested.

Once established, I sent letters to all the state's attorney's and probation offices, inviting them to forward any of their outstanding felony warrants to our office. Word then quickly spread through the small community of bail bondsmen, who were only too happy to have free help saving themselves money. Within weeks, referrals began pouring in.

While I was going around amassing fugitive cases from across the state, I received a call from FBI Special Agent Rich Teahan. Apparently the word had gotten out. The FBI had a fugitive task force headquartered in New Haven, and he invited me to visit, suggesting it might be mutually beneficial for me to join their "team," as they were already doing the same work. After receiving permission from Chief State's Attorney Bailey via Dave Best to make the visit, I was given the address of the off-site.

An "off-site" is what they call a law enforcement office that is not open to the public. This one was a flat-roof, one-story brick building with white-painted iron burglar bars on the windows, set back at the end of a fenced-in parking lot secured by an electronic sliding gate. After honking my arrival, the gate chugged open and I parked.

The room was an open, fluorescent-lit rectangle with a random assortment of government desks, file cabinets, and chairs. Detectives and troopers occupied several of the desks, and the FBI coordinator, Special Agent Ralph DiFonzo Jr., had his large wooden desk in a corner overlooking the room. Ralph was hard to miss; he was loud, big, and burly with abundant hair everywhere but on his head.

SA DiFonzo said that if it could be agreed upon by our respective agencies, he would like me to become part of the Connecticut Fugitive Task Force (CFTF), a compound unit composed at the time of him, three FBI agents, three state troopers, one detective from New Haven, and another from Bridgeport. Each member was responsible for acquiring fugitive cases from their respective agencies, as well as being available to assist team members in surveillances and apprehensions.

SA DiFonzo seemed eager to get me on board and had a well-rehearsed pitch touting the fact that "his" office could provide me a rental vehicle (which I did not need), overtime pay (which by contract I could not receive), and limited federal arrest authority (which was redundant as I already had statewide arrest authority). He noted their various successes, quoting the number of fugitives captured since the task force began and making it a point to say—as every member was volunteered by their agency—that he recognized it was important that each guy keep their department's brass happy.

I said my goodbyes and headed back to report to Best and Bailey, who decided I should join the CFTF. Although apprehensive about throwing in with a group of cops I knew little about, I also recognized that I was currently playing a very dangerous team sport without the benefit of a team.

This lesson would soon be painfully reinforced. One of my friends from the WFO SWAT team, SA William "Billy" Christian Jr., would be shot to death on May 29, 1995, while conducting surveillance during a fugitive investigation. Acting on a tip that Ralph McLean—wanted for ambushing and shooting several police officers in DC and Maryland—was supposed to meet an ex-girlfriend in Greenbelt, Maryland, SA Christian and others were conducting a surveillance from a middle school parking lot nearby. McLean, sensing a trap, conducted countersurveillance and ambushed Billy, approaching his car from behind and shooting him through his car window. Responding surveillance team members pursued McLean to a nearby mall parking garage, where—during the course of a gun battle—the fugitive committed suicide with his own weapon. Billy was forty-eight years old and married with four children.

Starting in the '80s, task forces became a popular way for law enforcement agencies to address certain criminal justice issues. The concept of combining federal, state, and/or local departments was a cost-effective and creative way of tackling vexing crime problems. This approach was applied most often to narcotics trafficking, fugitives, and gangs, and would later expand to identity theft, cold cases, computer crimes, sex trafficking, and child porn. It made sense, as various participants enjoyed certain advantages others did not. The federal agencies had large budgets and nationwide authority, while the state and local departments knew the players and geography, in addition to having established informants. As long as the egos could be kept in check and the bosses kept happy, it was an effective crime-fighting strategy. Many a career was catapulted by being assigned to a successful task force.

After filing the requisite paperwork, I was photographed for my new federal ID, given a pager and raid jacket, and assigned a desk in the bunker. I had already opened dozens of fugitive cases, so I lugged those in with me and set up shop. I was officially assigned to the CFTF on January 27, 1994, four years after leaving the FBI, and I was eager to prove myself once again.

On traditional work days, my hours were 8 a.m. to 4 p.m.: poring over reports, reviewing criminal histories, prioritizing investigative leads, updating notes, making and returning telephone calls, and using po-lice, public, and private computer databases. Some days there was also fieldwork, such as surveillance of an address the subject was known to frequent or a drive-by to run license plates of vehicles. Sometimes it was a trip to a parole or probation office, a correctional facility, or a courthouse where you would review and photocopy files. The more information you could assemble on a fugitive, the greater your chances of finding him or her in places that had previously been overlooked.

However, the other type of workday was the early wake-up. Everyone knows the prime time to find a person at home is when they are sleeping. Too early, and they might still be out; too late, and they might be gone for the day. The task force would assemble at a predetermined location at an ungodly hour, then drive caravan-fashion to the target location accompanied by at least one marked patrol car.

Once the fugitive has been located, he or she must be captured. Preparation of a safe and practical arrest plan is essential, as car chases and gunplay are frowned upon by management. My time spent on SWAT teams was a tremendous help when it came to making these preparations. First, the residence must be scoped for primary and secondary points of entry, location, and type of doors. Intelligence must be gathered as whether to expect children or dogs; you must also assign an entry team and perimeter team, determine what breaching equipment will be re-quired, identify the nearest emergency room in case things go sideways, and so forth. The pre-raid briefing would include copies of the fugitive's photo, physical description, criminal history, propensity for violence, and any other relevant information. The more dangerous the subject, the more critical it was to properly prepare for the raid.

Whoever's guy it was formed the plan, but not everyone on the task force was as meticulous. The hacks would simply pass around a picture, then pick three or four of their buddies to make entry while the rest of us were expected to surround the house. End of plan. From that point forward they were flying by the seats of their pants. More often than not, they would drag the group to a "dry hole," some address where the fugitive may (or may not) have stayed at one time. Sometimes when we got there it was just a vacant house or an address that failed even to exist. Anyone who screwed up this bad could expect to get their balls busted by the whole raucous crew at the group breakfast that always followed a raid, successful or not.

My first raid was on a Waterbury outlaw motorcycle club member. Twenty-six-year-old Alan R. Gamache, already a full patch member of the Helter Skelter motorcycle gang, had managed to accumulate three failure to appear warrants on five charges, all felonies: assault in the first degree, interfering with a police officer, carrying a dangerous weapon, threatening, and possession of narcotics.

The Helter Skelter Motorcycle Club was well known to Connecticut law enforcement. One of Gamache's fellow club members, Anthony "T-Bone" Sinchak, was arrested for the execution of thirty-nine-year-old Kathleen Gianni, shot twice in the head after club members suspected she might be a police informant. Waterbury, the ninth largest city in New England, was a blue-collar city on the skids. It once boasted a large industrial base and led the country in brassware production. Now it was a mishmash of various ethnic groups: Blacks and Puerto Ricans, immigrants from Italy, Canada, Portugal, Cape Verde, Lebanon, Ireland, Lithuania, and Albania, as well as Orthodox Jews. It was like Brooklyn, minus the cool restaurants.

One thing that made fugitive work challenging was that you never had home field advantage. Veteran police officers become quite familiar with their beats, not only the geography but the residents and pulse of the neighborhood. But because we covered all 169 cities, towns, and burgs in Connecticut, we were always the visiting team. Even though I grew up in New Haven and knew my way around, I did not have the intimate knowledge of the neighborhoods a beat cop would. I knew it would be a challenge to find a Waterbury guy if Gamache decided to go underground in his hometown, especially with a network of supportive club brothers and family members.

After getting the referral package, which included Gamache's initial arrest reports, booking sheets, mugshot, fingerprint card, and copies of his rearrest warrants, I went back to flesh out his file. This involved obtaining copies of any police reports in which he had ever been mentioned, all prior detention and corrections files, and all vehicle registrations in his name. Fortunately he had used a bondsman, which yielded his most current personal information.

Professional criminals don't live like your average citizen; they tend to move around a lot, change vehicles—and aliases—often, and go through life paying cash. This makes tracking them a difficult and time-consuming challenge. But they all have one thing in common: the need to sleep somewhere. If I could zero in on whom they were likely to stay with, it was much easier to find them.

After a careful review of my notes, I learned a few new things: (1) Gamache listed his emergency contact as his sister; (2) his girlfriend posted his bond; (3) he listed his occupation as a "Sheetrocker" (a drywall installer). Contacts at the Waterbury Police Department told me his girlfriend was a "dancer" at Mr. Happy's Cafe, advertised as a "total adult entertainment bar." I learned that while his girlfriend still performed there, Gamache had not been seen since he skipped bail. His bondsman—who had his own clients on the lookout and was eager to help—confirmed this.

Eventually I was able to track the girlfriend to an address in Waterbury, a quiet residential side street in a blue-collar neighborhood. After a few drive-bys, I knew any type of prolonged surveillance would prove near impossible. Most of the residents parked in their driveways, so any occupied vehicle parked on the street stood out immediately. I could not risk spooking him and driving him further underground. I was able to learn, through contact with the US Postal Service, that his girlfriend was receiving mail at that address and was supposed to be living in the third-floor apartment of the three-family home.

I finally decided to call the sister, posing as an old friend of Gamache, under the guise of offering temporary work. In 1994, cell phones were just starting to replace pagers (commonly called beepers). I called the sister from my flip-phone and made the call near heavy street traffic. This way, whenever I was asked a troublesome question, I could buy myself some stall time, claiming I could not hear over the noise. If things started going badly, I could always feign a bad connection and just drop the call.

"Hi, I'm trying to reach Al."

"Who's this?"

"Greg. He gave me this number a while back and said I could reach him this way. Who's this?"

"This is his sister. He doesn't live here. Why do you need him?"

"I used to see him all the time at Mr. Happy's. We worked a Sheetrock job a while back, and I'm running a condo job now and need some help. Is he still around?"

"I don't know. I haven't heard from him in a while."

"OK, well if you hear from him, give him my number. I can throw him a few weeks of work, cash under the table, if he's interested."

"Like I said, I haven't heard from him in a while. Let me have your name and number just in case...."

Within an hour, my cell phone rang. I ran out of the office to get outdoors before I took the call. Luckily it was a windy day, as it gave me several chances to tell him we had a bad connection and I couldn't hear him well. Every time my new buddy Al asked me a personal question, I would either talk over him and ask if he could hear me or just tell him I was having trouble hearing him. I finally told him to give me a number where I could reach him that night, and I would call when I got home. He did. Now I just had to hope the number would come back to his girlfriend's address.

It did, and now it was a matter of assembling an arrest plan and moving fast. That same afternoon, I notified Ralph DiFonzo that I was ready to attempt my first capture as a member of the Task Force and wanted to assemble an arrest team for an early morning raid in Waterbury. I gave a briefing that same afternoon to the task force members, then made contact with the Waterbury Police to expect us in about fourteen hours.

After a restless night chasing sleep, I finally got up at 4 a.m. to prepare for my debut. As a courtesy to my then fiancée (later my wife), I soon developed the habit of putting all my gear and work clothes downstairs to avoid turning on lights and waking her. After giving another quick briefing to the Waterbury patrol officers, we began the drive to our target location.

The parade of cars going to "hit a house" always reminded me of a funeral procession. In the predawn hours, we wove our way down empty streets until the final block, at which time we would roll up with headlights off. While a few team members positioned themselves at opposite corners of the house, I led the entry team up the outside wooden staircase to an enclosed porch on the third floor. I felt certain the creaking on the stairs from the queue of bodies would wake the entire house. Fortunately, the outside porch door was unlocked; we carefully spread out within the enclosed porch as I loudly announced our presence.

After several seconds of loud knocking, a female voice eventually asked who was there. She peeked around the drawn door shade, then said she needed some time to get dressed. This was obviously a stall, and I began kicking the bottom of the door, practically shattering the window glass. She was trying to buy time. I announced we would break down the door, ratcheting up my kicks. She opened the door slightly, and we pushed past her and fanned out through the small apartment. We quickly found Gamache at the bottom of an interior flight of stairs, hopping on one leg attempting to step into his skinny jeans. He was handcuffed at gunpoint, then brought back up the stairs so we could throw his jacket over him—it was a bitterly cold morning.

In their bohemian bedroom, we found the standard biker home decor: wax skull candle—check, Mardi Gras beads—check, oversized medieval knife—check, oversized dildo—check, police scanner—check, black leather vest with three-piece club patch—check. We also found— fully loaded and ready to go—a 12-gauge shotgun, a .357 magnum revolver, and a 9mm semiautomatic pistol loaded with Black Talon ammo.[18] Naturally, the girlfriend claimed she owned all the firepower.

After the evidence was seized and Gamache secured at the Waterbury Police Department, we headed back to the off-site before going out for breakfast.[19] The group was upbeat, and I was basking in the glow of success. Several of the guys asked how I got onto Gamache in the first place, and I explained the sequence of telephone calls leading up to the raid. Ralph, who was taking this all in from behind his desk, waited for a lull in the conversation.

"Don't forget: just because you hit a home run today doesn't make you a home-run hitter."

I realized right then that Ralph was stingy with praise and didn't want anyone getting too big for their britches. His sour comment should have been a warning that he was the kind of petty bureaucrat who was not about to share the spotlight; he wanted a pecking order in place. That's when it first occurred to me that signing on with his team might have been a mistake.

That suspicion was soon reinforced when I invited Ralph and some of the guys from the office to attend my "surprise" engagement party.

At the time, I was getting serious with a young lady who had recently moved from New York to accept a position as an illustrator at the Weekly Reader company. Vilma and I had dated exclusively for a few years, until I decided it was finally time to get married.

I wanted the engagement to be special, so I confided my plan to Terry, a close friend, and asked her to plant the idea in Vilma's head to give me

---

[18] Introduced by Winchester in 1991, the hollow point ammo was known for its unique construction and sharp petal-shape expansion post-impact, making for a gory and devastating wound.

[19] I would arrest Gamache two more times: four months later for theft of a firearm, possession of a firearm with an altered serial number, and larceny in the fifth degree (based upon the guns we seized), then again the following year for jumping bond on those charges.

a surprise birthday party. Then I would surprise *her* by dropping to my knee and proposing in front of the surprised guests. Terry thought it was a wonderful idea, and she and the unwitting Vilma immediately began preparations.

On the night of the party, my former Branford Police Department sergeant, Ray Wiederhold, and his wife, Cecilia (a prosecutor at the DCJ), took us out for dinner. When it came time for dessert, Vilma suggested we head back to my place, as she announced she had secretly prepared a birthday cake. I knew from Terry that in a few minutes, my neighbor Jeff was going to ring my doorbell and ask for my help; he would tell me there was some type of rowdy party at the clubhouse, and would I mind going over there with him? On cue, he came in and did a credible job with his lines. I made my apologies, said we would be right back, and left with Jeff—while Vilma and the other couple snuck out the back door and raced ahead of us behind the condo buildings to the clubhouse.

Jeff made nervous small talk, explaining how he felt more comfortable having a cop with him and so on, until we arrived at the clubhouse. One could see the decorations inside, but it was dim and quiet. I mentioned to him it certainly wasn't very noisy now, as we entered the foyer.

"Surprise!" yelled the group in unison, and I went through the act of first being shocked, then stupefied. The whole works: hands on top of my head, then on my hips, looking from face to face, overreacting the way people do when thrown a surprise party.

The party was well attended. Guests included my father and stepmom, my aunt Lucille, and my eleven-year-old godson, Brian, as well as his brother Jay and their parents. It was a wonderful mix of family, friends, and colleagues. Off to the side, at their own table, were Ralph DiFonzo and his wife—an FBI civilian employee—as well as several task force members and their dates.

After the kisses, handshakes, and awkward man-hugs were exchanged, I sat in front of the clubhouse fireplace and began opening my cards and gifts. The cops remained at their own table, drinking lustily and overtalking everyone, with Ralph presiding at the head. I knew when I got to the end, it would be my time to pull off the big surprise and drop to my knee. But first, Ralph had to upstage me with—of all things—a gift of an inflated sex doll and a lifelike dildo, together with a small box and a note he insisted I read out loud:

"To Mister Bailey's Bum-Boy

Altho [sic] you are not a real agent yet ever

If you drink from this cup you could be clever

I believe some day you may be the Man

But for now my friend you will always be our Girly Man"

It was signed "Linda & Da Man."

I then opened the small box and found a coffee mug embossed with the FBI seal. Ralph sat there, grinning stupidly. I smiled, raised the mug in a mock toast, then turned around, and placed it on the mantle over the fireplace. I then put the dildo into the mug head first so the ball bag jiggled up and down. Some of the cops found it hysterical, but Ralph sat there, arms folded across his chest, glaring.

After I opened my last gift, I stood and gave a thank-you speech, congratulating the guests for being able to keep a secret so well. Then—as I could see Vilma was hurt I had not mentioned her—I announced while this was indeed a great surprise party, the real surprise was on everyone *but* me. There were confused looks as I explained how I had approached Terry several months ago, asking her to convince Vilma to throw this surprise party for me, just so I could surprise *her*.

Vilma looked confused, but when I got down on one knee, it dawned on her—and everyone else—exactly what was going on. I asked her to marry me, and she tearfully accepted.

Attending the one week Survival Awareness In-Service with some members of the Connecticut Fugitive Task Force: (from left to right) Inspector Steve Kumnick, author, Bridgeport police officer John Cueto, Connecticut state trooper Rob Berry (deceased), New Haven police detective Joe Greene (kneeling).

CHAPTER 8

Sometime later, Steve Kumnick was hired as the second Fugitive Squad inspector. I had met Steve in 1993 when he was a Hartford homicide detective and we were both assigned to the police corruption grand jury. With a thick head of hair and even thicker glasses, he was not physically imposing, but he was a creative and tireless investigator with a mind like a computer. We were good partners. He was a welcome addition to the task force, as he knew Hartford inside and out, something the task force had been missing.

Steve and I were getting fugitive referrals from the Connecticut state's attorneys, probation and parole offices, and bail bondsmen from across the state. These fugitives were genuine badasses, accused or convicted of multiple felonies—mostly crimes of violence—who had already jumped bail and would pull out all the stops to elude capture.

Many of our investigations led to promising leads outside Connecticut, which was particularly important to Ralph, who needed to justify his budget and manpower to his bosses. Any case that went across state lines required federal authorities to obtain what was called a UFAP (Unlawful

Flight to Avoid Prosecution) warrant to arrest a defendant wanted on state charges. As the FBI is limited to investigating certain, or "special," federal crimes (hence the title "special" agent), the agency cannot involve themselves in common crimes that are simply state felonies. Thus the filing of the federal charge of Unlawful Flight to Avoid Prosecution, or its lesser known twin brother, Unlawful Flight to Avoid Confinement (reserved for those already convicted). The feds must show probable cause the fugitive has likely left the state in an attempt to elude capture by presenting a sworn affidavit articulating these facts to a federal judge or magistrate.

Once a state prosecutor authorizes nationwide extradition, a federal affidavit may be submitted to the jurisdictional US Attorney's Office. After prosecutorial review and approval, it is sworn before a federal magistrate or federal judge. When this process is completed, the FBI is then authorized to look for the fugitive anywhere in the world. At the time, 133 FBI-led fugitive task forces had been formed across the country, utilizing the UFAP violation to justify their efforts.

Everyone in the law enforcement and legal community understood this was a formality, because as soon as the fugitive was apprehended and returned to state custody, the federal charge was dismissed and never prosecuted. It was just one more statistic the FBI could show Congress to keep the money flowing.

Kumnick, always an independent thinker, would periodically question Ralph over why we had to jump through these extra legal hoops, when we could simply reach out directly to a local or state police agency and have them make the arrest in their state, without having to wait for the UFAP approval. As our state warrants were already entered into NCIC with nationwide extradition authorization, any law enforcement officer could legally make the arrest without a UFAP warrant. An exasperated Ralph would then explain that each FBI task force was constantly evaluated on how many UFAP warrants were filed, so obviously, the more the better. Even if we learned a fugitive likely had fled Connecticut and then returned, we were supposed to *still* file a UFAP warrant. This made absolutely no sense to any of us.

Ralph inexplicably insisted that *only* FBI agents file the UFAPs in federal court, something that was not done on other task forces. What this did was create a scenario where the case investigator was not the ultimate author of the affidavit; rather, he was to relay the facts to an FBI agent, who then filed the UFAP warrant as if it were *his or her* investigation. It was cumbersome, time consuming, and legally unnecessary, as all the investigators in the office were federally cross-designated and could therefore file their own affidavits in federal court (like they did on other task forces). But it turned out there was a method to Ralph's madness.

All federal agents are subject to periodic performance evaluations: subpoenas served, search warrants executed, arrests made, potential economic loss prevented (PELP), assets seized, informants registered, UFAPs filed, and so on. There's a form called an FD-515 that records these accomplishments. The FD-515 comes to assume an undue importance in the life of an agent trying to shine; you want as many "stats" as you can get in your personnel file. It impresses your supervisor and improves his or her performance rating, which is also good for you; plus you can earn a one-time bonus or even an annual salary bump. Having played this game in the FBI, I explained all this to Steve.

Even if a fugitive were to remain at large, a filed UFAP still counted as a documented accomplishment. As the UFAP stats piled up, agents cashed in: Incentive Awards (a one-time bonus—usually $1,000 added to your check plus a letter of recognition in your file) or a Quality Step Increase (QSI). A QSI is a faster-than-normal within-grade increase (WGI) used to reward employees at any general scale (GS) grade level who display high-quality performance. Ralph became a very popular guy within his office as he doled out these stat-enhancers to his favorites. By allowing agents to file UFAPS on cases not assigned to them (inspectors' cases), they were able to list those UFAPs on their FD-515s as their accomplishments, which often translated to financial gains. With the increase of press releases and ensuing publicity surrounding the jump in arrests, Ralph's stock within the New Haven Office began to rise as well.

Kumnick and I were temporarily popular, because most of the referrals we got from the state's attorney's offices involved serious offenders who fled the state—or even the country—resulting in the filing of many UFAPs. We sent leads everywhere, resulting in fugitives being apprehended in New York, Massachusetts, New Jersey, Pennsylvania, West Virginia, Illinois, New Mexico, California, and Canada. Each time, Ralph would insist on our preparing an affidavit outlining what the charges were, why the defendant knew he or she was wanted for those charges, and probable cause to show the defendant likely fled the state to avoid prosecution. Ralph then assigned the warrant application to another agent, who in turn lodged a UFAP complaint, swearing to the veracity of the information before a federal magistrate or judge.

This was good for Ralph and for our group's continued funding and support. We had become a profit center within the state's attorney's office as well. My office was getting a third of all forfeited bond money; soon the Bond Forfeiture Unit collected $1.5 million in bonds, of which our office received $500,000. For his part, Bailey was thrilled with the results of his brainchild (both the funding *and* the captures) and was not shy about taking credit in the press.

By December 1994, Bailey felt flush enough to create four new inspectors' positions, increasing our squad number to six, and buy us some new equipment and vehicles. The first hire, John Healy, was forced upon us by the fact that his younger brother was Chief Inspector Paul Healy. John had been an unpopular inspector at the Waterbury State's Attorney Office and was looking to leave. He had the reputation as the type of guy who would argue with a stop sign. With aspirations of being a supervisor, John recognized the addition of more inspectors would create the need for the supervisor's position he craved. The other three "outside" hires were Bob Hughes, a Naugatuck deputy chief; Jose "Joe" Marrero, a Spanish-speaking Hartford detective; and Steve Freddo, a South Windsor detective.

Now that it was a real squad, regulations required a supervisory inspector be selected to oversee it; at the start of 1995, the position was posted. Only two inspectors applied for the spot: me and—no surprise—John Healy. As John had spent less than two months assigned to the squad, I was officially promoted by Bailey on February 17, 1995. In hindsight, I was the perfect candidate for the position: smart enough to train, organize, and supervise five fugitive inspectors, and dumb enough to believe our work actually mattered.

I was now responsible for assigning cases to the inspectors, along with the administrative duties associated with my new position: equipment allocation, probationary evaluations, training, time and attendance records, annual evaluations, and so on. Now recognizing how insecure Ralph was, upon receiving the promotion I assured Ralph that it was still his task force, but I asked to be kept in the loop on any assignments he gave the inspectors. While Ralph was the coordinator at the task force, he was still only a special agent, not a supervisor. Initially, this worked well enough. However, working for Ralph wasn't easy. He was an odd guy, always needing to be the center of attention. He reminded us—more than a few times—that he was a hostage negotiator, fingerprint examiner, police trainer, criminal profiler, interview and interrogation instructor, *and* a master man hunter.

Ralph also tended to overshare, and it seemed the larger the audience, the more cringeworthy the stories. He talked openly about his drinking and once described how, as an agent assigned to the Los Angeles office, he hit a city bus with his bureau car, drunk midday. He bragged of how he got out of his car, flashed his badge at the driver, then drove home and passed out on the couch, where he was later found by the local police. According to him, this embarrassing episode precipitated his transfer to New Haven. Why he felt the need to boast of it was anyone's guess.

One good thing about conducting law enforcement activity as a federal agent was that when someone said "FBI!," you got a lot more respect and cooperation than you could expect as a local cop. When we would arrive at an address, most residents were indifferent—or even confrontational—with the local police in uniform. When these same people realized federal agents were involved, their tone—and attitude—changed. Because federal agencies have an almost limitless amount of money (with less accountability), damage done to doors was soon repaired and informants were paid quickly—and handsomely—for information.

As a result, the state and local guys on the task force adhered to the rules when it came to making forcible entries into homes, whereas the federal agents under Ralph's direction were far more cavalier. While we had to photograph the damage, write a report, submit an explanatory memo, and file a payment requisition, the feds simply handed the aggrieved landlord or tenant a business card and told them to submit a receipt for damages.

Of course, this card could be overplayed. One day we went out to the notorious crime-ridden, poverty-stricken Newhallville neighborhood of New Haven, known simply as "The 'Ville." New Haven Detective Joseph "Mean Joe" Greene, a veteran task force member, asked several of us to give him a hand looking for a local gangbanger who had missed a court appearance. We arrived at a shabby house with the front door displaying the scars of prior forced entries, frayed threadbare carpeting on the creaky staircase leading to the second floor, and the blended odor of cooked cabbage, stale reefer, and fast food.

The fugitive was not there, but a couple of his crew were hanging out, playing video games on a large-screen TV. After fanning out through the apartment and frisking the two young men, we seated them on the couch, first tossing the cushions. One of them wondered out loud if we needed a warrant to be there.

"We don't need a fuckin' warrant to be here asshole!" Jerking his thumb toward his vest, Ralph continued, "Read these numbers: F-B-I!" The teen looked up at me smirking. Even he knew the difference between numbers and letters.

The rule in Connecticut—as most criminals knew—was that when entering a residence without a search warrant, officers needed sufficient probable cause to believe (a) that the premises belonged to the suspect *and* (b) that he was likely there. If he was at the home of someone else, it was considered "a third party residence," and thus required a court-authorized warrant. Of course, Ralph's way of thinking was this: if we caught the person—even if we lacked the necessary search warrant—the court was not about to release the defendant, so what was the harm?

Obtaining a search warrant was indeed a time-consuming process: one had to draft the affidavit and warrant, have it approved by a prosecutor, then the author and a second affiant needed to bring it to a state judge, swear to the facts and sign it, then file a copy with the Clerk's Office, before finally being able to execute it. Because I worked for the State of Connecticut and had taken an oath to uphold the laws, I made sure my inspectors secured a search warrant whenever the requirement applied, just like I always had.

This quickly became a point of conflict with Ralph. We frequently clashed when I would instruct an inspector to obtain a warrant. Ralph would openly ridicule the suggestion, dismissing the idea as unnecessary and overly cautious. He claimed that he had never once had to obtain a search warrant in his entire career. This corner-cutting habit turned out to be a trademark in his slipshod approach to law enforcement protocol.

Fortunately, most people usually complied with our request to enter and search their home. If not, I would inform them we would secure the house and send someone to apply for a warrant. I also made sure to explain that if we then found the fugitive on the premises, two people would be going to jail, not just one.

Due to the inherent danger of the work, we seldom worked without a partner. Kumnick and I often paired up, as did the other four inspectors. So I was taken aback when I arrived for work one day to find Ralph had unilaterally decided to partner each inspector with a local officer or state trooper.

Ralph had opted not to notify me ahead of time, and I called him on it in private. He claimed he wanted more integration and felt it would be good for morale. Had he told me he planned on doing it, I would have likely agreed. Administratively, it made things harder for me. When the inspectors were partnered up, I only had to keep track of two or three pairs of guys working. If paired with other CFTF investigators, I would have to keep track of five inspectors running around the state on any given day—or night. I told him, as I was directly responsible for the management of the inspectors who already *had* assigned partners, that he should have notified me as a courtesy. He replied that he didn't need to check with me before making administrative decisions and added (gratuitously) that if I didn't like it, I could leave. This was troubling *and* ominous.

One week later I walked into the off-site to find my desk moved to the far corner of the office. My desk had been in the center of the bullpen since my first day; now I was removed from everyone, with a portable partition separating me from the rest of the office. When I asked why there had been a rearrangement, Ralph announced—to the office—that since I was now a supervisor, I was entitled to privacy and personal space befitting my position. No one, of course, bought this explanation. Ralph smirked, and work continued.

As the atmosphere deteriorated, I kept Chief Inspector Best apprised of both the good and the bad. He, in turn, passed along the information to CSA Bailey. I knew this because Dave would pass along Bailey's comments regarding the growing friction between the inspectors and Ralph.

Despite the limited contact between Dave and Ralph, it was apparent that neither man cared for the other. Ralph often referred to Dave as the "big-headed wanna-be cop," and Bailey as a "publicity hound who wants to be governor." This I did *not* pass along, as I knew it would only make matters worse. Over time, Ralph's resentment toward me and the inspectors grew, as did his passive-aggressive creativity in demeaning us.

While reflecting as to why DiFonzo was resentful of inspectors who were making his CFTF look good, here were the reasons as I see it: (1) Most of the inspectors were close to Ralph's age, while the agents and police were younger; the younger members tended to look up to Ralph, but we—the inspectors—saw through a lot of his bravado and bragging. (2) Inspectors did not need the FBI's perks of undercover cars, OT, and statewide powers of arrest—the inspectors had cars, did not qualify for OT, and had statewide arrest authority; therefore, the inspectors did not feel indebted to the FBI for these "gifts." (3) We knew the state courts' personnel and had better contacts than anyone in the task force, including Ralph. Most of the work in the office dealt with the state—and not the federal—courts; it seemed Ralph resented that we held the advantage. He often had to ask us to get things done for him and not vice versa. While we were making him *look* good, we were not necessarily making him *feel* good.

In fairness, Ralph could be comical at times, and sometimes his humor was self-deprecating. However, he could also be quite cruel, though he would attempt to disguise it as "just busting balls." For instance, he started referring to Kumnick as "Waldo," after the "Where's Waldo" character. Steve's glasses were round and thick, and with his mop of hair he fit the part. But it soon turned nasty. Freddo suffered from facial acne scars and had a ruddy complexion; Marrero was Puerto Rican. One day, I overheard Ralph loudly ask where were "Pimples and Pancho"? I told him in private that this was inappropriate, but he just laughed it off.

SA Rich Teahan was Ralph's right-hand man and had been assigned to the task force before my arrival in 1994. One day, Rich drafted a UFAP warrant and forwarded it to the US Attorney's Office for review, per office protocol. Routinely it was approved and returned to the agent to bring before a federal magistrate or judge, where it was sworn to, signed, and filed in the federal clerk's office, never to be seen again.

On this particular occasion, however, Rich informed Ralph his UFAP warrant had been declined for "insufficient probable cause." Ralph hit the roof. He was incredulous and threw a tantrum.

"This is bullshit! Give me that! I'll write it in such a way that they'll have to sign it! It doesn't make any difference anyway; they never prosecute these things! Like I always say, if you don't have it, lie."

I could not believe my ears. Every warrant I had ever prepared during my career was scrupulously accurate. In the rare instances when I had a warrant refused, I simply went back and shored up whatever weakness the judge identified, then resubmitted it.

In 1994, I had assigned myself two cases, both of which had out-of-state implications: Michael Thomas Rodriquez and Joseph James Dolan.

Rodriquez had been arrested several times by the Norwalk Police Department in 1993 for a variety of felonies, including firearms charges, assault, and interfering with a police officer. Norwalk PD considered him a badass, a notorious narcotics trafficker, a fifth-degree karate black belt, and known to be armed. At 6'3" and 260 pounds, it was rumored he regularly wore body armor. A dangerous man. I had a stack of warrants on him from the court.

At the same time I was also attempting to locate one Joseph James Dolan, a career criminal arrested for robbing and assaulting an elderly couple, then failing to appear for trial. Through the nationwide criminal record database, I had discovered that Dolan had already served a ninety-day sentence for auto theft in upstate New York. Based upon this information, I drafted a UFAP warrant with a request that the Albany FBI follow up with the local police.

I handed both drafts to Ralph, who then gifted them to Lisa Bull, an agent not even on the task force. SA Bull later filed both the Rodriquez and Dolan UFAP warrants on December 20, 1994, before US Magistrate Judge F. Owen Eagan. While I had seen SA Bull at the off-site to ferry paperwork to the main office, I had never seen her work fugitive cases or participate in a raid, nor had I ever had a conversation with her—work related or otherwise.

After witnessing Ralph's rant over Teahan's UFAP warrant—acting on a hunch—I went to the office file cabinet to retrieve the Rodriquez file. Once a file was closed by arrest, the "official" file was quickly removed from the off-site and returned to the main office, while the investigator retained his "working" file. Therefore, there were never more than a few dozen closed UFAP files within the off-site at any given time. Because the Rodriquez file was active—and it was my file—I was curious to see how Lisa Bull's affidavit read.

During my investigation, I had received a tip that Rodriquez's brother had died unexpectedly in Maryland and the family was planning on holding his funeral two days later in Norwalk. I scrambled a surveillance group together. A female agent and I posed as a couple, and we attended the church service, while others observed at a distance and photographed the graveside ceremony. "Miguel" was a no-show. We did, however, compile a list of license plates for future leads. Several of these plates were registered to addresses in the Bronx, where it was rumored he had family. I had also received information from the fugitive's parole officer that by happenstance he had spotted Rodriquez near a White Castle restaurant by the Bronx Zoo before the funeral. I prepared a UFAP warrant.

There is an old saying, "Don't ask a question you don't want an answer to." I found the Rodriquez file and examined Bull's sworn affidavit. The first irregularity I noticed was when Bull wrote that I "advised" her that Kevin Clifford, Rodriquez's Bridgeport PO, had told me that the fugitive "was living with friends at 459E, 185 Street, 1, Bronx, New York, according to Clifford." This was untrue on its face, as I never had a conversation with SA Bull about *anything*, never mind this case. Further, the facts themselves were untrue. I then noticed the words "according to Clifford" were in a different font, indicating that sentence had been added on a different typewriter. The airtel I had sent to the New York FBI Fugitive Task Force clearly stated that Clifford had seen the fugitive *near* the Bronx Zoo. The address on 185th Street was found as a result of running license plates recorded at the brother's funeral, *not* from his probation officer.

Remember, these applications are not simply reports. They are sworn federal affidavits and are legally admissible in court. In this case, the application stated facts—attributed to me—which were not true.

Because the Rodriquez and Dolan applications had been submitted by Bull on the same day, I decided to also review the Dolan case. I had retained the original typed draft of the criminal complaint/affidavit and now compared it to the one submitted and sworn to by Bull. She again attested that I had "advised" her of the facts, when we had never discussed this case. She then added: "Inspector Dillon told me Patrolman Garrett, Colonie Town Police Department, New York, believes Dolan is staying at 24 Clermont Street, Albany, New York. Garrett has seen Dolan at this address." Again, as in the Rodriquez warrant, the last line was in a different font.

My airtel to the Albany FBI office never made mention of a conversation with an Officer Garrett, and I was at a loss as to how his or her name even came up in my investigation. My airtel lead was succinct: "Conduct appropriate fugitive investigation at subject's last known address of 24 Clermont Street." This was the address listed on his arrest report for the car theft. No sighting of Dolan at this address was ever mentioned or even hinted at, certainly not by a police officer.

During my initial investigation, I had telephoned the Colonie Town Police Department to confirm Dolan had been in their custody. Nowhere in my handwritten notes was there mention of a conversation with an Officer Garrett. While I was at my other office at the OCSA one day, I decided to call the Colonie Town Police Department to see if such an officer even worked there. I called and was informed Garrett was assigned to the records section. As soon as I was transferred and Garrett answered, I quickly hung up. I mulled it over and decided it was conceivable someone had done some additional digging and added language to my original draft. I dropped it, hoping the Rodriquez file was a one-off and that the Dolan "addendum" was somehow valid.

I now knew the Rodriquez affidavit had been falsified.[20] I was on the fence with the Dolan affidavit.[21] What I didn't know was whether Ralph or Lisa Bull was responsible. That was my first problem.

My second problem was one that has historically plagued honest police officers: what to do when you discover wrongdoing by a brother (or sister) officer. By this time, I had been in law enforcement for fifteen

---

[20] Rodriquez eventually surrendered after he was seen at a relative's home in NY. Upon his release from prison, Rodriquez turned his life around, working as a self-employed carpenter and plumber. Sadly, he passed away on his forty-eighth birthday in 2013 (*Norwalk Hour*).

[21] Dolan, after his capture, continued his life of crime. He has since been arrested several more times over the years on charges including kidnapping, sexual assault, burglary, witness tampering, and violation of a protective order. He was last arrested in August 2019 on sexual contact charges.

years. I knew the backlash that came from throwing a penalty flag. Having been involved in prior police corruption investigations, I knew the vast majority of police officers were honest, but this was a blind spot. No one wanted to be "that guy."

I also knew that if I reported this, the falsified affidavit would be explained away as an honest mistake, a simple miscommunication. Meanwhile I would be branded a troublemaker, and Ralph would demand I be removed from the task force. I had observed Ralph in action for some time now and knew he would try to flip this back on me; he would claim it was an oversight and unintentional, and that I was capitalizing on it in an attempt to cast shade on him as the coordinator. After fifteen years on the job, I thought I had a pretty fair sense of how things worked in "cop land."

So I decided to tell no one. But it still troubled me, as I suspected this was not an aberration or a one-off.

Sure enough, it happened again: another UFAP was rejected, and again Ralph blew up. He now lectured us that a UFAP was a mere formality and that no one is ever actually prosecuted federally; as soon as the fugitive was returned to the state, the US Attorney's Office automatically dismissed the federal charge. Again, he pointedly announced that he would rewrite the warrant himself so that the probable cause would be sufficiently convincing.

Despite the friction at the task force, Chief State's Attorney Bailey was basking in the glow of our successes. Chief Inspector Best and I talked on the phone daily, and I made a point of seeing him at least once a week, both to keep him in the loop and to gauge the support for our squad now that things were getting rocky.

I was heartened by his performance evaluation, which deemed me "outstanding" in ten different areas of job performance, along with many flattering comments, such as that I served "as a 'peace maker' and spokesperson for the Chief State's Attorney's Office" and that I was "always thinking and acting 'ahead of the curve' keeping the best interest of the C.S.A.O. in the forefront of [my] actions."

Meanwhile I made regular visits to the home office and made sure my guys weren't strangers at headquarters either. I had seen officers join a task force and forget who their employer was. I also wanted to make sure CI Best was hearing from inspectors other than me about the goings-on at the task force. Best had known Kumnick, Freddo, and Marrero professionally before they were hired as inspectors, so he trusted them and their observations.

CHAPTER 9

When you work with people, you have to invite them to your wedding, so when Vilma and I were married in September 1995, I sent invitations to all the task force members, as well as to CSA Bailey and CI Best. Most everyone, including Bailey and Best, attended. Following a couple of gorgeous tropical honeymoon days in the British Virgin Islands, the island of Tortola was leveled by Hurricane Marilyn. After some time confined to our beachside bungalow with no running water or electricity, we were happy to evacuate.

Back at work, relations continued to sour. The inspectors and I began to notice we were getting fewer requests for help on surveillances and arrests, and when we asked for help in turn, there were fewer volunteers. By the spring of 1996, I found myself spending more time at my office in Rocky Hill and less time at the New Haven off-site. When I did go there, I would hear about it from Ralph and his sidekick Richie, "Oh, you still work here?" or "Nice of you to show up." It was apparent I was now rubbing both agents the wrong way.

Another issue that created division within the office was Ralph's insistence that everyone join him for the weekly Wednesday pizza night and Friday night happy hour. Ralph seemed intent on fostering the atmosphere of a frat house under the misguided concept of team-building. The problem was that all the other inspectors were married with children at home. This was not how my guys wanted to spend their off time, and I didn't blame them. After spending forty or fifty hours running around the state at all hours of the day and night, my guys wanted to get home and spend time with their families. Other task force members were either single, divorced, or married without children, so they were usually agreeable to indulging him. Ralph's persistent mentioning of the fact that the inspectors were absent just further highlighted the developing rift. If Ralph's intent was to unnecessarily divide the office into two camps though "team-building," he was succeeding.

This goes back to the earlier category descriptions of the Boy Scout and the Cowboy, and how the two can't play well in the same sandbox. DiFonzo distrusted me, as he knew I would never play along with his falsified affidavit scheme, and I resented DiFonzo, as he had put me in an untenable ethical dilemma. It didn't take a clairvoyant to predict this wouldn't end well.

There was plenty of work to do. Fugitive cases were now being referred to us daily. Reviewing, researching, opening, and assigning the cases to the inspectors took up most of my time, and I could just as easily work at my own office thirty miles away. In the meantime, Ralph rearranged the furniture yet again, placing me back in the center of the bullpen, just to show he was still in charge.

Even after several months, the questionable Rodriquez file still nagged at me. I was deeply troubled that someone had invented information and added it—quite carelessly—to the sworn affidavit. What bothered me more was that the information had been sourced to *me*. While I was troubled to see someone compromise his or her professional integrity just to get a warrant signed, it was a risk assumed by the liar. If the affiant chose to take such a foolish gamble and was found out, that person would suffer serious consequences, and rightfully so.

Nevertheless, I wanted nothing to do with it and did not want my name linked to the scheme, never mind being named as the source of the bogus intel.

The Dolan file also troubled me. At this point, I had not mentioned it to anyone, not even my wife. Initially, I had given Bull and DiFonzo the benefit of the doubt, but my gut told me otherwise.

I finally picked up the phone in my Rocky Hill office and called the Colonie Town Police Department again. However, this time when I was connected to Officer Garrett, I didn't hang up. I now explained who I was and that there was confusion over a report that mentioned his name. He retrieved the case file and confirmed that Dolan had been previously arrested for a stolen car. When asked, he told me he himself had no involvement in the investigation or the arrest, nor had he ever provided any information to an outside agency regarding Dolan, and he didn't even know what Dolan looked like.

I finished our awkward conversation by asking Garrett if he had ever seen Dolan at 24 Clermont Street in Albany. Slightly annoyed and not realizing the purpose of my call, he repeated he did not know Dolan or even Clermont Street, as Albany was several miles outside his town and therefore not even in his jurisdiction. Before ending the call, I asked, and he confirmed: he was the only Garrett on the police force.

Now I knew that Bull's signed and sworn affidavit stating I had told her about Garrett seeing Dolan in Albany was a total fiction. I had irrefutable evidence that two federal affidavits—both quoting me as the source of information—were submitted with the intention of deceiving the court. So what was I going to do?

I was in a precarious situation. If I left it unreported, I was complicit in this conspiracy; if I reported it, I would be a pariah within law enforcement circles. I could not confront DiFonzo, even though I was sure he was responsible for the falsification. I knew he would use it as a means of having me removed from the task force. FBI management was not about to turn on one of their own—certainly not on a complaint filed by a guy who had decided to leave the FBI for a state job. In short, the squeaky wheel wasn't going to get the grease; it would be replaced with a new wheel.

My other concern was the repercussions for those responsible. Since I had resigned from the FBI, Director William Sessions had been replaced by Louis Freeh, a former assistant US attorney from New York.[22] Director Freeh had emphasized his new "bright line" policy, which espoused a hard stance on unethical behavior by agents, regardless of seniority or position. All personnel had been put on notice that there would be "zero tolerance" for lying, cheating, and stealing. I did not wish to be the catalyst for an investigation that could jeopardize the career of a colleague.

I decided to call an agent whom I had admired and respected for years. Richard "Dick" Harrington had been the applicant coordinator at the New Haven FBI Office when I applied. Although he was no longer in New Haven, we stayed in touch and remained friends (to this day).

I explained in detail what I had discovered, and he told me I already knew what I needed to do. If I didn't, I would be committing "misprision of a felony," a term that I had never heard before. He explained that simply being aware of a crime—and he made it clear it was a felony—could put me in jeopardy of criminal prosecution, more so because I was an officer of the law and held to a higher standard. Shaken, I thanked him for his advice and said goodbye.

I thought back to Frank Serpico and his story. Like him, all I wanted to do was catch bad guys by any legal means necessary. He refused to partake in criminal conduct and thought he could maintain his integrity by ignoring it while it was taking place right under his nose. But he couldn't, as he knew that allowing it to take place was the same as condoning it. My concern was my name was now being used to facilitate a crime—an intentional deception upon the court—and that I was now involved just by my being *aware* this was being done. Worse, if a UFAP was ever legally challenged, I could be left trying to convince a judge or jury that

---

[22] Sessions, appointed by President Reagan in 1987, was dismissed midterm by President Clinton in 1993 after accusations he had used FBI planes for personal travel and had illegally billed the government for a home security system.

I did not provide the false information, possibly in conflict with an FBI agent who might testify dishonestly in an attempt to protect his or her career. But I also remembered the rest of Serpico's story: he was ignored, rebuked, ostracized, and almost died in the line of duty. Not exactly an incentive to take a hard stand and report my concerns.

I first decided to review my UFAP files. I would not be able to make a thorough search, because only the most recent files would be accessible. I did this one night, since it would have been too obvious to start pulling files and sit there in the bullpen comparing them side by side with my work files.

Some of the files had indeed been "enhanced" but not to a level of egregious falsification. But there was one that showed clear signs of being tampered with. While the rough draft of the UFAP warrant had not been returned to me, my notes showed it had been given to Rich Teahan, who gave it to Victor Treadway, a likable first-office agent fresh from Quantico. The fugitive in this case was another bail-jumper, and I had worked closely with his bondsman. SA Treadway's two-page affidavit was dated April 24, 1996, and sworn to before Judge Joan G. Margolis. It read in part:

> "I have been advised by Inspector Gregory B. Dillon of the Chief State's Attorney's Office that he had discussed the whereabouts of Kenneth A. Clark with members of Kenneth A. Clark's family. Those family members told Inspector Dillon that they have spoken to Kenneth A. Clark on the telephone. The family members further stated that Kenneth A. Clark has been calling them from an address in Dallas, Texas. The family members told Inspector Dillon that Kenneth A. Clark has told them that he is in Dallas and has provided them with a telephone number by which to contact him there. The telephone number that Kenneth A. Clark has provided

does, in fact, begin with a Dallas, Texas area code. The family members have also informed Inspector Dillon that Kenneth A. Clark has told them that he is aware of the outstanding felony warrant for his arrest and that he intends to remain in Dallas to avoid arrest."

This was all quite untrue. I had never discussed the investigation with SA Treadway and never contacted any member of Clark's family, so all of that paragraph was blatantly false. The airtel I had sent to the Dallas FBI Office confirmed this contradiction, in which I was quite clear about the source of the information: "Information was received from a confidential source that subject's brother, Jimmy Clark, is a reverend or minister living in Dallas, Texas, and has re-habilitated the subject, who is reportedly living with him at 6731 Day Street." That confidential source was in fact the bondsman with whom I had been working.

I sought out my partner, Stephen Kumnick, for a private conversation. Steve said he wasn't surprised, given the remarks Ralph had made in the office; he agreed to go through his open UFAP cases. Steve reminded me as most of his UFAP cases were closed, he would only be able to review a handful of open files. I asked him to do so discreetly, since we could not afford to tip our hand. The very next day, he showed me the file of Kendell Davis, wanted for sexual assault. Another first-office agent, Todd J. Brophy, had submitted a three-page affidavit outlining the reasons why he believed Davis had fled to New York, filled with false assertions attributed to Steve.

"Inspector Stephen Kumnick, Chief State's Attorney's Office, has informed me that his investigation has revealed that Ortega and Davis moved back to New York in June 1994. Ortega had told friends, who are still living in Connecticut, that she and Davis had to leave Connecticut because Davis had warrants active for his arrest.... Photographs of Davis have been distributed to the local authorities in New York City and they have confirmed that Davis is currently residing in the area."

Kumnick said this was all made up: he had not discussed the investigation with SA Brophy, he never reported that Davis's girlfriend, Ortega, told him that "she and Davis had to leave Connecticut because Davis had warrants for his arrest," and that he had never forwarded photographs to the NYPD. Steve confirmed—as he was the case investigator—Brophy had no involvement in the investigation, with the exception of filing the ginned-up UFAP warrant.

A pattern was emerging, and as an investigator the next step was clear: ask the other inspectors to review their files. Steve, my number two, said he didn't think Bob Hughes or Joe Marrero had many, if any, UFAP files. Bob was the best investigator we had; he would collar his guys so fast, they didn't have time to get far enough away for him to need a UFAP. Joe was no ball of fire, but he was dependable, spoke Spanish, and got along with everyone. We decided to meet with them and Freddo at my office in Rocky Hill.

We didn't invite John Healy. He was still miffed he had not been made the squad supervisor. His being older and senior to me, plus the fact that his younger brother was already a chief inspector, likely made the slight more painful. He aligned himself with Ralph, Richie, and the rest of the agents and now shunned his fellow inspectors with the exception of his partner, Bob.

I laid out the tale of the falsified affidavits to the other three and asked them to find any of their UFAP files that were still at the off-site and compare them to their work files. Bob Hughes and Joe Marrero said they only had a couple, and those had likely been closed out and returned to the main office. I asked them to double check anyway and not to mention this to anyone.

I knew the stakes were high. If Ralph suspected I was suspicious of his tampering with UFAP preparations, the remaining files would certainly by removed and a request made through office channels that I be rotated out. Ralph enjoyed a luxury few supervisors had: he could move personnel in and out of the task force as he saw fit. Ralph did not have to deal with unions, seniority, grievances, or any other labor issues that police management had to navigate. Because each member was "donated" by an agency head to the task force for a one-year stint, Ralph had built up his own team. There was a Connecticut State Police trooper assigned there almost from the beginning. He and Ralph went for their morning jogs together, barhopped after work, and socialized outside the office. Every time this trooper's "expiration date" came up, Ralph asked his SAC to request an extension, as Ralph misrepresented this trooper was a valuable asset to the task force. The truth was, the guy was an underperformer who rarely caught anyone. But because of his close relationship with Ralph, he was given special status. Other troopers, who worked harder but didn't shine up to Ralph, were rotated out annually. This lesson was not lost on anyone who wished to remain assigned to a task force that provided you with a take-home car and limitless overtime.

At the end of the week, Hughes and Marrero reported they could not find any of their files, but Freddo found three and said he couldn't believe it: not only was his name listed as the source of false information in *all* three cases, but all three warrants were currently on file and active at the New Haven federal courthouse. Freddo's immediate concern was his liability if the misleading information in the file was used as justification to raid a residence. If something went sideways, could he be sued? I asked him to photocopy the paperwork and meet me right away, and he walked me through each falsified affidavit.

Freddo's first case was a bad guy named Michael A. Williams, convicted in a Hartford court for assault in the first degree and criminal use of a firearm. Out on bond, Williams was to have been sentenced on August 22, 1995, but he got cold feet, then got fast feet. He never showed. Freddo handwrote a rough draft of a UFAP warrant and provided it to SA Brophy, who filed a ten-paragraph affidavit before the Honorable Donna F. Martinez.

"I have been advised by Inspector Steven C. Freddo of the Chief State's Attorney's Office that he had discussed the whereabouts of Michael A. Williams with his former girlfriend. The former girlfriend informed Inspector Freddo that Michael A. Williams is aware of the fact that he has outstanding warrants for his arrest and that he left the state of Connecticut to avoid arrest. The former girlfriend also informed Inspector Freddo that Michael A. Williams telephoned her on November 28, 1995 and told her that he was residing in Boston, Massachusetts."

The real Inspector Freddo had not spoken with Brophy and knew nothing about any telephone call putting the fugitive in Boston. His rough draft quoted the fugitive's girlfriend as saying, "Williams may be staying with a girl, Angela, in Boston, MA, but she could not provide an address, telephone number or last name for Angela."

Freddo's next file concerned a young lady named Erica Jefferis, accused of dealing drugs, who had skipped her court appearance and jumped bond. Freddo worked the case with a Glastonbury officer, who discovered that the fugitive had relocated to Holiday, Tennessee. Freddo handwrote a rough draft for Brophy, but the two-page affidavit presented to Judge Martinez contained the following addition: "Further investigation by Inspector Steven Freddo, Chief State's Attorney's Office has revealed that Jefferis has left Connecticut specifically to avoid the aforementioned pending charges. This information was provided to Inspector Freddo by a close relative of Jefferis who currently resides in Connecticut." This, again, was news to the real Inspector Freddo.

The final case was that of Alika Wright, sought by Bloomfield police for a 1995 robbery and assault. Steve had prepared a two-page typed affidavit, which contained sufficient probable cause to show that Wright lived in Massachusetts, traveled to Connecticut to commit the robbery, and had likely returned afterwards. Additionally, Freddo noted Wright's coconspirators were Massachusetts residents. Freddo's prepared affidavit even included SA Todd Brophy's name—all Brophy needed to do was sign it. But again it was changed: "Inspector Freddo has also advised me that he has interviewed a known associate of Alika Wright. The associate has told Inspector Freddo that he/she has spoken to Alika Wright on a regular basis from the Summer of 1995 through present. The associate has told Inspector Freddo that Alika Wright has informed the associate that she is currently living in Massachusetts and that she is staying there to elude police and avoid arrest and prosecution for the robbery." There was no associate, Freddo said, and no conversation. It was all made up.

That brought the total in hand to seven falsified affidavits. In each instance, someone had fabricated investigative facts and attributed the falsehoods to me or one of my inspectors. The way it was written, we were the sources of the false information. If we left them uncontested, we would bear the blame if the lies were exposed. If the affiant agent of record decided to claim we had actually provided the false information, then we could be answering to a judge, after first losing our jobs. Ultimately, this is what forced our hands.

After consulting with Freddo and Kumnick, we decided I would personally meet with Chief Inspector Best, as he was my direct supervisor and next in the chain of command. In June 1996, I told him there was a serious problem concerning our involvement at the Fugitive Task Force which required immediate attention. CI Best told me to meet him at his office the following day.

When I arrived, also waiting there was Deputy Chief State's Attorney Dominick Galluzzo. There were two DCSAs at our office: one oversaw "operations," the other "administration." Galluzzo oversaw operations, which meant he monitored all active prosecutions being handled by our office. Galluzzo physically resembled Alfred Hitchcock, but with the voice, dress, and manner of a New York mob boss. Killing time until he was eligible for his pension, I suspected he was sitting in mostly out of protocol and curiosity.

I explained my initial concern about the first falsified affidavit, then recounted how more affidavits were discovered, totaling seven. Galluzzo naturally inquired what proof we had, and I explained that in most instances, we had the rough drafts, along with corresponding copies of the filed affidavits. I then turned over a notebook I had prepared, which contained the questionable warrants. I had highlighted the sections we contested and included copies of the truthful rough drafts as proof.

Both men seemed to be waiting for the other to say something. Galluzzo finally broke the silence, telling me the information needed to "be considered." I asked what I—and the inspectors—should do next. The response was to continue working our cases but not to file any more UFAPs. Before adjourning, they reassured me I would be contacted soon.

I relayed the gist of the meeting to Kumnick and Freddo, and we continued playing our respective roles. I was now working from my Rocky Hill office more than the New Haven off-site, which was plainly an annoyance to Ralph. As weeks went by, I kept asking CI Best when we would have some indication as to what happens next. CI Best would tell me it was being discussed with "the Boss." This delay made me more uncomfortable the longer it went on.

I was learning firsthand how bureaucrats tend to handle troublesome matters. First, when in doubt, dither—which was better than the follow-up: do what is politically expedient.

At last, in order to protect myself and the other inspectors, I decided I needed to "go on paper," formalizing my complaint with a memo to CI Best and DCSA Galluzzo. I submitted a two-page memorandum on July 12, 1996, that began:

> "In recent months, the relationship between the Fugitive Squad Inspectors and the host agency of the CFTF has deteriorated to the point where the atmosphere at the New Haven off-site is fraught with suspicion and animosity. We have exposed a continuing pattern of false affidavits being filed by several FBI agents in federal court. This practice is largely attributable to SA Ralph DiFonzo, Jr., who displays an antagonistic attitude toward the DCJ and it is my strong belief that no DCJ Inspectors should remain in the CFTF until this practice has ended. I have documentation pertaining to seven instances ranging from 1994 to just last month where FBI agents have filed Unlawful Flight to Avoid Prosecution affidavits before federal judges/magistrates which contain false and fictitious information attributed to DCJ Inspectors."

The memo closed:

> "I am very uncomfortable with the role I have been thrust into, but this is an ugly issue that needs to be addressed at the first opportunity."

I felt I had been backed into a corner, first by the FBI, then by my own office. As soon as I met with CI Best and DCSA Galluzzo—who likely had fifty-plus years of criminal justice experience between them—this should have been a no-brainer. You simply cannot allow subordinates to continue to work at an office outside of your control after making the kind of allegations we had just made. This rose far above any type of personality conflict or interagency friction; these were crimes that were ongoing, by the fact that false affidavits were on file and pending in a federal courthouse. Agonizing over it was not going to make anything better, and swift action should have been taken. We were looking for direction, and they were trying to read tea leaves.

I didn't have any confidence in Galluzzo, as he had no skin in the game, appeared indifferent to our predicament, and was a short-timer. Best, I knew, was conflicted and fence-sitting. He empathized with us, but his ultimate allegiance was to the guy who took him to the dance, Bailey. I recognized if I did not formalize my complaint, it was apt to be handled like a personality dispute and not as serious misconduct, which it clearly was.

I was promptly notified to appear in Bailey's office to discuss my memo and the notebook. I stood alongside the seated Bailey at his glass-topped desk.

As he thumbed through the notebook, he scowled, shaking his head and clicking his tongue. He acknowledged this was indeed a "serious matter" and needed to be addressed immediately "at the highest levels." He thanked me for having the best interests of the Division at heart and my having the good sense to call his attention to it. He concluded by saying we needed to get our group out of the off-site until this issue could be resolved.

I believe at this point Bailey was being sincere but short-sighted. Bailey considered the head of the New Haven FBI office, Merrill Parks, a friend. Bailey failed to recognize how much damage this could do to Parks and his beloved task force. Bailey likely thought he was doing Parks a solid by low-keying the discovery so that it could be quietly addressed and remedied. In his shortsightedness, Bailey did not grasp the gravity and ramifications of withdrawing active federal warrants that were already approved by assistant United States attorneys and sworn to before federal judges.

Soon after, I was sitting in my office in Rocky Hill when the phone rang. It was Steve Freddo, who simply said, "He's in the building."

"He" was Merrill Simpson Parks Jr., special agent in charge (SAC) of the FBI's New Haven Division, come to meet with Chief State's Attorney Jack Bailey about the problem I was causing him. I hung up the phone and walked out of my office to the second-floor balcony that overlooked the lobby of the Connecticut Division of Criminal Justice. It offered a commanding view not only of the atrium but also the parking lot through the three-story glass façade.

As I leaned on the railing, Freddo sidled up to me. "Did you see him?" I asked.

"One of the secretaries recognized him and gave me the heads-up," he whispered back.

Steve moved along, not wanting to be conspicuous. Normally I would have done the same, but now I was beyond. Relations were not just strained, they were fractured.

Knowing I would never get an honest answer about the details of their meeting, I opted to keep my vigil until the summit ended. Before long my patience was rewarded with a scene that told me everything I needed to know. The electronically activated security door swung open and SAC Parks strode through the lobby, traditional FBI dark business suit, white dress shirt, and conservative necktie, the heels of his custom cowboy boots clicking briskly on the tile floor—a farewell gift from the boys in Houston, where he'd previously been assistant special agent in charge (ASAC). His hand-tooled boots bore the colorful Bureau seal and the motto "Fidelity, Bravery, Integrity" stitched on the front.

At his stacked heels followed the frazzled Bailey. Parks shoved open the glass double doors, leaving them to swing back on Bailey, as he headed straight for his government car. They were quickly out of earshot, but it was obvious the state's chief prosecutor was pleading his case to a deaf juror.

Bailey caught up with him at his car, and an angry Parks turned on him, poking at his chest with two stubby fingers that pinched a cigar. The chastised Bailey looked at the ground, hands spread at his sides in an inverted surrender. Parks got into his car and sped off, while the rebuked Bailey sulked back to his office, head down.

I had taken enough body language courses during my career to pretty much know what had taken place. Parks had punked Bailey down. Parks dug his heels in, somehow putting Bailey on the defensive, which meant now we would be at odds not only with the FBI but with our own office. Things were going from bad to worse, and quickly.

When I got back to my office, the other Fugitive Squad inspectors were already assembled. Steve Kumnick broke the silence. "So?"

I pursed my lips, took in a deep breath, and exhaled a longer one. "We're screwed."

I began to hedge my bets. I assembled a notebook with six dividers; each section contained photocopies of each falsified affidavit. Luckily we were able to find six of the seven original drafts of the falsified warrants, which was the strongest proof they had been changed. I also included a synopsis describing what information had been falsified. I had made three copies, and submitted one to Bailey along with my memo. Once I sensed a shifting of the tides, I made an additional four copies. One I kept in my briefcase, another I secreted in my house, another I gave to Kumnick. The last one I sealed in a waterproof folder and asked a long-time "non-police" friend to hide it—and not to tell anyone, including me—where.

Knowing we were certain to be removed from the task force, I had quietly begun to transfer my files from my New Haven task force desk back to Rocky Hill. Just before submitting my memo and notebook to Bailey on Friday, I had cleaned out my desk, leaving no doubt I was transferring myself and depriving Ralph of the opportunity. Basically, "You can't fire me, I quit."

Steve Kumnick walked into the off-site later that Friday, July 12, and found FBI "tech" agents working on the front door.[23] He asked if the lock was broken, but no one even acknowledged him. A short time later, Agent Teahan arrived and began to berate him: all the inspectors were "out," and we needed to turn in our pagers, keys, and electric gate openers immediately.

Offices were hastily set up in Rocky Hill to accommodate the banished Fugitive Squad, with the exception of Inspector John Healy, whom the FBI now decided they wanted to keep. He had distanced himself from the rest of the inspectors and—more importantly—still had access to the twelve state's attorney's office files.

Bailey next ordered us to clean out our files and equipment from the FBI off-site. Dave Best briefed us on what we could remove: our breaching equipment, radios, and gun safe containing our shotguns. We were not to go searching for files but should confine ourselves to whatever remained in our desks. And he did not want any conversation or banter in the unlikely event anyone else was present. Dave greatly misjudged that part.

Best and I drove down together. The mood was already tense; the inspectors were picking up the vibe we had done something wrong. I fumed in silence until we got about halfway to New Haven, but I couldn't contain myself. I began to question Dave as to what was being done about the false affidavits, why Bailey had capitulated to Parks in leaving an inspector on the task force, and why we were getting the cold shoulder from Bailey and his staff. Dave gruffly replied that all we had done was make allegations, and it was our word against theirs.

Stung by this implicit criticism of the case I had meticulously assembled, I angrily replied that the FBI's own documents proved we were telling the truth, and this should be evident to anyone who bothered to read them.

---

23   "Tech" agents are responsible for not only installing and updating office security equipment, they are also used for clandestine operations, also known as "black bag jobs": court-authorized burglaries and installations of eavesdropping equipment in residences, businesses, and vehicles.

"I don't see the initials J.D. after your name," said Dave.

As the remark sunk in, I slammed the palm of my right hand against the dashboard, turned my head, and yelled directly at him: "Goddammit! I don't need a law degree to know the difference between right and wrong!" Dave was clearly stunned, but there was no stopping me now. "I knew the difference between the truth and a lie when I was five years old! You think I need a law degree to know right from wrong? Do *you* have a law degree? What the fuck kind of horse-shit remark is that?"

After several seconds, he blinked a few times while avoiding my stare and finally spoke. "Okay, okay. Calm down. Please." I was fuming. After a long, uncomfortable silence, Dave said he was just trying to say all our information would need to be examined, and it was in the hands of the attorneys to figure out what to do next, and we needed to let the system do its job.

As soon as we pulled onto Olive Street, we saw that the parking lot was almost full. It was never full in the middle of the day. Obviously Ralph had ordered everyone to be there to witness our expulsion: he wanted to make our departure as humiliating as possible.

After blowing the horn to alert someone to activate the gate, we waited several minutes on the street before they decided to let us in. With all the parking closest to the building taken up, we had to park at the far end, making every trip to our vehicles as inconvenient as possible. We marched in with Dave in the lead to find almost all the task force members at their desks, some with arms folded across their chests, others looking away. Some seemed embarrassed; others openly displayed their contempt.

As our guys packed their files and desk items into cardboard bankers boxes, I opened the electronic keypad on our gun safe, then hefted the door from its hinges and carried it to the van. After the safe was emptied of the Mossbergs, we had to lug the still-heavy safe to our van.

Ralph was ensconced at his corner desk, leaning back in his swivel chair and smirking, with his hands behind his head. It was the last time I ever saw him.

John "Jack" Bailey attending a banquet with unidentified table mate.
(Photo courtesy of Journal Inquirer archives)

CHAPTER 10

Within days, the attorneys in the Bond Forfeiture Unit were getting besieged with phone calls from bondsmen, wanting to know how come we were no longer looking for fugitives. There was much speculation in the courts and police departments as to what had happened. Rumors (no doubt started by DiFonzo and the agents) circulated that we had been terminated due to ineffectiveness, were no longer in that line of work, and other such nonsense.

This obviously did not sit well with us, as we were still actively working our fugitive cases—just in a different office. We made our protests to CI Best, who told us to focus on our work and ignore the "drama."

On July 30, 1996, we got our first gag order from Chief State's Attorney Bailey:

> "Merrill Parks, Special Agent in Charge of the FBI
> in Connecticut is very concerned about statements

allegedly being made by members of the State of Connecticut Fugitive Squad regarding the truthfulness of certain statements in UFAP warrants to other law enforcement agencies and personnel. This issue is being addressed by Mr. Parks based on a memo prepared by Inspector Dillon and given to him by me. I do not want any further discussion of this issue with any outside law enforcement personnel or other state or federal agencies. If I do hear of any continuing discussions, I will take appropriate action."

It was not lost on me that I was now being referred to as an "inspector" and not a supervisory-inspector, even though I had already finished my probationary period. I thought it unlikely this was an oversight and more likely a subtle attempt to remind me that something that could be given could also be taken away. And it would not be the last time that threat would be made.

The Fugitive Squad had been formed independent of the FBI and would now continue to operate independently of them. Except now, instead of it being a squad of one, it was now a squad of six; we had picked up Joe Howard, a streetwise retired New Haven detective, through an intraoffice transfer. Healy was now the only token FBI task force inspector. Meanwhile, the referrals continued to pour in, as well as the forfeited bonds.

The only thing to do now was go on doing our jobs as though nothing was wrong. Every Monday morning at 9 we held our Fugitive Squad meeting, with CI Best usually in attendance. I would assign new cases, and each inspector would give a quick update of promising leads, followed by the scheduling of any upcoming raids or surveillances for the week. Following the meeting, I would then head upstairs to Bailey's third floor conference room, where the weekly office-wide supervisors meeting was held at 10 a.m.

Naively, I had thought we could regain Bailey's confidence if we worked hard as a team, played well with others, and produced consistent results. Even though we were now down to me and five inspectors, we were more motivated than ever. In just the last two weeks of June, we arrested a New Britain absconder who was wanted for attempted murder, weapons possession, narcotics violations, and failure to appear in court; a Hartford drug dealer for three counts of failure to appear in court on narcotics and weapons charges plus a probation violation; and a Bridgeport Latin King—whom we tracked to Hartford—wanted for violation of probation, several assaults, threatening, and failure to appear in court.

Our successes continued, as we wanted to prove we could do just fine without the FBI. In a single day in September, we apprehended three fugitives—all wanted in different parts of the country. The first, Edward Duffy, we arrested in Derby, who was wanted out of the Bronx for multiple counts of kidnapping, robbery, assault, and larceny. Next was Tina Jones, whom we located in New Haven; she was wanted in Ohio by the Cuyahoga Sheriff's Department for various forgery and larceny charges. Finally, we again beat the Task Force at their own game, arresting Louis Morris West Jr., who was wanted on a UFAP warrant by the FBI's Cleveland office. Better yet, we caught West in the FBI's home field of New Haven. A convicted bank robber with thirty-two prior arrests in New Jersey, Virginia, and Ohio, West was on the run for receiving stolen property, forgery, and theft. At the end of that day, there were high-fives all around the squad.

By week's end, we also captured a Hartford armed robber in New London—and as a bonus arrested his wife on a bad check warrant. Steve Kumnick's leads to New Jersey resulted in the arrest of a sexual predator in Newark, while from my computer I identified and located two fugitives who were serving time under aliases: a drug dealer locked up in Bridgeport, Connecticut, and a rapist who had been wanted since 1991 and was currently doing time in Georgia.

Although the CFTF had twice the manpower, we were bringing in more referrals, and—more importantly—more captures. We all knew Ralph had been inflating the task force's statistics (known as "juking the stats") for years. When a police officer or trooper assigned to his task force opened a fugitive file on a defendant—but the criminal was arrested without direct involvement of the task force—Ralph would count it as a task force apprehension, even though no one from the task force was involved. Our group, on the other hand, would mark the case successfully closed but not count it as our own capture. Again, once you compromise your integrity in one area, it becomes easier to cheat in others.

Despite these successes and Bailey's celebratory press release blitz, I was not getting any warm fuzzies from my boss. Upon the return of our group to Rocky Hill, we were initially welcomed, with promises of our own off-site, a toll-free number to be answered 24/7, and a boost in manpower. After all, we had surplus funds from all the bonds being collected.

When none of this began to materialize, and there was no action on our UFAP complaint, it slowly dawned on me that we were being hung out to dry.

I recognized the importance of leaving a paper trail. Meetings and conversations did not seem to move any agenda forward. More troubling was how recollections differed, even over the span of just a few days. Based upon my initial revelation of the falsified affidavits to Galluzzo and Best, it seemed that to make anything happen, I had to put it in writing. Now within my weekly progress report of apprehensions and referrals received, I would often mention how we were having difficulty keeping up with the case load, how we were still not in the promised off-site, and how we were in need of additional inspectors. I began sending my memos directly to the attention of the chief state's attorney, with courtesy copies to others. Further, I began to keep detailed notes of pertinent conversations, even if they appeared innocuous at the time. These later paid dividends.

At the end of September of 1996, after Steve Kumnick was temporarily reassigned to a homicide trial, my first memo read in part:

> "This (Kumnick's reassignment), coupled with Inspector Hughes' injury leave (Bob required a second knee surgery after assisting Det. Joe Green) and Inspector Howard's temporary re-assignment, has hampered our investigative efforts. Without an off-site location, we are unable to explore obtaining an 800 or 888 number, which is essential if we are to request the public's assistance via wanted flyers and media releases."

If it sounds like I was complaining, it is because I was. In October, another of my memos to Bailey read in part:

> "When the Fugitive Squad was associated with the Connecticut Fugitive Task Force, we were conducting surveillances and executing arrests and/or search warrants with as many as 12 investigators. We are now attempting to undertake the same activities with 4 or 5 inspectors. This is impractical and tactically unsafe, making an already dangerous assignment more dangerous…. Finally, as you are well aware, we are in dire need of an off-site location space. Some of the Fugitive Squad inspectors have now made their 4th intra-office move in 2 months."

During the first week of November, leads we had sent out to various police and sheriff's departments across the country began to pay off. In one week alone, our investigative requests resulted in the arrest of four Connecticut fugitives: Manhattan Beach, California; Bangor, Maine; New York City, New York; and Puerto Rico. During that same week, we located four more in Connecticut: two in New Haven, one in Bridgeport, and one in Waterbury—all this accomplished without the cumbersome UFAP process. My hope was our activity level would make us indispensable to Bailey.

When Bob finally recovered from his knee surgery, I assigned him a particularly interesting case. We had received a referral from the Bridgeport probation office on a Steven Necaise for three counts of violation of probation, for the original charges of stalking, harassment, threatening, criminal trespass, and interfering with an officer. While attempting to learn more about him, the criminal database showed Necaise was also wanted by New York authorities—under the name Rashaan Wiggins—for a parole violation related to illegal possession of a firearm. Prior to this, he had been nabbed in Ohio—this time using the name Stephen Alexander—for robbery and receiving stolen property. One of his problems, apparently, was he couldn't figure out what he wanted to do in life or what he wanted to be called.

I had just finished congratulating Bob on his previous day's pre-dawn captures (one in Bridgeport and another in Waterbury), when he asked if I was busy. He wanted me to join him running down a lead. We were still shorthanded, so I pushed my paperwork aside and said let's go. On the way to Bridgeport, he explained how he had located Necaise's last-known address, shown the fugitive's photo to the landlord, who in turn showed Bob the one-bedroom apartment Necaise had vacated—without notice of course—just a week earlier. Bob was a bloodhound. While looking through the empty apartment, he had spotted a plastic garbage bag tucked into the back of a closet. Rummaging through the trash, he had found a torn-up report card from the Housatonic Technical Community College—but the name on the report card was female. Bob had pocketed it and left. On the drive to Bridgeport, he explained he wanted to stop at the school and see if we could locate and interview the female student.

Bridgeport was always a good place to go looking for a fugitive. Business Insider ranked it at the time as the fourth most dangerous city in the country; certainly it was one of the ugliest cities in the nation, block after block of ruined neighborhoods, rows of two- and three-story homes either fire damaged or abandoned. With decrepit low-income housing, fifteen different identifiable gang sets, and a quarter of the population living below the poverty line, there was no shortage of work for our squad in the Park City.

We introduced ourselves to the dean of the school and explained how we found ourselves on his campus. After confirming Necaise was never a student at the school, we gave him the name on the report card. As luck would have it, he knew the student quite well. He explained she was one of his favorites, as she was also a part-time tutor at the school. While we were still in his office, he had his secretary contact the girl and asked her to stop by.

When she arrived, we introduced ourselves and explained the nature of our visit. We could immediately see she was a very proper, refined young lady, hardly the type you would expect to associate with a career criminal. She was quite confused when we asked her if she knew Steven Necaise. She demurely shook her head no, and then Bob showed her his mug shot. The look on her face gave her away, and we both knew he was now using yet another alias. She told us his new last name and asked if he was in any trouble. We could tell he was more to her than just a guy she was tutoring and that we needed to proceed delicately. We explained he had neglected to show up at court "for a matter," and tried to let it go at that. Now quite concerned, she pressed for more details.

We knew this was no act and that she didn't know with whom she was dealing. She eventually conceded she had met him on campus and that he had told her he had recently dropped out of school and was thinking of returning. She admitted they had been meeting for lunch once or twice a week—between her classes and tutoring sessions—but were not technically "dating." She added she would break it off now, however, as her church would not condone her seeing someone who was "in trouble."

While we were trying to get more details, her pager went off. She looked at it, and we saw that same expression on her face as when we showed her his photo. She clipped the pager back on her purse strap and pretended it was only an interruption. Bob said gently, "That was him, wasn't it?" She nodded but firmly replied she would not return his page. I asked her if he was supposed to meet her today for lunch, and she looked away and shrugged. While she was polite to a fault, it was apparent she was not about to make any effort to lure him in. When Bob asked if he usually met her on campus, she shrugged again and nonchalantly answered "sometimes," then asked to be excused. I asked her to please not contact him about our meeting, and she assured us she would not be contacting him—for any reason—ever again.

Although we thought it was a long shot, Bob and I decided to give it an hour and positioned ourselves on either side of the large double-doors of the busy lobby vestibule. Our subject was described as a light-complected black male, six feet tall with a medium build, which seemed to fit the description of about a quarter of the student body of the inner-city community college. Almost every student was African American or Hispanic; Necaise could pass for either. To add to the challenge, most of the students on this bitterly cold day were wearing hoodies, ball caps, or ski hats. The one thing in our favor was the fact our guy was supposed to have a "gold grill," a mouthful of gold-plated teeth. At the time, this was a popular look and did not guarantee uniqueness, but it did make things easier—if we could see his teeth.

Every few minutes, Bob and I would spot a student who resembled the black-and-white mugshot. And Bob, ever the quick study, would make eye-contact with the look-a-like and yell, "Steve!" If the student responded—usually with a quizzical "Who?"—we would see his teeth and rule him out.

We had been in these scenarios before, trying to spot someone in a crowd based on a photo. It could get maddening how many look-a-likes you could find, but whenever you spotted the actual person, there was no mistake. It was that "ah-ha" moment. And that's just what happened next. I spotted him walking in with a group of students on my side of the doorway and quickly made eye contact with Bob, who picked up on my raised-eyebrows facial alert.

Necaise was wearing an oversized, silver, puffy down jacket with the hood partway up. As soon as he entered the lobby, we moved to either side of him and I said, "Steve, let's be cool about this." He knew what time it was and immediately started to back out the door. We braced him on either side, trying to be discreet, but nearby students began to sense trouble. We steered him toward a wall, while he kept trying out various excuses: "I'm not Steve," "You've got the wrong guy," "I haven't done anything wrong." As soon as we asked him to put his hands behind his back, it was game on. He began to wildly flail his arms and kick off the wall, while we attempted to pin him against the wall. The security guard stood there with his mouth open, frozen in place, and I yelled to him to call 911.

Necaise was a strong guy, wiry, fast, and desperate, and soon had wriggled right out of his slick nylon parka. Like a human tug of war, he was trying to pull us out the door to the street, while we were trying to pull him further into the building. The security guard was trying to usher us down the hall to an empty office, where he stood like a doorman at a hotel, holding open the door and pointing. Bob told me to use my pepper spray, which—after several attempts—I was finally able to fumble off my belt and into my hand. I announced, "Spray!" to alert Bob as to what was coming. Pepper spray is a great tool, but it is not perfect. In close quarters, everyone gets a taste. And so we did, along with the student onlookers within the first ring of spectators. The burst cleared out most of the crowd in our vicinity, making it easier to steer our potential escapee into the small office.

We bum-rushed him into the office so fast the three of us fell over the first desk in the dim room. Bob was like a pit bull at this point, locked onto Necaise in a bear hug around both of his arms. I could see Necaise attempting to dig into his pants, and I told Bob, "Watch his hands; he's trying to get rid of dope!" I repositioned myself alongside them and noticed a custodian standing in the doorway. In a low voice, the janitor calmly asked me if I had my gun. I quickly pressed my right elbow into my holster and was relieved to feel the polymer butt of my .40-caliber Glock.

I then asked Bob the same question as I snaked an arm around our fighter's neck; Bob said he did. He answered so fast that I asked him again to make sure. Annoyed, Bob gave me the same answer, at which point I looked up to see the custodian pinching the grip of a chrome-plated 9mm Smith & Wesson as if he were holding a dirty diaper.

I constricted my arm around his neck and told him to put both his hands behind his back. We could hear the sirens getting louder in the background, but I wanted Necaise in custody before the cavalry arrived. We were all spent by this point, wet with sweat from grappling in a heated building wearing our winter clothes. Necaise, who had borne the brunt of the pepper spray, had a hearty blend of tears, saliva, and snot running down his face but was still not giving up. I began to really crank on his neck, repeating that he needed to put his hands behind his back. Only when he was on the verge of passing out did he surrender, relaxing just enough to allow Bob to pull his hands behind him to be cuffed.

It is quite hard to subdue a motivated opponent safely. It is one thing to practice a choke on a semi-cooperative partner in a gym or dojo, quite another to do it when you are all wearing winter clothes, breathing pepper spray, and sprawled out on the floor between furniture, wondering if the subject still has access to a gun or knife.

We were finally able to roll off him and sit up, trying to catch our breath. Between the coughing and gasping it sounded like an asthma ward. Bob sat on top of Necaise while I went to the custodian to retrieve the handgun. He was plainly relieved to hand it off. We got Necaise to his feet and walked him into the hallway, where a larger crowd had now gathered. Uniformed Bridgeport officers were running into the building, and I asked them to call off responding units, as everything was under control.

The officers took custody of our prisoner, but I held on to the pistol to tag as evidence. Meanwhile the fire department arrived with large fans to ventilate the school of the lingering pepper spray vapor. Bob and I then drove to the police station to begin the paperwork.[24]

---

[24] Within weeks of being paroled from a Connecticut prison in 2001, Necaise was back behind bars. Following a minor fender-bender, he viciously attacked the other driver with a box cutter. Although his victim survived, he suffered a foot-long scar from his forehead to his throat and almost lost an eye. Following his trial and conviction, Necaise was once again paroled in 2017.

CHAPTER 11

I n December, I got a call from Best, telling me that Kumnick, Freddo, and I needed to be at the office the following day in jackets and ties. We were finally going to be interviewed by the FBI regarding the falsified affidavits, nearly six months after filing our complaint.

The Office of Professional Responsibility is the FBI equivalent of "internal affairs" in police departments. I thought back to my Alexandria posting, where I remember the hat being passed around the office for a veteran agent who had received a thirty-day suspension. OPR had dinged him when it was determined he had driven his take-home car on an errand that was not official government business. Thankfully, I had never had any involvement with that unit during my brief career as an agent, but their reputation as the bogeymen of the agency was legendary: no nonsense and all business.

What had troubled me the last few months was how long it was taking OPR to contact us. When I had first spoken to SA Harrington (the former applicant coordinator from New Haven), he opined OPR would be all over this fast, due to the seriousness of the allegations. When I spoke with him over the Thanksgiving break, he was shocked to learn we had not yet been interviewed.

I knew Ralph and his crew were in a box. While the evidence was stacked against them, they could not afford to tell the truth, not even a little. Their best chance of avoiding harsh punishment was to lie their asses off and point fingers. Like my old FBI partner, Dennis, used to joke: "Admit nothing, deny everything, and make counter-allegations."

The following morning, our suits drew the attention of our colleagues, used to seeing us dressed in "soft" clothes: cargo pants or jeans paired with sweatshirts or hoodies in the winter, polo shirts or "guayaberas" in the summer, worn outside our pants to conceal our equipment.[25] I was the first to be called into Bailey's conference room, where the two OPR agents waited. Both had file folders and notebooks between them, and when they introduced themselves, I recognized one. He asked me if I had been in the Alexandria Division, and I remembered him as a fellow first-office agent who arrived several months after me. My spirit was somewhat buoyed by this fact. I knew both had been briefed I was a former agent, but I felt the fact one had seen me hustling on the criminal squad in Alexandria should count for something.

After these brief formalities, they informed me the allegations were "very serious" and that criminal charges were being "considered." I walked them through the narrative: how I first came to discover the inconsistencies in the UFAP affidavits and the discrepancies in the filed federal affidavits. I was buoyed by the fact the agent from Alexandria astutely noticed that two of the affidavits appeared to have been amended, based upon the differences in the type font.

After finishing with the notebook, they asked me if there were any other questionable affidavits. I told them I would be very surprised if there were not, as I was only able to review the most recent open files. I told them that twice in my presence, DiFonzo had announced to the office: "If you don't have it, lie." I added that if they really wanted to get to the bottom of this, all they needed to do was pull a random selection

---

[25] A "guayabera" is a short-sleeved, summer-weight, collared sport shirt, worn outside of one's pants, popular in tropical climates.

of UFAP cases, comparing the affidavits to the information contained in the corresponding airtel lead. If the information did not match up, the affiant should be asked why.

The interview then took a different tack. I was asked if I would be willing to provide a written, sworn statement as to what I had just said. I agreed. They exchanged concerned glances, but neither made a move to take my statement. Then the agent I did not know, Supervisory Special Agent (SSA) Tom Mayhall, asked if I would be willing to testify in a criminal proceeding. Now this was tricky, because if I said no, the investigation would stall and likely go no further. However, if I said yes, it might appear I wanted to see former colleagues of mine face termination, federal prosecution, and possibly even prison. After some thought, my response was measured: if subpoenaed, I would testify truthfully.

I was next asked if I was comfortable with the idea of people being criminally prosecuted on this complaint. I replied it was not my call to decide how this should be handled—that it was ultimately a DOJ decision. Would I be willing to submit to a polygraph examination? My answer was straightforward and without hesitation. "Yes." They again exchanged glances, thanked me for my time, and asked me to send Freddo in.

The three of us met later in my office to compare notes. We had all been asked about our willingness to testify, and much to my relief, we had all agreed. The same with the offer to be polygraphed; Kumnick had said he would take a polygraph if the accused agents also agreed to take one.

The two Steves asked me how long I thought the process would take, but I honestly had no idea. I guessed it would be a matter of weeks—at best a month—depending on how far they wished to pursue it. I suspected that as much as they wanted to deep-six the investigation, our agreeing to provide sworn statements, testify in court, and take polygraphs would force OPR to fairly examine the evidence, expand their search, and hold people accountable.

All through Christmas and into the new year our squad relentlessly hunted felons. Kumnick located a Hartford fugitive wanted for jumping bail on several assaults, robberies, and firearms offenses; the defendant was incarcerated under an alias in Selma, Alabama, and would have been released within days had Kumnick not located him. Next he tracked a Hartford murder suspect to Puerto Rico, where local authorities arrested him. Freddo located a New Britain murder suspect locked up in a Dominican prison, while another of his fugitives was arrested in Philadelphia. Bob Hughes took our squad to Waterbury, where we apprehended a probation violator who was wanted for five counts of first degree failure to appear in court. Later that same week, Hughes arrested a twenty-four-year-old female wanted in Pennsylvania by the Erie County Sheriff's Department as a fugitive from justice. All these captures were made during a one-week period, December 16–23. While most of our office mates were out doing last-minute Christmas shopping, we captured six felons the week before Christmas.

At year's end I received a glowing performance appraisal, prepared by CI Best and approved by DCSA Galluzzo. It concluded: "Supervisory Inspector Dillon is an asset to both the Division of Criminal Justice and the Fugitive Squad. He is a stellar role model and spokesperson for the Division."

At the end of January the *Hartford Courant* announced that Bailey had been offered a job as head of the criminal division of the US Department of Justice. Now it became clear why he had been so careful not to rile the FBI or the Connecticut US Attorney's Office: he needed both agencies' recommendations to land his dream job. If his own people were in the way, then they were just in the way. It was a real step-up in his career. The head of the Department of Justice (DOJ) criminal division supervises US attorneys throughout the United States and its territories, sets policy, and approves and supervises sensitive investigations. Bailey told the reporter he was surprised by the call and added that his sister, US Rep. Barbara B. Kennelly—a close ally of then-President Clinton—"had nothing to do with the call, and was the only person more surprised than he was by the offer." In a poker game, that would be called "a tell."

This was pretty wild, but it paled in comparison to what happened next: Bailey had not actually been offered the job, only sounded out to see if he was interested. The *Courant* ran a follow-up story where a White House source called it "a mischaracterization from the start," and was unable to disguise his annoyance with Bailey for having rushed to tout it in the press. If this was a test of Bailey's ability to keep a secret, it was a spectacular fail, and his name was not mentioned in connection with a federal position ever again.

We continued to dig in and grind away. We located or arrested so many fugitives—working at a construction site in Hartford, hanging out at a "homie's" home in New Britain, strolling down a Bridgeport street we were watching, locked up in a New York prison under an alias, and a Florida fugitive literally "chilling" at the Hartford morgue—that the FBI was getting jealous. They demanded a sit-down.

I was not invited. The brass went instead. Deputy Chief State's Attorney Galluzzo, accompanied by Executive Assistant State's Attorney Tim Sugrue, met with Assistant Special Agent in Charge Gary Rohen at the New Haven FBI Office. Afterwards I received a copy of Sugrue's memo to Galluzzo, memorializing the meeting.

"Mr. Rohen made it perfectly clear that he placed the blame for the breakdown of relations between our office and the Connecticut Fugitive Task Force entirely upon Inspectors Dillon, Kumnick and Freddo and that these three men were 'persona non grata' at the CFTF. Mr. Rohen also questioned the physical fitness of Inspector Marrero and the 'philosophical' fitness of Chief Inspector Best."

Rohen had tremendous chutzpah, and he wasn't done. He proposed Inspectors Bob Hughes and Joe Howard be reassigned to the Task Force along with Inspector Healy, while the "persona non grata" were to refer all incoming fugitive cases "to the CFTF, which would be the exclusive street apprehension team."

Fortunately, Sugrue was able to see this for the insult that it was and recommended that our office take no action until OPR had completed its investigation: "Mr. Rohen's proposal serves primarily the FBI's interests and ignores concerns raised by our own people. I am not at all comfortable with agreeing to a proposal which, in essence, punished several of our Inspectors for reasons that are not at all clear to me." Moreover, the FBI was attempting to control "what is primarily a state concern: the apprehension of fugitives facing state criminal charges...not federal crimes." Instead Sugrue made a counter proposal, whereby the task force would be run by our office, with three state troopers, detectives from New Haven, Bridgeport, and Hartford, and two FBI agents at our proposed future off-site in Newington. Needless to say this went nowhere.[26]

News of the meeting with ASAC Rohen did not sit well with the Fugitive Squad. The task force still had one of our inspectors, even if it was one we didn't trust. Now the FBI had the audacity to request two more, while telling the chief state's attorney how to run his own office.

During the first week of March, I opened and assigned seventeen referred fugitive cases. I'd already lost Healy to the task force, and Kumnick was again on temporary assignment to the Hartford State's Attorney's Office on a murder trial. This left me with three inspectors for over one hundred fugitive cases.

Meanwhile, the FBI task force continued to mislead callers who specifically asked for us, telling callers that we no longer worked fugitives. Police officers who knew us reported rumors were being spread that we had been asked to leave the task force due to incompetence and ineffectiveness. Since we were still under Bailey's gag order not to discuss the falsified affidavits with anyone, the accusations went unrefuted while we steamed over it.

Additionally, there was still no news from the FBI's Office of Professional Responsibility. Steve Kumnick had received a telephone call from SSA Mayhall, the OPR investigator, shortly after our interviews, asking him to clarify one of his answers. After that, nothing for three months. Kumnick called Mayhall in mid-April and asked him for an

---

[26] To show Mr. Sugrue his appreciation for his candor, Mr. Bailey later demoted him from executive assistant state's attorney (the number three position, just below a deputy assistant chief state's attorney but above a supervisory assistant state's attorney) and flopped him back to the Appellate Division at a lower pay grade.

update on the investigation, only to be told he could not comment on the status of the case.

This was bewildering and ominous. I had never heard of a law enforcement agency telling victims that they could not reveal the status of an investigation into their complaint. I began to suspect that OPR had no intention of conducting an actual investigation. If they were, they would have pulled *all* our previous UFAP cases and met with us in a follow-up interview. We would have then had the opportunity to review and recognize any other instances where affidavits were embellished with fictitious information, thereby showing a long-standing pattern of misconduct.

Further, despite having our ears to the ground, we never heard of any other current or former task force members being interviewed about the issue of falsified UFAP affidavits. Had the FBI been looking into misconduct of a police department under similar circumstances, they would have pulled files and reports going back at least a year and interviewed everyone who was working or had worked there. This notable lack of curiosity suggested they were trying to do damage control rather than get to the bottom of things.

Dave Best would simply throw up his hands in exasperation and shake his head, not wanting to hear it. He was in a tough spot: publicly loyal to Bailey, privately angry that OPR was giving us the runaround, unable to do anything about it.

The mystery was solved when we learned that Special Agent Ralph DiFonzo had been promoted to Supervisory Special Agent Ralph DiFonzo while still the target of the OPR investigation. Promoting Ralph sent a clear message to the FBI investigators that HQ would not support any finding of criminal wrongdoing, hence there was no need to research other UFAP warrants or expand their interviews. It also meant that the other FBI agents who had signed the falsified affidavits had no reason to be forthcoming during questioning; no one in their right mind was going to implicate the person who was now their immediate supervisor.

It was lonely out there in the wind, and the three of us decided we needed to provide a copy of the falsified affidavit notebook to our union. It was clear our own agency didn't have our back.

As far as our union went, they were historically a toothless lapdog, only active when they thought that pay or take-home cars were at issue. The union president at that time was Larry Skinner, who was originally hired by Bailey back when Bailey was the Hartford state's attorney. Because of that alliance, Skinner deferred to Bailey in most union issues and did not want to rock the boat. Skinner also took a dim view of the Fugitive Squad. I suspect most inspectors resented us getting to dress down, having special equipment issued exclusively to us, and seeing press releases issued weekly because of our successes. This was atypical of the traditional inspector role, which had normally been low key, low profile, and behind the scenes.

On March 28, I got a call from Bryson Hull, a cub reporter for the *New Britain Herald*. Hull had accompanied us at Bailey's invitation the previous month. He had written a glowing profile of our fugitive squad, noting: "Founded in late 1993 by Chief State's Attorney Jack Bailey, the elite, six-man fugitive squad has annually brought in more than 100 repeat offenders back to justice — at no cost to the taxpayer." During Hull's ride-along, he witnessed us capture a fugitive in a Bridgeport basement apartment. I was shocked when Hull now asked me about the falsified federal affidavits and even more shocked to learn that he had copies of all the documents.

After several seconds, I recovered enough to be guarded in my response. As much as I wanted to speak the truth, I had to be careful not to violate Bailey's directive. I told him I did not feel comfortable discussing the matter and asked who had put him onto the story. Like any good reporter, he declined to name his source. I then contacted CI Best and put him on notice of the conversation, in case he was the next name on Hull's contact list.

Kumnick went public. With OPR avoiding his calls, Bailey's indifference to our manpower shortage, and DiFonzo being promoted in the midst of the OPR investigation, Steve had had enough. When Hull called him back in April and told Steve he had photocopies of the falsified affidavits, Steve met with him, confirmed they were real, and spoke on the record. But that did not explain who leaked the affidavits in the first place. I had not provided the paperwork to anyone outside our office, and Steve swore he had not been the source of the leak.[27]

I could tell we were in for it right away, and while I knew it would be a shit show, I was secretly pleased it was being exposed to public view.

Unbeknownst to us that Friday, Hull had contacted CSA Bailey regarding this breaking story. While it is unclear if SAC Parks learned of the impending article from Bailey or from Hull himself, it apparently upset him so much he "suffered a near fatal asthma attack" as reported by *the Herald-Press* and was fighting for his life in a New Haven hospital.

With all this excitement, we rushed out to get the Sunday edition of the *Herald-Press*, and there it was on the front page, above the fold: "FBI Fabricated Warrants, Complaint Says…State inspectors allege seven incidents of changed information."

Kumnick walked the reporter through all the facts, and Hull had the files. It was pretty damning. For context, Hull interviewed a Hartford federal public defender named Gary Weinberger, who explained to readers, "A UFAP is just a gimmick to allow the FBI to join in on the search for someone, because it is dismissed as soon as the suspect is arrested." Weinberger added he had never seen anyone prosecuted on this charge in his fourteen years as a federal attorney.

Kumnick told Hull about DiFonzo's remark advising his agents to lie to the court if they didn't have the facts. "At the time," said Kumnick, "I thought it was a joke but as things turned out, I don't think it was."

The article recounted the lockout from the New Haven off-site, our eviction, and the OPR investigation. "As of Friday, neither Kumnick nor Bailey knew the status of the nine-month old investigation."

In his interview with Hull, Bailey tried—but failed—to walk a tightrope: "'I have every confidence in the internal affairs department of the FBI,' said Bailey, who would not comment on whether he believes the allegations to be true. Despite the allegations of his employees, Bailey said

---

27 Years later I discovered our union was actually the source of the leaked documents.

that he still has confidence in the FBI office and their leadership. 'I would have not kept an inspector there if I had felt that there was a problem with the affidavits,' Bailey said, referring to Inspector Healy."

This was the real news in the story for us. Our boss was publicly throwing his support behind the men who were telling lies about us and obstructing an investigation into their behavior. Bailey knew us, he had seen the evidence with his own eyes, and knew we were telling the truth. By saying he did not feel "that there was a problem with the affidavits," he aligned himself with SAC Parks and against his own men. That changed everything for me.

In the article, Kumnick's indignation came through loud and clear: "He (SA Brophy) lied, but he lied using my name as the source of these creations of his mind. In this business, meaning police business, you have your word and your name, and I cannot allow my name to be associated with that." Kumnick nailed it. As a law enforcement professional, Steve recognized your reputation is everything. One begins to build one's reputation the first day of the academy, and it continues from that point on. Before you start your first tour of duty, your reputation follows you *and* precedes you. And this is why DiFonzo never asked me or my guys to "amend" our UFAP affidavits to comport to his version of the truth: he knew I would not tolerate it. Ralph had seen me conduct police business day-to-day, obtaining search warrants for third-party residences, not playing fast and loose with the truth. So he knew not to tip his hand and ask for a "rewrite"—he knew he would be rebuked. I had spent years building my reputation in the court system and in law enforcement circles, and was not about to allow it to be compromised so that an FBI agent could pad his or her statistical accomplishments for financial gain.

As an example, when I first left the FBI and was assigned to the Economic Crime Bureau, I was assigned a complex financial crimes case with multiple victims. After preparing an arrest warrant for the defendant, the affidavit was over thirty pages long. I presented it to Judge Martin L. McKeever in New Haven, a no-nonsense judge I had worked for as a courtroom sheriff years earlier. After greeting me in his chambers, he asked me about my time at the Branford Police Department and the

FBI. I was flattered he already knew I had worked at both places. But he was caught off guard by my new assignment at the Chief State's Attorney Office. After we caught up, he hefted the warrant, fanned through the multiple pages, and looked at me: "Is it here [meaning probable cause]?" I confirmed that it was and added it was a very solid case. Knowing me and my reputation, he began signing and dating the bottom of each page, while continuing to ask me about my career. After signing the last page, he put me under oath, handed me back my warrant, shook my hand, and wished me well. And the only reason that happened was because of my reputation.

With Bailey's position clearly articulated in the article, he had chosen his side. The shadow war had begun. Two sides diametrically opposed, operating in secrecy, housed within the same agency.

CHAPTER 12

irst thing Monday morning, CSA Bailey ordered us into his conference room for an emergency meeting. We all did our best to sit as
far as possible from the head of the table. Not by coincidence, I had
approved a vacation request for Kumnick the previous week, so Steve was
out of state. Just late enough to keep us guessing, Bailey's office door flew
open; he strode in and stood at the head of his conference table, staring at
each of us in turn with face flushed and nostrils flaring, then lit into us.

He told us the *Herald-Press* article would set back relations with the
FBI "for years." Kumnick "would be subpoenaed by every attorney in the
country because of his remarks, and could very well be subpoenaed to the
Unabomber trial."[28] This bizarre remark was followed by another: This
"could affect federal funding that the state was receiving." It had "made
it all the way to the Governor's office." He announced there would now
be an investigation into who spoke to the reporter. Of course, it was no

---

[28] Referring to Theodore "Ted" Kaczynski. Kumnick was never subpoenaed to
that trial, or any other federal trial for that matter.

mystery as to who had spoken to the reporter; Kumnick was quoted and his name used no less than twenty-five times in the article.

Bailey added that this was "a personal embarrassment" and "a black eye for the Division." We sat there and took it. There was nothing else to do.

The internal investigation would begin right away, led by Chief Inspector Steve Grasso and attorney Cornelius Shea, a trusted associate of Bailey's and a family friend. "Neal" Shea was a retired prosecutor with a reputation as a hard ass. He had a gravelly voice and an Irish sunburn from years of chain smoking and heavy drinking.

Bailey demanded to know who violated his orders and the Division's media policy. The report was due in thirty days, and Kumnick was to be transferred to the Litchfield State's Attorney's Office, effective immediately.

Litchfield County is a lovely area in the rural northwest corner of Connecticut where very little happens in the way of crime, or anything else for that matter. The informal nickname "the quiet corner of the state" is well deserved. Due to its remote location and lack of activity, it was an office an inspector could be "temporarily assigned," if one fell out of favor. It was commonly referred to as "Siberia," the "Land of the Lost," the "Penal Colony," or Kumnick's favorite: the "Island of Misfit Toys." While Steve was collecting his Hartford police pension at a relatively early age, he had two boys who had plans for college, and he was terrified of losing his job.

Bailey knew he could get away with this in the short-term, as our union contract allowed an inspector to be "temporarily assigned" for up to 120 days within any calendar year. What this meant for Steve was a ninety-mile round trip commute from his home in Rocky Hill. With little to do in the way of actual work, he now had all day to obsess over what his fate would be at month's end.

I was worried too. We had provided Bailey with seven documented examples of falsified affidavits being sworn to before federal judges—with our names as the sources of the false information—and he was content to let the FBI bury it, while Kumnick was made the target of an internal investigation and given an immediate thirty-day nonvoluntary transfer.

The office became a hostile work environment. We had been led to believe we would be moving to our own off-site, but once promised, this never came to pass no matter how many official and unofficial requests were made. Meanwhile, I was determined to keep the inspectors engaged in our work. I still felt if we continued to prove our value by bringing fugitives to justice, we could secure our position within the office as an indispensable asset. Even after I recognized this was a naïve hope, I still kept busy. As bad as office politics got, police work never got old.

There was a small sign in our office with a quote attributed to Sophocles: "He escapes who is not pursued." A bail jumper has two options: run or hide. News of police efforts come as no surprise, but often the heat works to our advantage. Sometimes the pressure from family and friends forces the subject to surrender. While this pressure may be out of concern for the criminal's safety, other times it is self-serving; they don't want the additional scrutiny of the police, which may be bad for their lifestyle or business.

In other instances, forcing the fugitive out of their "comfort zone," whether it be their "block," their "hood," or even their state, exposes them to make mistakes and burn through their cash even faster than usual. In turn, this draws the attention of the local police, who now see a strange face in their town or city and want to know who this newcomer is and what they are up to. In some instances—especially for drug dealers—this attracts the unwanted attention of rivals, who historically do not embrace competition or the free market. This was the case with one of Kumnick's fugitives, Takesha Burton, who was wanted in Hartford for murder and second-degree assault with a firearm. She was in turn murdered, gunned down on the streets of Indianapolis. Whether playing sports or slinging drugs, the visiting team is always at a disadvantage.

The same week Kumnick began his rural exile, our downsized squad still made seven collars. Bob Hughes received a call from a CI (confidential informant) on a Friday night, reporting he had spotted one of Bob's fugitives hanging out on a street corner. Bob immediately contacted the Bridgeport Police Department and provided a clothing description; they caught the subject, who was wanted on a gun beef and probation violation. A few days later, Inspector Joe Howard interviewed family and friends of a Bridgeport probation violator—also wanted on gun charges—who then opted to surrender himself at the New Haven Police Department.

Bob and Joe next began a neighborhood canvass for another probation violator, this one wanted for robbery. They recognized him sitting on a front porch in Bridgeport and had their third capture of the week. Bob Hughes then brought our dwindling squad out to a Waterbury address to locate a wanted rapist and drug dealer. We discovered his aunt had evicted him the previous day. That evening, his mother brought him to the Waterbury police station to surrender. Joe Howard next teamed up with the Yale University Police Department and scooped up a wanted burglar in New Haven. At the same time, Bob was attempting to locate a Bridgeport probation violator wanted for the sexual assault of a minor. Yale University police, unaware of his fugitive status, recognized this subject as a local panhandler. They took him into custody for Bob and notified us.

To end the week, Bob and I were surveilling a New Britain address while Joe Howard was simultaneously watching a Newington address for the same subject. Bob and I lucked out, stopping him as he was taking his pit bull for a walk. While waiting for New Britain police to arrive, we persuaded the fugitive—at gunpoint—to secure his dog in his pickup truck. We couldn't afford to take any chances with this guy. Even though he was "only" wanted on a probation violation for a pair of burglaries, he had already done a twelve-year bid for homicide.

Within a seven-day span, Bob Hughes and Joe Howard had been responsible—directly or indirectly—for the apprehension of seven wanted felons captured in four Connecticut cities.

The following week Steve Freddo tracked a Willimantic probation absconder to Bangor, Maine, where Penobscot sheriff's deputies took him into custody. Bob Hughes pinpointed the whereabouts of a Waterbury fugitive, wanted on firearms and narcotic charges, to Cobb County, Georgia. Bob contacted the Georgia Bureau of Investigation, who discovered the twenty-two-year-old hiding under a bed in a second-floor apartment.

To round out the week, Joe Howard, accompanied by two Stratford police officers, wrestled a wanted robber into handcuffs at a motel where he had been hiding out. Joe then took the squad to Bridgeport late one night after receiving an after-hours call from another informant. After failing to find the fugitive in the residence, we expanded our search and found him concealed under a woodpile in the backyard. The thirty-seven-year-old pedophile was wanted for a probation violation, stemming from a 1985 conviction: the sexual assault of a nine-year-old boy.

Even as he had us investigated, Chief State's Attorney Bailey continued to issue press releases taking credit for our growing list of captures.

I knew I had done nothing wrong: I had not disclosed any documents to anyone outside our office, I had declined to be interviewed by Hull, and I only learned of Kumnick's "media policy violation" at the same time as Chief Inspector Best. As a result, I knew I had little to fear from Chief Inspector Grasso and former prosecutor Shea.

Kumnick, on the other hand, had been read his Miranda warnings by Shea and Grasso, and was rattled to the core. He was convinced he was going to be terminated—and possibly arrested—although for what no one could fathom.

Our fugitive work continued through the summer with us clearly in the boss's doghouse; we still had not been moved into the empty off-site in Newington. We did get a new inspector to bring our number back up to six, a likable guy named Mike Malchik who had been on the prestigious major crime squad at the Connecticut State Police. Malchik stood out for two big reasons: he had gotten his law degree from Quinnipiac University Law School, and he also had arrested Michael Ross, a serial killer who terrorized New London County for five years. Ross confessed to Mike to raping and murdering eight women, the youngest a fourteen-year-old girl. Ross would be the last inmate put to death in Connecticut, and Mike was there to watch it.

Sadly, Kumnick was never the same after his thirty-day reassignment to Litchfield. While he was always there when needed, he did not have the same zeal for the work. Everyone was affected by the treatment Steve had suffered, and we collectively lost confidence in the support of the administration. We felt that in the event of an incident, if we hit the wrong door or had to shoot someone—which was a possibility every day we worked—we would be hung out to dry. In the event of a police-involved shooting, the Department of Justice would often open their own inquiry under the guise of a possible civil rights violation, where we could find ourselves answering questions from the FBI once again.

I did a lot of worrying about keeping my squad together, afraid of losing Bob, Joe, or Mike to the task force. They all said they would refuse the assignment, then file a union grievance if ordered to join the FBI group. Another problem was that Chief Inspector Grasso was in charge of the move to the Newington off-site. He resented my lack of cooperation with his internal affairs investigation, which was another reason why it was moving at a glacial pace. The two-story house was actually deteriorating from lack of use.

Our successes continued throughout the summer, and Ralph DiFonzo and his men fumed as we continued to set out leads across the country. At one point DiFonzo actually had an FBI teletype sent out to all the FBI fugitive task forces in the country advising them not to act on any Connecticut fugitive leads unless they originated from *his* task force. Joe Howard discovered this when he sent out a lead to my old office in Washington, DC, and I confirmed it with a telephone call to an agent I knew who still worked there.

Our group was persistent and imaginative. Research, interviews, informants, and street smarts generated intelligence, which in turn developed leads to out-of-state addresses. Through contacts and networking, we sent out requests across the globe, resulting in the arrests of Connecticut fugitives in California, Georgia, Hawaii, Kansas, Massachusetts, New York, North Carolina, Pennsylvania, South Carolina, Texas, and Washington, in addition to Canada and Puerto Rico—all without once utilizing the UFAP process.

We were showing up the task force, while at the same time proving we did not need the pretense of a UFAP warrant. In August 1997, likely at the urging of his personal friend SAC Parks, FBI Director Louis J. Freeh sent each member of the FBI task force a personal letter of commendation for their work. It was announced in *The Investigator*, the FBI's in-house publication, which naturally we read after I obtained a copy from a colleague.

In my weekly status report to CSA Bailey, dated September 22, 1997, I reminded him of a very significant milestone: "The Fugitive Squad has initiated 200 investigations (in 1997) as of this week." I then put it in perspective: "211 investigations were initiated during calendar year 1996 and 179 were initiated during calendar year 1995."

CSA Bailey continued his press releases: "Sweep Nets 3 in Bridgeport," described how our squad arrested three wanted felons at three separate addresses in a single morning. The charges ranged from robbery to weapons and narcotics violations, probation violations, and failure to appear in court. One week later, we received a tip from an informant that a most wanted fugitive was staying at a motel somewhere along the Berlin Turnpike. The problem was, the turnpike spans ten miles through five towns and cities, littered on both sides with seedy motels, flop houses, and short-stay inns. With only a general description of his vehicle, we methodically worked our way from motel to motel and only found the car several hours later at the second to last motel we had on our list.

After showing the photo to the desk clerk and confirming the room number, we discovered the door unlocked and our subject seated on the toilet, pants at his ankles. This was a big catch, and not just because of the fact Kenneth M. Edwards weighed over three hundred pounds. Edwards was being sought by the Connecticut State Police; the Bristol, Naugatuck, Waterbury, Watertown, and Wolcott Police Departments; and the Waterbury Probation Office for a total of forty-five felonies.

There were always rumblings our squad was destined to be axed. Kumnick had a source, his brother, Gerry, who worked as an inspector in the Gang Bureau, run by Bailey favorite Chris Morano. Morano was an ambitious scamp with a big mouth and often knew what was going on "upstairs." Still, Chief Inspector Best confidently reassured us we were doing a great job and would be in the new off-site by year's end. Showing me a budget proposal, he pointed out funding for six inspectors, plus my position and a secretary, in addition to monies for specialized training, equipment, cell phones, pagers, a toll-free hotline, laptops, computers, and an informant payment fund. Despite this, Steve Kumnick was convinced we wouldn't make it to year's end.

In October I learned our squad had been nominated to receive a certificate of recognition at the State Capitol for our achievements and our cooperation with other state agencies. Kumnick scoffed: "Is this a memorial service or what?" Sure enough, the invitation was rescinded at the last moment, and no one could tell us why. I began to suspect Kumnick might be right.

*Deputy Chief State's Attorney Chris Morano being
congratulated by Chief State's Attorney Jack Bailey.*

We kept hoping things would get better, and it seemed promising when Galluzzo retired as operations chief and Chris Morano took his place. While Morano was "Bailey's boy" and we knew he was ambitious, he could also be irreverent, spontaneous, and witty. Short in stature, with wire-framed glasses perched above chubby cheeks, he sported a dark mop of "slightly-too-long-for-his-age" hair. He looked a bit like Mike Meyers as Austin Powers: International Man of Mystery, both physically and in the way he fancied himself a bit of a dandy. While his predecessor, Galluzzo, had taken a passive role as Bailey's number two, Morano as deputy chief state's attorney was prepared to flex his muscles, and Bailey seemed fine with it.

We met him within a week of his appointment, in Bailey's conference room. Morano sat in Bailey's chair at the head of the table, but at least he showed more empathy than Bailey. He wanted to know everything about the history and acrimonious breakup of the FBI task force, and so we told him. He told us he was tasked by Bailey to meet with the FBI, which he planned to do on November 25, but wanted some background information and statistics prior to the sit-down.

He seemed open minded, so we shared our concern over the widespread rumor that Bailey was looking for a reason to disband our group in an attempt to appease Parks, who was obviously upset that we continued to exist. Interestingly, Morano reassured us that there was no such plan he was aware of and that he personally supported our continued existence.

Before Morano's meeting "to discuss the co-existence" of the rival fugitive squads at the New Haven FBI office with SAC Parks and ASAC Rohen, I provided him with a memo outlining our accomplishments for the year to date:

- Fugitive Squad arrests within the State of Connecticut: 131
- Arrests made outside Connecticut at our request: 45
- Arrests made by the Fugitive Squad at the request of another state: 4

Morano met with SAC Parks and ASAC Rohen for over an hour. In his report to Bailey, Morano accurately noted our belief that the root of the conflict was the falsified affidavits and our concern at the hostility of the FBI to our continued existence, "even though the Federal Investigation into the complaint remains unresolved."

Parks told Morano he had no problem with the existence of the unit "as long as it did not involve Inspectors Dillon, Kumnick or Freddo." Rohen was of the opinion our squad should be disbanded completely, and the state's attorney should send two new inspectors to join the Task Force.

This was an outrageous demand, and to Morano's credit, he rejected it, saying the Fugitive Squad "has been a productive and valuable resource to the division…an efficient operation that not only locates fugitives but also apprehends them in a professional and operationally safe manner. In fact, I could not discover any situation where a target has filed a complaint related to the operations of the Fugitive Unit."

It was true; operating on our own, we did not have a single instance where a shot was fired, a lawsuit or complaint filed, or anyone—inspector, police officer, defendant, or civilian—injured. There had been no vehicle pursuits, no car accidents, and no claims of property unjustifiably destroyed or damaged. Luck certainly favored us, but proper planning, training, experience, and cool heads also played a big part.

Morano pointed out that the elaborate and time-consuming process of the FBI's UFAP application procedure contrasted unfavorably with our streamlined ability to deal directly with other state law enforcement agencies as soon as a state's attorney verbally authorized extradition. He officially recommended against abolishing the unit: "It would be a shame to dissolve a unit that is providing a valuable service to the Division as well as local police departments and state agencies. In addition, dissolution of the squad could give the impression to some that it was done to appease the F.B.I. completely ignoring the many successes it (the Fugitive Squad) has enjoyed."

Morano's compromise solution was to place the fugitive squad at the Newington off-site, assign a prosecutor as a liaison, reduce CI Best's involvement, and send one inspector to the Task Force instead of two.

I felt buoyed by Morano's memo. Best agreed. Kumnick still believed we were doomed. The rest of the guys were on the fence. We continued to sulk around the office, analyzing every bit of scuttlebutt we could glean. Everyone was hoping Bailey would hang tough and support us, but the rumors persisted we were "dead men walking."

Despite our funk, we still made captures. The Fairfield State's Attorney's Office was trying a defendant for a homicide, and a key witness could not be found. The Fairfield state's attorney's inspectors had been unable to serve the subpoena on the eighteen-year-old; he was not only on the run as a reluctant witness, but also as a probation violator and bond jumper on a drug charge. I assigned the case to Joe Howard right after Thanksgiving. On Wednesday, December 3—the last day of the homicide trial—Joe Howard, Bob Hughes, and I, along with Bridgeport probation officers, gave Marshawn Spruill an early morning wake-up call. After a quick trip to the Bridgeport lockup for processing, Spruill was taken directly to the courthouse, where he testified on behalf of the prosecution.

Simultaneously, Mike Malchik, Steve Kumnick, and Steve Freddo were at the opposite end of the state. There, with the assistance of the New London, Groton City, and Waterford Police Departments, they went to a New London address and were told by Mildred Guzman—quite adamantly—that she was home alone. Upon entering the house, they located Luis A. Davila hiding in Guzman's bedroom closet. He had been wanted since 1993 for sexually assaulting a minor. Guzman, for her Oscar-worthy performance, was also arrested and hauled off for hindering prosecution.

The following day, Howard hit pay dirt again. Joe was tracking a guy whose record was as big as he was in size: Richard J. Jenkins Jr.—6'3" and 290 pounds—had fifty-three arrests in Connecticut, plus criminal histories in New Jersey and New York. Joe believed Jenkins had relocated to Dobbs Ferry, New York, and provided that department with a description of Jenkins's vehicle. Dobbs Ferry authorities spotted the vehicle in front of a house. They then had to physically restrain the combative Jenkins, who was not hard not to miss. Jenkins was wanted by thirteen Connecticut police departments, with additional outstanding arrest warrants in New York and New Jersey.

An aside that Morano shared with Dave Best was that during his meeting with the FBI, SAC Parks—in a fit of pique—had threatened to assign "fifteen agents" to follow us around. Incredulous, I asked Dave what was supposed to be the purpose of that, and he guessed "to see if we were working." Steve Kumnick quipped that Parks should, then maybe they could learn how to catch fugitives.

I could not believe my ears. The head of the New Haven FBI was threatening to have inspectors surveilled because we had truthfully accused his agents of falsifying federal affidavits. Dave recognized his mistake in sharing this when I asked if the surveillance was to be directed at the entire squad, or just me, Kumnick, and Freddo. He said he didn't know anything more, and suggested I ask Morano when I saw him.

On Thursday, December 11, DCSA Morano poked his head into my office. Catching him off guard, I immediately asked him if SAC Parks intended to have the entire squad surveilled or just his three personal targets. Morano grinned, then frowned and asked, "Where did you get that?" I asked what did Parks think he was going to discover with his surveillance? Morano replied, "I think he would do anything he could to try to find one of you guys screwing off." Then quickly added, "If in fact he said that." And with that, he left my office, obviously regretting the exchange.

This is when I decided to begin documenting *everything*. I had been keeping copies of all the memos and emails that were being exchanged. Starting on this day, I began taking notes of every pertinent conversation the same day while they were fresh in my mind.

Not only was Mike Malchik a lawyer, he also possessed keen insight into office politics. He suggested I consult with an attorney, and he introduced me to a friend of his. After I had walked him through what had transpired to date, Mike's lawyer friend sat for a minute mulling it over. Finally, he said that while he found the tale highly disturbing, he could not think of any grounds to file a lawsuit. Mike and I looked at each other in disbelief; how could it be we had no civil recourse? The attorney sat back in his chair, pinched the bridge of his nose, and shrugged. "I just don't see where you have a case." He patted us each on the back sympathetically as we left his office.

The hammer finally fell, but I was not there; I was on a rare day off. Fortunately, Freddo took notes. The entire squad was summoned to Bailey's conference room. Bailey and Morano entered the room, and Bailey announced the "suspension" of the squad due to a loss of funding and manpower issues. Bailey, trying to take a palliative approach, quickly added how he was not doing away with the Fugitive Squad but temporarily shelving it until he could get the state legislature to pass a bill making us a "statutory unit."

"Rest assured," he said, Parks and the FBI had nothing to do with it. Again, the poker "tell." Which meant, of course, that Parks and the FBI had *everything* to do with it. Money and manpower had never once been mentioned during the last year, and now it was supposed to be the reason behind our "suspension." Nobody was buying a word of it. While our funding had been changed, we were still a cash cow. The legislature—finally realizing how much money was being brought in by the efforts of the office—had changed the wording in the original bill; we now received a percentage of the monies, not the full amount. However, the money more than made up for our cost, so we knew we were part of the upcoming budget.

Bailey then asked everyone to give some thought as to what they would like to do while he worked on getting the "money back." He reminded them not to open any new cases and to close out all our active files, and wrapped up by adding that he planned to write a letter of commendation for each inspector's file.

Bailey formalized the announcement the following day, by faxing his edict to all the state's attorney's offices. I took the afternoon off; I went to see a different lawyer.

After Mike Malchik and I suffered through his attorney's disappointing assessment of our plight, I discreetly began asking my contacts who was the best labor law attorney for employment actions and civil rights cases. Karen Lee Torre's name came up, although I was warned she could be ornery. I wanted someone formidable, someone who would not wilt in a courtroom when our adversaries would be the Division of Criminal Justice, the Office of the Attorney General, and the Federal Bureau of Investigation. With my career on the line, I needed a juggernaut, a barrister with sharp elbows and a sharper tongue. I was not looking to get into a gun fight outgunned.

Her office was in downtown New Haven within walking distance of the federal courthouse. She sat behind an antique wooden desk piled with papers in an exposed-brick, high-ceilinged room. Her manner was as rough as her office walls. She chain-smoked Virginia Slims and kept the large window open behind her in a losing attempt to clear the air. One got the impression from her coughing and squinting she did not actually enjoy smoking but rather tolerated it; nonetheless, we both suffered through it together over the next hour while she reviewed my documents.

She was a tough, Catholic school girl from New Haven. She'd attended Yale Law School. She was sharp. And we got off on the wrong foot. "All cops lie," she said as she thumbed through the notebook of falsified affidavits. My stony silence eventually made her look up.

"What if I said all lawyers are greedy ambulance chasers out to make a quick buck at the expense of their clients?"

"Point taken," she deadpanned.

I explained to her that everything I told her was the absolute truth, and throughout my career I had never submitted any warrant that was not accurate. I then walked her through the entire debacle. She asked blunt questions, interrupted often, and didn't waste time. At the end of the hour, she said her interest was piqued, but she wanted to see what happened next, now that the Fugitive Squad was kaput. If there were to be a free speech case, she added, it would be stronger if all the aggrieved parties filed together. My one hour with her cost me $300.

The next day I was asked to see Mr. Bailey in his office. All of a sudden he was full of praise, about how I had begun the unit from nothing, what a great job I had done, what a huge success it had been, and how he was going to put a letter of commendation into each inspector's personal file, including mine.

"It was too bad about the funding," he said, adding that the other state's attorneys never fully supported our work. This was news to me but not surprising; the dozen state's attorneys felt most of our bureaus and units were either redundant or simply not needed. He quickly went on about how we needed to figure out how to get our funding back so we could get the squad operational again. "I need you to rally the troops" and to be prepared to "testify before the legislature" as to the need for this type of unit. He mapped out his plan of our meeting with all the bail bondsmen and their lobbyists in an effort to guarantee its passage. Of course, none of this ever happened.

Meanwhile, he suggested I should think of something I would like to do, "something innovative and interesting," but not to get "bogged down" as he needed me available to "testify before the legislature, schmooze bondsmen, and get ready to start the Fugitive Squad back up with at least six people."

There was no mention of the FBI and their falsified affidavits. Bailey finished by shaking my hand and asking me to meet with DCSA Morano to work out the details.

As soon as I left Bailey's office, I saw Morano lurking in the hallway. He invited me into his office and asked me how my meeting went with "the Boss." I told him, and he said he would be meeting with each inspector to determine new assignments.

It was "pretty much agreed" that I would be able to retain my current salary and title, said Morano. Again, the veiled threat. I replied I hoped so since I'd held the supervisor's job way past the probationary period, and all my evaluations had been quite favorable. Morano observed that the issue could still be contested but quickly added he did not want to see me go through the trouble of filing a prolonged grievance before the labor board.

After this subtle exchange of threats, he asked me where I wished to be transferred. My response was blunt: "Nowhere." He was visibly taken aback. I explained I had been hired at the Chief State's Attorney's Office and had worked there for eight years, I had more seniority than any other inspector in the squad, and I did not expect to be transferred to another location. Our inspectors' contract read that when involuntary transfers are to be made, seniority must be considered. I was the most senior of all the inspectors except for Healy, who was not being transferred because he was still on loan to the FBI.

Completely ignoring my answer, he matter-of-factly said there was a need for manpower in Fairfield, Hartford, New London, and Litchfield. Did I still want to be the supervisor of the Fugitive Squad at a later time? Again, the not-so-subtle threat. I was intentionally noncommittal, as I knew the Fugitive Squad was never coming back. "Perhaps. I'll think about it. *If* it ever happens."

Did Morano expect me to work as an inspector and not a supervisor? He did, but at a supervisor's pay. He said he would get back to me with a list of offices to choose from. I informed him I would challenge any transfer through a union grievance. He wryly observed that by the time my grievance was filed, heard, and decided, the four-month transfer would be over. "I figured you would grieve it." Apparently Bailey's definition of me finding something "innovative and interesting to do" contrasted greatly with Morano's marching orders: assign me to a nonsupervisory inspector's position at a distant judicial district for a third of a year.

Bailey and Morano, taking a page from police movies, thought they could play "good cop/bad cop." They did not figure on my strategy, which was "worse cop." There were two other big differences they forgot to consider: first, they were not cops; and second, I was not playing.

Now that the gloves were off, I asked Morano why the squad had not been allowed to move into the Newington off-site eight months ago, and how did the funding suddenly run out on our self-funded operation when we were recovering so many bonds? Morano softened. "Read between the lines—they didn't want you to get entrenched." Morano then said he hoped nothing we discussed or anything he handed out (obviously referring to his December 8 memo) would ever be used against him. He admitted he was put into a "shitty situation and was not happy with the way things turned out."

As I was later recounting these conversations with Dave Best, he told me he overheard the director of financial services express her surprise at the suspension of the Fugitive Squad for financial reasons, since the positions were funded through the following year. We considered the meaning of this and agreed that Bailey needed an excuse to justify sacking our squad, and the only credible reason he could come up with was the nebulous "lack of funding" excuse.

Kumnick, Freddo, and I stepped into a vacant office to talk, as we suspected our offices were now being bugged. I told them about my meeting with Karen Torre and asked how they felt about a joint lawsuit. Kumnick was a quick no. He'd already come close to losing his job and could not risk it again. Freddo also begged off. He needed his pension and had no money to pay a lawyer. It was warm in that office, but there were cold feet in the room. The team was beginning to disintegrate.

CHAPTER 13

O n New Year's Eve day, Morano found Kumnick and me sitting in my office. He was all business and came right to the point: where do you want to be transferred? The Statewide Prosecution Bureau, I said. I reminded him no supervisor was currently assigned there.

"There is no posting for that spot."
"That's my choice."
"If not there, then where?"

I pointed out there were no postings for any *other* offices either, that he was attempting to assign me outside of my official duty station and outside of my job classification. He walked away, openly taking notes.

Later that week, Bob Hughes and I were exercising at the Newington Gold's Gym before work. We ran into Tim Seery, a National Guardsmen who was still assigned to the FBI Task Force as an intelligence analyst, which was a fancy term for coffee and lunch delivery boy. He was stand-offish, no surprise, but as he was headed out the door he said to me in passing, "When do you start in Litchfield?" Before his remark even registered, he was in his car and gone. Although I felt there was little possibility of me actually being sent to Litchfield, the idea that a nobody like Seery was even aware of this threat had me furious.

All the guys were back in the office after New Year's with nothing to do but talk. Kumnick had been humiliated at having been read his Miranda warnings like some common criminal and had been cowed by his one-month transfer to Litchfield. Freddo—as mad as he was—wanted nothing to do with provoking Bailey or Morano any further.

Later that afternoon, Morano called me into his office and asked if I had made my decision. By now he left me with only two choices— Fairfield or Litchfield—and said he would let me pick first, as I was senior to Hughes. I pointed out there were six inspectors that needed to be placed, and I was senior to everyone, so I wanted the spot at headquarters, and according to our union contract I should be entitled to it. I wanted to force them to get rid of me; I was not going to make it easy for them.

Morano looked at me. "OK, I've considered it." (Long pause for effect.) "Now make a different choice."

"Statewide Prosecution Bureau."

"Not a choice."

I asked him to provide me—in writing—my list of choices.

"Why, so you can grieve it?"

"Yes."

"I'm too busy."

He ended by telling me to work it out with Hughes; figure out who wanted to work in Litchfield and who wanted to work in Fairfield and tell him in the morning. The following day I typed out my request at 8:30 a.m. and handed it to Morano's secretary, who told me Morano would not be in. Ten minutes before my workday ended, Morano unexpectedly walked into my office and handed me a sealed envelope. I opened it to find I was to report to Litchfield, forty-five miles from my house, for 120 days. Starting Friday. The next day.

Shocked, I asked Morano why I had not been given my written choice of Fairfield, and he snapped, "Because you never got back to me." I corrected him, pointing out I had left him a memo at 8:30 that morning. He nonchalantly replied he hadn't gotten around to looking at his mail yet and walked out.

Mike Malchik was as angry as any of us, even though he'd only been assigned to the squad for six months. With too much time on our hands, we kicked around the idea of taking the story to the media. We all knew how Bailey prized his public image; it was his Achilles' heel. He was extremely sensitive of negative media coverage, and we were now his dirty bastard children.

Bailey's world revolved around Connecticut's capital, Hartford, and all the important people in his circle read the *Hartford Courant*. But we had witnessed firsthand how deferential the *Courant* could be toward Bailey. We were also concerned a reporter there might not protect our confidentiality. While we recognized we would be the prime suspects behind any news story, we also recognized that just like in police work: knowing something is one thing, proving it another.

Mike knew a reporter he trusted at the *Journal Inquirer*. Although it was published in Manchester, it was distributed throughout Hartford County and beyond. Better yet, it enjoyed a reputation as a real investigative newspaper; it did not shy away from controversial stories or play favorites. Mike reached out to the reporter to see if she would guarantee us confidentiality in exchange for a scoop.

We met Rhonda Stearley that weekend at a McDonald's parking lot. Mike, sitting in the back seat, made the introductions. After Rhonda repeated her promise to never reveal a source, I walked her through the entire story. At the end of the interview, Mike gave her a copy of Morano's December 8 memo to Bailey, in which Morano recommended retaining the Fugitive Squad. She was interested.

There was nothing for me to do now but drive to Litchfield every day, starting the trip first by highway, then over scenic country roads with little traffic for an hour and a half. My first day there, I located the office, found the doors locked, and waited for someone to arrive. Soon enough, another state car pulled into the lot, and my old colleague Ron DeNuzzo got out.

We had both started together in January 1990 in the Economic Crime Bureau. In 1994, Ron had transferred to Bailey's newly formed Gang & Continuing Criminal Activity Bureau, headed by Morano. He soon found himself at odds with Morano, who had him involuntarily transferred to Litchfield for 120 days for an attitude adjustment. The Litchfield office treated Ron so well he opted to stay, far away from the vengeful Morano, despite his four-hour round-trip commute.[29]

Ron gave me a tour of the tiny office, introduced me to the staff as they came in, then showed me the local sights, the state police barracks, the courthouse, and the coffee shop. It being January, it was already dark when I left for the day. I walked through my front door Friday night at 6:30. I still had 119 days left.

On Monday, the second official day of our new assignments, the entire former Fugitive Squad was summoned back to Rocky Hill for a mandatory emergency meeting called by Bailey. We were simultaneously paged, telephoned, and faxed at our new offices. "There are no excuses for missing this meeting," the fax ominously read.

Malchik and I knew what the meeting was about. The other inspectors were calling my cell phone for my take on it. I was intentionally vague. "Let's wait and see," I said.

The last time we had been called into Bailey's conference room, we had assembled like frightened school children before a stern headmaster. We had all taken seats as far away as possible from Bailey's head chair. This time I brushed a picture askew as I entered and sat down in the chair typically used by Morano. All the other inspectors followed suit. Bailey's treasured photos were all hanging crooked, and now the only empty seats at our end of the conference table were Bailey's and a side chair for Morano. By me taking Morano's reserved "right-hand man" chair, I was hoping to unnerve both men.

---

[29]   Ron DeNuzzo remained at the Litchfield State's Attorney's office for twenty-three years, until his retirement in 2017.

When they came in, it took Bailey and Morano a few seconds to get their bearings. Morano reversed direction and moved to Bailey's left. I could tell Bailey thought about correcting the tilted frames, until he realized that almost all of them were haphazard. Both men then took their seats, while Dave Best opted for the opposite end, where there was plenty of room.

Bailey and Morano were livid. Instead of looking away, as we did at the last dressing-down, we made a point of making direct eye contact. Bailey was rattled, but then regained his composure and dove in. He announced the *Journal Inquirer* was about to publish an article about our break with the Task Force and the disbanding of the Fugitive Squad. It was being held until Saturday, the paper's largest circulation day.

We all looked surprised. Most of us actually were. "I am not hurt by the publicity personally, but the Division of Criminal Justice is embarrassed, as is every state's attorney's office in the state." Again, the "tell." Translation: he was absolutely mortified by the publicity. He then announced that the newspaper had been provided "stolen memos" which had been prepared by Deputy Chief State's Attorney Morano and Executive Assistant State's Attorney Sugrue.

"Never in the history of the DCJ has this ever happened. There will probably be quotes in the article. And I have no problem with any employee sharing their personal opinions with any reporter…as long as they are willing to resign first!"

Bailey's nostrils were flaring like a bull's. He was struggling to keep his breathing under control. He kept up the diatribe, saying this article would "ruin relations with other agencies, both federal and the state police." Bailey told us Rhonda Stearley asked SAC Parks if the FBI could ever trust any employee from the Division of Criminal Justice again. This was just laughable, considering the circumstances.

Next up was Morano, seated directly across from me. "I tried to treat you like human beings, not workers, and this is the thanks I get? I am not embarrassed about anything I wrote. Now I've had it stuck up my ass!"

Everyone was now ordered to turn in our keys to the building *and* the keys to our personal offices. It was no longer feeling like a temporary transfer.

That Saturday morning, I met Steve Kumnick at a diner for an early breakfast. He had already bought two copies of the *Journal Inquirer*, as they were not carried in my area. He showed up, flashing the copies with a big grin. Pictures of Bailey, Rohen, and Morano were on the front page.[30] We did not even make it into the diner, so eager were we to read the article; we sat in my car, hooting and hollering over various quotes.

Reporter Stearley nailed it. She quoted Bailey justifying the disbanding of his own Fugitive Squad as "primarily financial," then explained how this was not so. One law enforcement source described the financial justification as a "smokescreen," while a second source said, "Bailey is trying to appease the feds." Stearley used the leaked memo to show how Parks and Rohen wanted the CFTF to be solely responsible for fugitive apprehension in Connecticut; "Morano writes that 'Mr. Parks makes no bones about it, he is very upset with the situation….'" An unnamed law enforcement source of Stearley (to this day I still don't know who) was quoted as saying the FBI task force was to blame for the problem: "Of course they're to blame," the source said. "They were accused of criminal behavior, and they're upset about that. That's the whole thing here. Prior to that, everything was fine. Are they too small to admit some of their people could be wrong?"

Bailey took the opposite view as he attempted to minimize the issue between the rival groups as "a misunderstanding." Asked about Sugrue's memo to him that criticized the FBI for attempting to take control of the apprehension of fugitives facing state criminal charges, which was "primarily a state concern," Bailey said he didn't agree with Sugrue's assessment, then bizarrely claimed he "never received the memo."

Bailey now imagined a new proposal: he was going to ask the legislature "to tack on a $25 surcharge to all criminal bonds, thus creating a fund for the resumption of his fugitive squad. But Bailey wouldn't comment on the makeup of a new squad. 'Some of these people, after working in the field, may want to stay there,' he said." Bailey skirted the actual issue of the falsified affidavits this way: "He attributed the

---

[30] ASAC Rohen's photo was mistakenly published, misidentifying him as SAC Parks.

problems between the state and federal squads to personnel and 'a misunderstanding.' 'There was the Connecticut Fugitive Task Force, and then our squad grew, and we never really coordinated the differences between the two squads,' Bailey said." He was doing the limbo in an attempt to mention everything *but* the falsified affidavits.

Four years later, I was finally able to read Bailey's apology letter to Parks—dated just three days after the article appeared (released under a Freedom of Information request by the same newspaper). It reveals the extent of Bailey's indebtedness to Parks that surprised even me. "Again I apologize for the stories which have appeared in the various newspapers…. I would hope that in no way did these articles effect (*sic*) our personal and professional relationship. I have always held that relationship with very high regard. Again, I apologize for all of this." Attached were documents showing how he intended to pursue through an internal investigation whoever was responsible for the media leak. It was obvious Bailey was prepared to sacrifice anyone in an attempt to keep his hopes of a federal position alive.

My adjustment to Litchfield was not easy. Where previously I had grown accustomed to the hustle and bustle of bouncing from city to city chasing bad guys, I now found myself sitting in an office where little happened day to day. One of the three prosecutors would actually leave the office at lunchtime each day to check his beaver traps.

Not that I was idle. They had sent me to the perfect location to work on my lawsuit. I prepared for Karen a detailed chronological narrative, the players, the events to date. I photocopied and indexed the falsified affidavits, emails, memos, and newspaper articles. My claim was the violation of my First Amendment right to free speech, and it would be filed in federal court. Karen needed proof of Bailey's "gag orders" and adverse employment actions, which I now chronicled in detail.

Litchfield State's Attorney Frank Maco had the smallest staff in the state: three prosecutors, a secretary, and an inspector (or two, on a thinly disguised temporary reassignment). State's Attorney Maco was a pleasant fellow, if seldom seen. One day he poked his head into the lunchroom to say that even though all the temporary inspectors had arrived "with a cloud over their heads," he was always happy with their performance and demeanor, and I was no exception.

Mr. Maco was a country gentleman. He graciously extended me the option of staying on if I liked. After all, he added, that was how he had secured Ron DeNuzzo as his inspector. I was told that once the weather got warmer and the golf courses opened, we would actually see him even less.

The weather is changeable and varied in Connecticut, and the Litchfield hills enjoyed its own brand of winter. Some mornings I would leave my home under light rain showers, find it flurrying at the halfway point in Waterbury, then witness a full-blown whiteout at the office. Often I would clear more than a foot of snow from my car and return home at night to find only a dusting.

The CSP troopers were friendly at the Troop L barracks where I went to gas up my state car, an almost daily occurrence. One day at the pumps, Captain Lynch asked what I was doing in his neck of the woods. I gave him a summary, and he handed me a key to the basement gym. While spartan and dank, the gym was free and open 24/7 whenever I needed to work out my anger. I'd play James Brown's greatest hits. "Hey! Gotta gotta pay back!" hollered the Godfather of Soul.

I went for long walks in the woods. The nearby four thousand–acre White Memorial Foundation property was a short drive from the office, a beautiful nature sanctuary with thirty-five miles of trails. January through March, I had the place to myself.

On April 17, at our semiannual firearms qualifications, I caught up with Dave Best. Out of earshot of the other inspectors, he told me he'd been in a meeting with Morano, and my name came up. Dave said Morano broke up the room by observing, "If we allow him (Dillon) to stay at Litchfield, where do we send people when they fuck up?"

During these four months, I also had my broken nose fixed. An old sports injury made it hard to get air on one side. I took three weeks of sick leave and spent time walking with Vilma, strategizing out loud, trying to anticipate various scenarios once the lawsuit was filed. While I had little experience in civil litigation, Vilma had none, so we could only speculate on how much it would cost, how protracted the process could be, and discuss the possible outcomes.

Naturally, we were both anxious about me losing my job. I was only eight years in and needed two more before I was vested—twelve more before I was eligible to retire and collect a pension. If I were to lose my job, I'd have to figure out something else to do. It would be nearly impossible to get a job in law enforcement, especially in Connecticut, with the stigma of having sued my employer in federal court.

I thought going on the offensive actually increased my chances of keeping my job and repairing my reputation. The passive approach hadn't worked. All my experiences with bullies told me I had to take a stand, bring the fight to them. Vilma gave me her full support. She trusted my instincts and would back whatever decisions I made.

I recovered from my surgery and returned to Litchfield. Winter turned into spring, and I began preparing for my return to Rocky Hill, even though Bailey made it clear that he would rather I stayed put. His pro forma letter reminding me that my temporary transfer would be up soon asked me "whether you would be interested in remaining at your temporary assignment on a permanent basis." On April 22, I informed him in writing that I intended to "return to my official duty station."

Before departing Litchfield, I wrote one more letter, this one to the director of the FBI, Louis J. Freeh. I wanted to make sure the New Haven FBI Office hadn't been successful in burying our complaint. I was bringing it straight to the director's attention.

I told him I'd first been an FBI agent, then an inspector for the Connecticut chief state's attorney. I told him about the falsified affidavits and the investigation by his Office of Professional Responsibility, whose outcome I was unable to determine despite my status as the complainant. "As a proud former Special Agent, I hope there is a timely and fair adjudication concerning this matter."

I eventually received a non-answer answer from Assistant Director Michael DeFeo at OPR, FBIHQ dated May 6, 1997. In it, he confirmed my letter of complaint was received and referred to OPR. He went on to

THE THIN BLUE LIE

state: "I want to assure you that all misconduct allegations against FBI employees are taken very seriously, and that when those allegations are substantiated, appropriate action is taken." He then concluded the letter by saying he could not provide any specific information.

Unexpectedly, I received a telephone call from Michael Isikoff from *Newsweek* magazine. The October edition of *Newsweek* published this article:

Newsweek: FBI Officials Failed to Tell Congress, Freeh of Doubts in Wen Ho Lee Espionage Case; Lenient Treatment for Ethics Abuses at High Levels, Agents Claim. The article noted:

"In another instance, FBI agents in Connecticut were found to have signed false arrest warrants — a serious breach. The senior agent on the task force, who had a reputation as a tough gumshoe with several high-profile arrests, was given just a five-day suspension and then had his pay restored by an internal FBI review panel. Gregory Dillon, the Connecticut state investigator who exposed the false warrants ('They were pure fiction,' he told Newsweek) wrote Freeh, hoping he would enforce his 'bright line.' Freeh did nothing; he declined to be interviewed by Newsweek."[31]

---

[31] Wikipedia: "In June 2001, he [Freeh] resigned amid criticism that the FBI needed stronger leadership.... He was replaced by Robert Mueller."

CHAPTER 14

I returned to Rocky Hill, as did Mike Malchik and Bob Hughes. Our squad had been scattered to the four winds. Kumnick and Freddo opted to remain in Hartford, and I couldn't blame them. I was now a polarizing figure in the office, damaged goods. No one wished to be seen chatting with me if management was nearby. Some of my colleagues openly gave me the cold shoulder, while a few went out of their way to show support and encouragement. Most were keeping their heads down. Outside, they would be as cordial as ever, but within the confines of the building, most coworkers were formal.

The office paging system announced the three of us (me, Mike, and Bob) were to report to Chief Inspector Dave Best's office. When we arrived, Dave handed each of us an envelope with our new assignments. Mike and I were now assigned to Statewide Prosecution, Bob luckily landed in Gangs. Next, Morano walked in, and he was all smiles: "Welcome home! Last time I spoke to this group, I was upset. That is all in the past. I do not intend to hold any grudges. I'd like a fresh start."

This got our attention, as Morano usually had the sincerity of a used car salesman.

After a brief pause, he continued. "Let's face it, this whole thing [apparently referring to the termination of our Fugitive Squad] was never about money—no one here ever got laid off or missed a paycheck, right? When I left here that night [referring to December 16], you guys looked like you were going to make it. Something happened overnight; I suspect a phone call was made, and the next morning you were history. I don't know what happened; this thing became a political football, and you guys got screwed. I was thrust into a shitty position as soon as I got this job [deputy chief state's attorney]; I was basically appointed to be the executioner except I didn't have the luxury of a hood. I'd like to try to make it up to you guys, get you assigned to a place you want to be, doing work you want to do." With that, the impromptu meeting was over.

Mike and I returned to our new offices, located side by side. We discussed this latest twist: I was still a supervisor, and we were now assigned to a bureau without a supervisor. We agreed I was in a unique position that needed to be explored further with the administration.

And immediately, a supervisor's position was indeed posted. I asked Morano about it, and he encouraged me to apply. I asked him why I needed to apply, as I was already a supervisor and now assigned to that bureau. Morano informed me I was "a supervisory inspector in title and pay only, but with no supervisory authority or responsibility." Why was that? "Because your unit was eliminated."

I could see Morano was making a concerted effort to not get into an argument with me. His tone changed, and he cautioned me sincerely about challenging the issue. He mentioned Deputy Chief State's Attorney Sellers (in charge of administration) was of the opinion my supervisor's position could simply be eliminated. This, of course, would mean a loss in pay, something Morano said he would rather not see happen. He told me how impressed he had been with my supervision of the Fugitive Squad and how CI Best was still pushing to have the squad resurrected, with me in charge again. He said he "personally felt you have been emasculated enough by the way things were handled."

I responded in kind. Despite what had taken place, I said I did not hate him and felt he did not hate me, but circumstances compelled me to protect myself. Morano said he understood and was hoping to find me some assignment I might enjoy. I responded that without wanting to sound cynical, the last person who told me that was Bailey.

Morano told me there were two other well-qualified candidates for the supervisor's position, both with more seniority in that particular assignment. What he conveniently failed to acknowledge was that neither was a supervisory inspector, yet I was. "As there are only three candidates, you stand a thirty-three and a third percent chance of being selected." When I observed that Bailey got the final say, he quipped, "Your chances just dropped to ten percent."

I added, "Which would be true if both candidates died before Friday."

I was duly interviewed and of course did not get the job. Dave Best called me at home that night and said "the Boss" had asked him to give me a "heads-up." He and the others on the selection panel had gone to lunch before they ranked the three candidates for Bailey, but when they got back, they found the boss had already made his decision without their input.

The following morning, I ran into the successful candidate, Chuck Coffey, walking to his office. I shook his hand and offered my congratulations. Coffey looked confused; I told him for getting the promotion. "This is the first I'm hearing of this," he said. Neither of us knew what to say for a several seconds. How did I know? I told him about the telephone call from Best. Coffey was nonplussed. "Wish they'd been nice enough to let me know," he said before walking away.

Mike Malchik and I digested my latest setback in my office. We had seen this one coming, as the "office line" had Coffey as the runaway favorite and me a distant third. I was still a supervisor, still senior to Coffey, but now receiving assignments and taking direction from him.

Of the various economic crime cases Coffey assigned us, most were nothing more than civil disputes in which one party was looking to leverage our office as a collection agency. Any time Mike would approach Supervisory Inspector Coffey for investigative guidance, Chuck would look up at him from behind his desk over his glasses and flatly say, "You're a smart guy—you figure it out." Needless to say, not a lot of progress was made.

I dug in. My feeling was that I was hired and employed by the Office of the Chief State's Attorney, not by the chief state's attorney himself. My loyalty was to the agency and its mission, not the individual. My allegiance was to the principles, not the principals. Bailey was not in the office when I was hired, and God willing, would not be in the office when I decided to retire. Therefore, I did not feel any sense of obligation to him, personally or professionally. I was determined to outlast him, if it was the last thing I did. Bailey's capitulation to the FBI only diminished my poor opinion of him.

I told Karen Torre about the latest development with Coffey, now as *my* supervisor, while I was still employed *as* a supervisor; she told me she was now satisfied we had sufficient grounds to file a federal lawsuit against Bailey. It was clear to her that Bailey was violating my right to free speech by taking a series of retaliatory employment actions against me. She asked me to draft an affidavit detailing all the events to date, while she began preparing the necessary filing papers.

We went over the nineteen-page complaint in painstaking detail. We sought an "injunctive and declaratory relief to redress the deprivation of my rights." We also asked for a declaratory judgment declaring Bailey's media policies unconstitutional; an injunction prohibiting Bailey from enforcing his media policies; an order I be reinstated as a supervisor; compensatory damages and punitive damages determined by a jury; attorney's fees; and "any and all such further relief as this Court may deem just."

As we prepared to file the lawsuit, part of me was giddy with antic-ipation. This one-sided beating was about to become a fair fight—or at least as fair as we could make it. But another part of me dreaded it as a point of no return. I was already a modern-day leper at the office. Once the lawsuit became public, I would be radioactive.

I steeled myself to be the stoic, stand-up cop, taking pride in my work, doing things by the book, careful of my image and reputation. I had kept a low profile, had never been disciplined, and went above and beyond what was asked of me. When I joined in 1990, I was the youngest inspector in the Division of Criminal Justice. I fully expected, after making supervisor within five years, I would one day retire as a chief inspector. Now my career was going backwards, without my ever receiving a negative evaluation or disciplinary action.

Initially Karen was charging me by the hour, but at the rate we were progressing, I could see the case was going to last far longer than my savings. After already borrowing money from my father, I asked Karen if she would take the case on a contingency basis. She agreed but told me it would have to be a 40/60 split, not the standard 30/70 arrangement—with no refund of the already paid legal fees. Karen explained employment law cases typically did not see high payouts and were notoriously drawn out and time-consuming. She insisted upon her 40 percent cut, and I reluctantly agreed. With skin in the game, she'd go straight for the jugular; plus, I couldn't afford her otherwise.

Karen called me at home one night to tell me a sheriff would serve the lawsuit on Bailey at his office the following day. I watched from the second-floor balcony when the plainclothes sheriff arrived with a manila envelope, signed in at the visitor's logbook, and was escorted to the third floor. He left within minutes. It was all rather anticlimactic.

Dave Best would not be happy with me; I had not given him advance notice because I knew he would be obliged to tell Bailey, and I did not want to blunt the first blow. I wanted Bailey to be thunderstruck.

CHAPTER 15

"I nspector Suing Chief State's Attorney" announced the *New Haven Register* on August 8, 1998.

In the story, Bailey defended his media policy. "We're doing criminal investigations," he said. "We just can't have everyone making statements (about) what we're doing." This made no sense, as the investigation in question was not ours but rather OPR's. Unless he had made a Freudian slip and now thought himself part of the FBI, Bailey had yet again misinterpreted his own policy. The article went on: "'Employees are free to speak publicly about matters that do not concern the criminal justice division,' he said." Unfortunately, the reporter did not question Bailey on this contradiction. We—the inspectors—had filed a complaint about the conduct of the Federal Bureau of Investigation, not the Division of Criminal Justice.

Karen cleverly filed a motion for a preliminary injunction of my agency's media policy, as it petitioned the court for "immediate relief." The term "immediate"—by court standards—is relative. While this ensured we would jump to the head of the line, it would still be a three-month wait before we would set foot in Judge Janet Bond Arterton's federal courtroom.

Within weeks, Karen informed me that we were to appear at the Bridgeport federal courthouse for a settlement conference. This was a surprise, as I had no interest in settling. Karen explained how it would be considered disrespectful to the court if I refused to participate. I insisted I wanted a trial, not a payoff. Karen persisted, so we went. I cooled my heels outside while she haggled with "the other side."

She related to me their offer was in the area of thirty thousand dollars. I told her that was great. She looked shocked. It was so ridiculously low, I said, I was not even tempted to consider it. She explained the perils of going to trial and how humiliated I would be if we lost, how disappointing it would be to receive a "nominal award" from the jury, which legally could not be *more* than ten dollars. The public exposure of Bailey's shameful behavior was worth it to me, I said. And that was that. For now.

Over the next few days, the offers increased incrementally. The figures seemed arbitrary, almost random: "Thirty-three thousand dollars; they may go as high as thirty-seven thousand dollars; forty thousand dollars is out of the question." Despite Karen's dire admonitions of the risks of going to trial, a trial was exactly what I wanted. It made for some hard feelings between us; she told me at one point the other side had chided her because she had lost "client control." I had to constantly remind myself that even though this was her field of expertise, she worked for me, not the other way around.

What was lost on Bailey, then apparently on Karen, was the fact this was a matter of principle, not expediency. I had been—and still was—protecting my integrity, the integrity of my subordinates, and the integrity of my agency, as well as upholding the oath I took when I was sworn in. Once Bailey knew—by our statements and evidence—that the FBI had likely committed crimes, he became a bad guy in my view. Stuck in the Boy Scout mentality, I was determined to see this through to its conclusion.

Federal Magistrate Judge William I. Garfinkel of the US District Court in Bridgeport was selected to facilitate a settlement negotiation.

I liked Judge Garfinkel immediately, a great bear of a man with an affable, humble demeanor. He was one of the few people I have met in life who "actively listened." While I used to joke that Karen would have been a popular parole officer—she never allowed anyone to finish a sentence—Judge Garfinkel was just the opposite. I never felt rushed in his presence. He was deliberate, thoughtful, and considerate, and listened while I vented.

He was patient with my stubbornness and made an honest effort to broker a fair compromise. At one point, in an effort to sweeten the offer, the vainglorious Bailey suggested shaking my hand on the courthouse steps in front of reporters. The magistrate advised me of the offer. Summoning all my powers of self-control, I said, "Your honor—and I mean no disrespect to you—I would rather eat a bucketful of live worms than shake that man's hand. If that is their latest condition, than my counter-offer just doubled."

Karen let out an exasperated sigh, but the judge was pensive. After several quiet seconds, he agreed, acknowledging this only benefited them and did nothing for me. There would be no settlement.

The State Attorney General's Office was representing Bailey, as he was being sued in his capacity as a state official. One of the primary responsibilities of Attorney General Richard Blumenthal's office was to provide legal counsel and representation to state agencies and its employees. Assistant Attorney General Terrence O'Neill, now assigned to the high-profile case, wisely instructed Bailey to stop talking about the case, finally. The New Haven FBI office also declined comment. Karen, however, did not let the opportunity go to waste. The *Connecticut Law Journal* published an article about our case:

> "'I think sometimes these agency heads forget they are public officials, accountable to the citizens and taxpayers who fund their agencies,' Dillon's attorney, Karen Lee Torre, says in an interview. 'They believe they are some

kind of czar. Agency heads are not czars. They are not entitled to whitewash or sweep under the carpet controversies that erupt in their agencies.'"

"'Mr. Bailey,' Torre writes in Dillon v. Bailey, 'has misused the power of his office to indulge his desire to avoid public scrutiny at the expense of his own inspectors who were not the ones who committed wrongdoing, but were the ones who had the backbone to report it.'"

Assistant AG O'Neill swiped back, "A preliminary injunction is not warranted in Dillon because the inspector has neither suffered irreparable harm nor shown he is likely to win on the merits. It is 'simply absurd' for a law enforcement veteran like Dillon to expect he can speak to the press about a pending FBI investigation."

The Richard C. Lee United States Courthouse is a fine example of early twentieth-century Classical Revival architecture in downtown New Haven, overlooking the sixteen-acre Green. It was to this magnificent white marble courthouse I had dragged Jack Bailey on October 26. We finally had our injunction hearing before federal Judge Janet Bond Arterton.

Bailey was flanked by a phalanx of attorneys: two from the Attorney General's Office beside him and an assistant US attorney and an FBI attorney behind him. The federal attorneys were not there to represent Bailey; they were there to assess damage and report back to their bosses in Washington, DC. Once Bailey took the witness stand, though, he was on his own.

Bailey had always lived by the sound bite and wasn't good on his feet. Because he had so little courtroom experience, he relied heavily on prepared scripts and struggled with spontaneous remarks. When pressed for details by reporters, he would sometimes wing it with inaccurate off-the-cuff remarks causing nearby prosecutors and inspectors to cringe. If pressed, he would retreat behind vague answers, citing confidentiality issues or concerns about jeopardizing "the ongoing investigation." In a press conference it worked all right, but this was different; this was a courtroom, he was under oath, and Karen Lee Torre was definitely not a deferential reporter.

The other side expected Karen to call me as her first witness to set the stage for Bailey's testimony. But at the last second, she brilliantly decided to call Bailey first, surprising everyone. As proof of how little time Bailey had spent in a courtroom, he left his defendant's table and walked hesitantly toward Judge Arterton's clerk. He then realized his mistake and began scanning the courtroom, bewildered. After several seconds, Judge Arterton caught his attention and pointed to the witness stand to her left. Chagrined, Bailey found his place and was sworn in.

Karen's plan was now to expose how Bailey's media policy was not only overly broad, it was never enforced, at least until the time came when Bailey was offended; then, it was exhumed and vigorously applied. Karen was intent to expose the double standard and that Bailey was using it as a cudgel to silence first Kumnick, then me. The policy prohibited DCJ personnel—with the exception of the CSA—from publicly commenting on pending state criminal investigations and prosecutions. Thus, it did not apply to pending federal matters or state matters that had been adjudicated.

After the opening questions used traditionally by attorneys to identify the witness for the record, things got rough. Once Bailey was forced to go "off script," he struggled mightily, and those in the courtroom struggled equally to understand his answers. Bailey was not used to being questioned, certainly not under oath. He was rattled, and it showed. He began prefacing almost every answer with "I believe" and "I think" and "to the best of my recollection," which made him sound uncertain at best, deceitful at worst. He struggled to formulate a logical response to even the most straightforward question from Karen. His attorneys assumed expressions of concern.

> Q: Mister Bailey, what in your opinion would be the risk to Greg Dillon if this practice [the falsification of affidavits] was, in fact, taking place as he alleged it to be?

A: I don't understand the question.

Q: You understand that Mister Dillon claimed that there were perjured statements in seven different affidavits with respect to seven different suspects filed with a magistrate or judge of the district court, correct?

A: Correct.

Q: You also understand that Mister Dillon was claiming at the time that the perjured statements were attributed by the affiants to him or to his fellow inspectors?

A: Correct.

Q: Do you agree that Greg Dillon was justified in being alarmed by this practice because it posed a risk to his career?

A: No.

Q: You don't?

A: No, because I think Mister Dillon did what he probably should have done if he thought there was a problem, an allegation of a crime, which it was, that he should bring it to my attention. I'm the one who supervises—I mean, I'm the head of the Division of Criminal Justice and if he didn't bring it to me, then I would ask him why he didn't bring it to me. But, no, I don't think that would play in his future in the Division of Criminal Justice.

Q: I'm sorry, sir, I think you may have misunderstood my question. I'll ask it another way. At the time Mister Dillon discovered what he believed to be an ongoing

practice of falsifying affidavits and attributing the falsified information to him and his fellow inspectors, do you
agree that he was justified in being concerned that his
career was being placed at risk by that behavior?

A: I stand by my other answer, my last answer.

Bailey dressed the part of a high-stakes litigator, but listening to him
recall events under direct examination was like listening to Mike Tyson
explain trickle-down economics while on a crack binge. Karen tried to
focus him on the conversation with Parks that blew up so spectacularly.

Q: I'm asking what Mister Parks told you.

A: I'm trying to refresh my recollection on reading the
statement I gave two years ago.[32] Again, I think it was
one that there is—I turned over the matter to them and
they were investigating. Second—

Q: I'm sorry, sir, are you quoting yourself now or Mister
Parks?

A: I think Mister Parks.

Q: You're quoting Mister Parks?

Befuddled, Bailey looked away from Karen and turned to Judge
Arterton for help.

The Witness: I'm trying to remember, your Honor, and
that's the best recollection I have. He may remember it
differently, but that's what I remember.

---

[32] It was actually two months earlier, not two years.

The Court: So your recollection is that Mister Parks told you that Mister Parks was investigating?

The Witness: No. No, that I turned over my matter—my exhibit, Plaintiff's Exhibit 1 [the notebook] to Mister Parks. Mister Parks had forwarded it to their professional standards or internal affairs people and it was being investigated and this is not helping the situation of the investigation.

The Court: And that is your recollection of what Mister Parks told you?

The Witness: And I—that's what I think, your Honor, and I think also concerning a relationship between the—this statement about the investigation or the truthfulness of the statements by the FBI was not helping the relationship with the Division of Criminal Justice and the FBI.

Legal observers call this yammering and stammering. Asked about his gag order on the Fugitive Squad, Bailey channeled his inner Yogi Berra:

Q: My question to you is, did you not by issuing this directive prohibit any member of your department from letting other people know that these agents are potentially dangerous people to work with and that they lie on affidavits?

A: I don't know that they lied in affidavits. I have an allegation that they lied in affidavits. This was issued, what is it, ten days after we gave it? I don't know if they lied in the—the allegations are that they lied. Did they lie? I don't know. B, it was being investigated and, three, which I think is important, the investigation should not be jeopardized.

At every opportunity on the stand, Bailey suggested Karen direct her questions to someone else: Special Agent in Charge Parks, Chief Inspector Best, Deputy Chief State's Attorney Morano, Chief Inspector Grasso, Cornelius Shea, Fairfield State's Attorney Benedict, and at one point even *me*. Bailey faltered as Karen continued to expose the hypocrisy in his application of the media policy. She gave examples of how it was rigidly applied to the Fugitive Squad inspectors and contrasted that with how it was *not* adhered to by others in his office, as well as the other state's attorney's offices under his purview.

Bailey kept repeating how his intent was to protect the integrity of the FBI's internal investigation, even as it was suggested that was not his role. Judge Arterton, known for her poker face, grimaced at Bailey's convoluted answers and was forced at times to step in and simplify a question. When Bailey attempted to rewrite the media policy on the stand by explaining that each of the twelve state's attorneys operated independently, Judge Arterton quickly corrected him, pointing out the media policy applied to *all* DCJ employees, not just those assigned to the Office of the Chief State's Attorney. The chastised chief state's attorney conceded the point.

Christian Miller of the *New Haven Register* explained the issues:

> On Monday, Bailey's motives in the controversy were called into question by New Haven attorney Karen Torre, who questioned whether the state's top prosecutor coddled the FBI to further his own political career.

> Bailey had been publicly interested in pursuing a position with the federal Department of Justice — an appointment that requires an FBI background check.

Bailey testified all day and still he was not done. After court adjourned, Bailey and his posse of attorneys realized they had a problem. The US Department of Justice attorneys, after watching Bailey defend his still in-force gag order the entire day, decided it was finally time to inform him the "ongoing" OPR investigation he kept referencing had actually concluded five months earlier and that discipline had already been imposed on SSA DiFonzo and others.

The following morning, before Bailey returned to the witness stand, Attorney O'Neill asked to address the court and made the embarrassing admission that his client's previous testimony was inaccurate. O'Neill explained that after court had adjourned, he and Bailey were invited to a meeting at the federal building where they were finally updated. Bailey—by his own admission under oath—had never once made inquiry as to the status of the FBI's internal investigation; he was now brought up to speed, along with the rest of us.

Judge Arterton was visibly taken aback by the revelation. Neither Bailey—the head of his agency—nor the complainants/victims had ever been advised the OPR inquiry had ended, or that discipline had been imposed as the result of our complaint. Further, Bailey testified under oath while DOJ attorneys were present and did not correct him, even though they were aware he was testifying inaccurately. Quickly regaining her composure, Judge Arterton announced she would now like to postpone the injunction hearing and let the civil action go forward. Without hesitation, she informed the attorneys that a trial—scheduled for next month—had unexpectedly settled, and she wanted to try this matter in its place. The attorneys on both sides, stunned, both bluffing, readily agreed.

The judge explained she was doing this for the sake of judicial efficiency; in a combined proceeding with judge and jury, the lawyers would only need to present their evidence once. The jury would decide the facts and determine any damages, while the judge would weigh the constitutional issues of the media policy. She set jury selection for November 4, the following week.

Rhonda Stearley had since left the *Journal Inquirer*, and Alex Wood was now covering the trial. Where we as police officers—and victims—had been completely stonewalled by the FBI in our attempts to determine the status of our complaint, Wood had better luck; he managed to learn that the internal affairs investigation resulted in DiFonzo being "disciplined." But the FBI spokeswoman would provide no further details, "since it can be appealed." And appealed it was.

Wood was also able to obtain a copy of the DOJ letter deciding against criminal prosecution. "'We have determined that prosecution of the agents is not warranted." wrote Lee J. Radek, the chief of the department's Public Integrity Section, in a letter to Richard M. Rogers, acting counsel to the department's Office of Professional Responsibility. Radek's letter gave no explanation of the decision, and none was forthcoming from a spokesman for the U.S. Justice Department either—hiding behind the tried-and-true company line: department policy.

Karen had no choice but to agree to the speedy trial and had less than a month to prepare. Bailey had all the resources of his office and the attorney general's office at his disposal. Karen had her associate (fresh out of law school and not yet a licensed attorney), a paralegal, a receptionist, and me. But after witnessing Bailey's performance on the stand, I was invigorated.

What followed was a month of frenzied preparation. Karen was in scramble-mode: getting continuances on all of her pending state and federal cases, submitting briefs, filing motions, and staying up late in advance of a courtroom showdown. No doubt her life would have been a lot easier with a negotiated settlement.

I, by contrast, was elated. After being marginalized and gagged for two and a half years, I was finally getting a chance to tell my side of the story in public, while compelling the other side to do the same under oath.

Settlement discussions continued. Karen would say things like, "This is their last, best offer." "After today, it's off the table." "What do you feel the case is worth?" "Once we start the trial, there's no going back." She mentioned more than once how we were at a huge disadvantage in seeking monetary damages, as I had never lost a single day's pay nor was my pay rate ever reduced, despite the not-so-subtle threats by Bailey and crew.

And the worst: "You are going to feel like a fool if you go to trial and lose." The jury could side with me on the law but award me a nominal amount of money due to my lack of proven loss—as little as a single dollar. If my compensatory damage award was nominal, then any punitive damage award would have to be comparable, by law. She repeated the phrases "hollow victory," "publicly humiliated," and "Pyrrhic victory."

I listened to her, ruminated, and decided I still wanted a trial. I sensed weakness in my opponent. Bailey cringed at the exposure. He'd just suffered a severe reversal. Karen said careful consideration of a settlement was in my own best interest, but I believed we were winning. The show would go on.

Christopher L. Morano attending a retirement dinner.

CHAPTER 16

"Lawyers," says Jeremy Bentham, "are the only persons in whom ignorance of the law is not punished." As a sequestration order was in place for the trial, the witnesses scheduled to testify were not allowed in the courtroom until after their testimony had concluded. This is a common and sensible precaution to ensure their testimony is not influenced by the testimony of other witnesses. It also prohibited witnesses from discussing their testimony prior to the trial in an attempt to "get their stories straight."

Oddly enough, the only witnesses who violated this order were the ones with law degrees: Chief State's Attorney Bailey, Deputy Chief State's Attorney Morano, and Deputy Chief State's Attorney Sellers. To what extent could never be determined, but after Bailey was deposed on October 26, 1998, a sixty-six-page transcript was prepared. Two weeks later Bailey admitted under oath that his secretary had photocopied his deposition, and a copy was provided to Deputy Chief State's Attorney Steven Sellers, who inexplicably loaned it to Morano, who then had to admit reviewing it while being questioned by Karen.

"I skimmed through it," he said, "but I did not go through it in great detail. As soon as I heard there was a problem, I sealed it in an envelope and I gave it to Mr. Bailey's secretary." Such an admission from a man who had been a state prosecutor for over twenty years must have been incredible to Judge Arterton.

In pretrial depositions, Morano came across as a smart aleck; SAC Parks was smug, condescending, and short-tempered; and Bailey was frequently confused by simple questions and tried his best to stick to a memorized script. We both picked up that Bailey was concerned he had been secretly recorded during his tirades. I had taken very detailed notes during Bailey's meetings, and Karen used this information when preparing her questions, but he let something slip when Karen asked him about his remarks.

> A: I said—what I think I said, and you know, someone may have taped that meeting, I don't know, what I'm saying to you is if you have information you developed as an inspector of the Division of Criminal Justice...

Once Bailey had tipped his hand to his fear of secret recordings, I recognized an opening.

"Law Agencies Find Selves In Courtroom," was the headline in the *Hartford Courant* on November 14. Stories ran in all the local newspapers and on the TV news announcing the start of the trial. The courthouse was crowded with reporters. The whole state was now watching.

"Next week, some of the state's most senior law enforcement officers will begin appearing in court, mostly trying not to be embarrassed by a potentially embarrassing lawsuit," the story in the *Hartford Courant* read. "It is a First Amendment suit filed by an employee against Chief State's Attorney John M. Bailey, one of the most media-savvy public figures in the state. On its face, the suit claims that Bailey's media policy amounts to an illegal restraint on speech for everyone at the Chief State's Attorney's Office except Bailey."

Dillon v. Bailey kicked off on Monday, November 16. The gallery of the courtroom was divided by a center aisle. Like at a church wedding, Bailey supporters sat on one side, mine on the other. Interestingly enough, Bailey's side did not contain a single person from our office, even though only a handful were listed as witnesses and therefore banned from the courtroom. Instead there were FBI agents, including Rich Teahan; his brother Ted, also an agent assigned to the New Haven office; Lisa Bull, the affiant on the Rodriquez and Dolan files; and Todd Brophy, the affiant on the Williams, Jefferis, Wright, and Davis files.

On my side were my father and stepmother, my aunt Lucille, some close friends, Inspector Mike Malchik, and Steve Kumnick's wife, Eloise. Later, after they testified—and were no longer bound by the sequestration order—my wife, and Inspectors Kumnick and Freddo would sit behind me. Karen and I both noticed that all the reporters sat on our side.

The agents glared at me and my group with such hostility that Judy Chong of WTNH News said live on the air: "His [Dillon's] fellow agents who served on the fugitive task force were in court. They gave Inspector Dillon icy stares throughout his testimony."

Even getting called out on TV was not enough to make them stop. After several days of this crap, Mike Malchik and I were heading outside for some fresh air at a recess, and I spotted Rich Teahan smirking in the corner with his crew. I veered off suddenly and walked up to him, asking if he had something he wanted to say. Flushed, he did an about-face and looked away. Mike averted a crisis, taking me by the arm and guiding me outside, where I was able to collect myself.

Less than a year later, SA Rich Teahan would kill thirty-four-year-old Hector Colon by shooting him in the back while he was running away—unarmed and in broad daylight.[33] And, of course, get away with

---

33   *Hartford Courant*: "As Colon got out of his car carrying a grocery bag with his lunch in it, Teehan [sic] jumped out of the [surveillance] van and identified himself as an FBI officer, sources said. Colon dropped the bag and started to run. Teehan [sic] fired two shots that missed before hitting Colon in the lower

it. Under similar circumstances today, it would be national news and he would likely be indicted.

As you entered the cavernous courtroom, the jury box was along the left wall, the judge's bench at the back, and the witness stand on the right side facing the jury. The defendant, Bailey, sat on the jury side, while Karen and I sat by the witness stand.

Unlike at the preliminary injunction hearing the previous month, I testified first this time. Karen went over the details of every medal and letter of commendation I ever received. Over the continual objections of Bailey's lawyer, Terrance O'Neill, my career passed in grand review, from the local force to the FBI to my eight-year tenure in the Division of Criminal Justice, my glowing performance evaluations, never a disciplinary action. This is called establishing the credibility of a witness. It went on for over an hour.

Next, methodically, Karen had me tell the story of the Connecticut Fugitive Task Force and FBI Agent Ralph DiFonzo. I walked her through the preparation and application of a federal Unlawful Flight to Avoid Prosecution (UFAP) warrant and my subsequent discovery of the false affidavits.

> Q: Inspector Dillon, with respect to the rejected Dolan warrant application, what did Ralph DiFonzo say?
>
> A: He made the remark that this was bullshit and [said], "Give me the warrant; I will write it up so they will have to sign it. It doesn't make any difference anyway; they never prosecute these things." And then he made some remark as to his motto or his slogan is, "If you don't have it, lie."

---

back with the third shot, sources said…. Teehan [sic] told investigators he fired because Colon made a move toward his waistband for what Teehan [sic] thought was a gun, sources said. But Colon was unarmed and was carrying a cell phone on his belt, sources said." In less than ninety days, Teahan was exonerated and the killing ruled as "justified."

Q: Is that the motto you wanted to abide by?

A: No, ma'am.

Q: Did you, in fact, do any such thing? Did you ever lie in one of those draft UFAPs?

A: Definitely not.

The following day, Karen walked me through our eviction from the task force office, Kumnick's interview with the *Herald Press*, Bailey's "gag order," and his ordering of an internal affairs investigation. We covered Kumnick's thirty-day transfer to Litchfield, Bailey's second "gag order," the disbanding of our squad, my 120-day transfer to Litchfield, and finally my being passed over for the supervisor's position in Statewide Prosecution.

When all the facts were on the record, she asked me if I'd do it again:

Q: [A]s you sit here now, if you were to become aware of any public corruption or bribes or any misconduct on the part of a law enforcement officer, what are your thoughts about how free you would feel to blow the whistle on that?

A: I still believe what I did was right, but I would have to seriously consider ever putting myself in that position again because it resulted in two and a half years, the worst part of my career as a law enforcement officer, and I would have to give it some serious thought whether it would ever be—the risk of doing something similar again.

Now it was time for cross examination. Terence O'Neill grilled me about my knowledge of the purpose of media policies in law enforcement agencies, my issues with Ralph DiFonzo, and why I had not reported the very first discovery of an alleged falsified affidavit. O'Neill proved Emory R. Buckner, a former US attorney, correct: "More cross-examinations are suicidal rather than homicidal."

> Q: Is it your testimony that you did not believe that the FBI was investigating the matter?
>
> A: Correct. Based upon the fact that when we supposedly violated a directive of Mister Bailey, within eighteen hours we were being investigated for an internal affairs investigation, and the entire month of August, September, October, November, and part of December we were never contacted or interviewed, by anyone from the FBI.

The core of our First Amendment case was of course Bailey's gag order. O'Neill and I clashed over the issue of whether Bailey's order had required me to lie, at a very real cost to my reputation, since without knowing what had actually happened at the Task Force, other people were allowed to think the worst about me and my colleagues.

> Q: And the reason it put you in an awkward position was because you feel you had to lie; is that your testimony?
>
> A: I felt I could not be truthful when asked what the circumstances were that resulted in our leaving the task force.
>
> Q: If you were—did anyone ever ask you why you were no longer with the task force?
>
> A: Yes, numerous occasions.
>
> Q: And couldn't you have just said I can't talk about it?
>
> A: That's what I had to say.

Q: Okay. That's not a lie, is it?

A: It's not the truth.

Q: Well, it is the truth.

A: The truth was we had accused agents of falsifying affidavits and using us as the source of information. That was the truth. The fact remained that Mister Bailey put out a memo that prohibited us from saying this.

Q: That's the truth, that's right. Mister Bailey put out a memo saying do not discuss this?

A: That's not the truth, that's a fact.

Prior to Bailey's testimony, Steve Kumnick had his chance on the witness stand. Karen elicited the following from Kumnick:

Q: And did Mister Bailey, however, make any statement in that meeting which would suggest that you and others might lose their jobs if they speak out?

A: Yes.

Q: What did Mister Bailey say?

A: I'm going to paraphrase because I don't know the exact words. It was a meeting that was called regarding an upcoming article that was going to be published by the *Journal Inquirer* newspaper and the gist of it was if we want to comment to the media about anything, business, personal, anything else, we should resign from the Division of Criminal Justice.

Q: And is your recollection pretty clear on that?

A: Oh, yes.

Q: Thank you, sir. I have nothing further.

Chief State's Attorney John M. Bailey wasn't a real prosecutor. He just played one on TV. He stood to be sworn in by the clerk, then went to take his seat and banged his forehead against the live microphone, which sounded like a gunshot in the courtroom. Everyone, including Bailey, jumped. Inspector Clouseau couldn't have done it better.

There was a nasty but persistent rumor that Bailey had tried only a single case as a prosecutor, early on in his career. It was a traffic violation trial and he lost. The story went that after the embarrassing setback, Bailey never attempted to try a case again—criminal or motor vehicle. Rather, he stayed as far away from a courtroom as professionally possible. On the witness stand, it showed. Here's how it read in the *Hartford Courant* the next day:

> His accuser, Supervisory Inspector Gregory B. Dillon, smiled as Dillon's lawyer, Karen Lee Torre, frequently admonished the glib career prosecutor to answer her questions, not make speeches.
>
> "Listen to the question, Mr. Bailey!" Torre said.
>
> With an increasingly hostile line of questioning, Torre tried to portray Bailey as a hypocrite — a man who frequently tells reporters about investigations, then punishes his employees for doing the same thing.

Oddly enough, one thing Karen did get Bailey to acknowledge was SAC Park's infamous temper.

Q: And I take it Mister Parks wasn't happy at all to learn that this kind of thing was going to be brought up by his officers, was he?

A: He did not express that.

Q: He didn't express that?

A: No.

Q: Does he have a hot temper, in your opinion?

A: I think he does have a temper.

Q: And you know from personal experience because he's a good friend of yours, that he tends to get explosive sometimes, right?

A: Yes.

The longer Bailey was on the stand, the further flustered he became. Even when a question was not pending, he looked like a man trying to chew his own teeth. After mistaking, misplacing, and dropping several of the documents that were in evidence, even the judge grew impatient.

The Court: Every time the exhibits get over there next to you, Mister Bailey, they get all mixed up. What's going on here?

A: They do, your Honor.

Things were not going well for the state's top prosecutor, clearly uncomfortable in open court. Bailey's year-round tan, expensive suits, and silk ties were all right for playing the part of the crime-fighting prosecutor and state-agency head, and he could even act with a script in his hand; but under oath and off-script, he bombed.

Karen Torre was good. We knew Bailey was concerned he had been secretly recorded during one of his tirades. O'Neill, slow to recognize this, had me served with a subpoena just before the start of the trial, demanding I turn over a variety of materials—including any pertinent audio and/or videotape recordings in my possession.

I had none, but O'Neill didn't know that, and he had to wait another day to find out. O'Neill asked the court to enforce his poorly timed subpoena. When Karen cleverly pointed out that due to the late service—and the fact that weekends don't count against legal deadlines—our side still had one more day to comply. Bailey, now convinced that I had him on tape, was forced to hedge his answers and concede that his recollections might be faulty for fear of triggering a federal perjury charge.

Just to keep them guessing, I kept several cassette tapes in a manila file folder that had a clear cellophane window and carried them in and out of the courtroom each day, leaving it on our table in full view. The ruse de guerre worked perfectly.

Every time Bailey tried to evade her, Karen pinned him down. Here they are on another of his gag orders.

> Q: [N]evertheless, at the time or at about the time you agreed to grant an interview to this newspaper reporter for the *Journal Inquirer*, you at the same time instructed your staff that they may not express their opinion to a reporter?
>
> A: On criminal matters.
>
> Q: Mister Bailey, you just told us a moment ago that you have a failure of recollection of sorts as to what you said at that meeting, correct?
>
> A: Correct.

Q: You do not mean to suggest to the jury now that you have a specific recollection of having said at that meeting that you were only talking about speech on criminal matters?

A: That's what I thought I said, what I thought I meant I said at that meeting. Do you want me to try that again?

Q: No, I would like to have the answer read back.

(Testimony read).

Q: That's what you thought you meant you said at that meeting. Okay, I don't understand that, Mister Bailey.

A: What I was trying to express to the individuals at that meeting was while a criminal investigation is going on that there should not be any comments on it.

Q: Mister Bailey, I want to know and I want everyone to understand what your recollection is as you sit here now about what you in fact said. Not what you think you should have said or what you intended to say, but what you said.

A: I said I don't exactly recall what I said.

Q: Okay. So, if you don't recall exactly what you said—

A: I recall the intent of what I wanted to say at that meeting.

Q: But I'm not interested in your intent, I'm interested in what you said.

A: And I said I don't recall the exact words of what I said.

Q: I understand that, and my point is that you do not mean to suggest that you have an absolute recollection that you confined your remarks only to expressions on a criminal matter?

A: My recollection is that that's what—when I went into that meeting that is what I wanted to express.

Q: But you can't testify under oath that that's what you said?

A: No, I cannot.

Q: So, Mister Dillon's account of what you said may, in fact, be accurate, correct?

A: It could be.

CHAPTER 17

O'Neill and Karen were barely on speaking terms at this point, and things didn't improve the next day when she made a fool of him in court on his subpoena for the mysterious tapes. Before the jury was called in, O'Neill stood and again repeated his demand for subpoena compliance. I found it difficult to suppress my grin as Karen stood up and announced we had nothing to turn over. Bailey looked up at O'Neill, bewildered. O'Neill realized he had been played and now had to explain it to his client. The only thing that had kept Bailey from vehemently denying his tirades of the previous two years was his fear of a federal perjury charge if an audiotape surfaced and contradicted his sworn testimony.

Bailey didn't look happy taking the stand for his second day. Karen asked him why his internal affairs investigators had read Stephen Kumnick his Miranda rights after Steve gave the *Herald Press* interview. Bailey said he believed an employee who took photocopies of documents from a government office could be guilty of "seventh degree" larceny.

Q: I'm asking you what the basis is for your own sworn testimony that Mister Kumnick could have been guilty of a larceny?

A: As I said, if there is—in my mind larceny would be the paper, which I believe would be larceny in the seventh degree.

Q: Larceny in the seventh degree?...is it your position that if Mister Kumnick had taken a division document, Xeroxed it, and gave the copy to somebody else, that piece of paper on which it was copied constitutes the property on which the larceny is based?

A: That would be the only crime I could think of.

Q: That's my point. The only crime you could think of that Mister Kumnick committed was stealing the piece of paper that was used to copy the document, correct? That was your testimony?

A: That was my testimony.

Q: Do you think there was anything at all about that statement that is ludicrous?

A: Yes, because the—I did not do that interview.

Connecticut law has never had more than six degrees of larceny, as the news reporters all pointed out in their stories the next day.

Karen began questioning Bailey about the Litchfield transfer. When she asked whether the FBI controversy had anything to do with his decision to transfer me to Litchfield, Bailey replied it did not, only to be reminded that during his November 9 deposition he had answered that question: "Not to my recollection."

Q: Has your recollection improved since November 9?

A: Not to my recollection.

The media policy also came in for scrutiny. On direct examination, Karen was able to show that it had never been applied to anyone and was routinely violated, as in the famous Martha Moxley homicide investigation, a high-profile Greenwich murder that had riveted the state—and the rest of the country.[34] Bailey, a self-described "religious" reader of the *Hartford Courant*, had somehow missed all but one of the articles written about the cold case, despite his employees being quoted throughout all the articles in clear violation of his own media policy.

Before the trial began, Karen cautioned me to guard my reactions in court, even when a witness testified falsely. When that happened—and it did—I either scribbled out a note to Karen explaining why the testimony was false or searched my binders to find a document that refuted the lie. I tried, though not always successfully, to maintain a "poker face." In contrast, Bailey reacted like a silent film actor each time testimony did not go his way.

Karen called Stephen Kumnick to corroborate my testimony:

Q: Did Ralph DiFonzo ever make any statement in your presence regarding the process by which UFAPs were to be drafted which in any way caused you concern?

After a flurry of objections from Bailey's attorneys, Kumnick gave the following response:

---

[34] Fifteen-year-old Martha Moxley was murdered in the posh town of Greenwich in 1975; Michael Skakel was eventually arrested twenty-five years later after the case was reopened. The case drew national attention in large part because Skakel is the nephew of Ethel Kennedy, widow of Senator Robert F. Kennedy. After his conviction, Skakel successfully appealed, and the case was overturned. The State of Connecticut elected not to retry the case on October 30, 2020, forty-five years to the day of the murder.

A: Regarding UFAPs: "If you don't have it, lie because they never prosecute them anyway."

And regarding this particular UFAP warrant prepared by the FBI? "It contained lies."

When court resumed Monday morning, O'Neill had Bailey back on the stand for a well-rehearsed dance to establish the justifications for his actions: the media policy, the Rules of Professional Responsibility for attorneys, the reduced budget, and the FBI's internal investigation. Bailey explained he had not lifted his gag order only because of the fact that the FBI had failed to notify him their investigation had concluded.

Karen took another shot at him as well, making it clear that he was sitting on our heads in order not to jeopardize *his* chance of being promoted:

> Q: Isn't it true that at the time of these events as they unfolded in 1996 and early and mid-1997, that you were under consideration for appointment to a federal post in the Department of Justice of the United States?
>
> A: I was from January 23 to February 6, roughly about fifteen days.
>
> Q: And isn't it true, sir, that during that time you had some discussion with the office of presidential personnel in Washington regarding whether or not you might be considered for appointment as an assistant or deputy attorney general?
>
> A: Correct.

Q: And that deputy attorney general position would be with the Department of Justice?

A: Yes, it would.

Q: The same department the FBI is in, correct?

A: Yes, it is.

Q: And isn't it also true, sir, that you were considering that career opportunity at that time?

A: I was considering it.

Q: And isn't it also true that that position was a pretty prestigious position?

A: Correct.

Q: And it was high up in the justice department?

A: It was.

Q: And isn't it true in order to get such a position you could not be approved and appointed unless you underwent an extensive FBI background check?

A: Counselor, as I said, it was for fifteen days. As Mister Dillon said, the Washington bureau would do the background investigation that you're asking. Was it in my consideration? Absolutely not.[35]

---

[35] Bailey's testimony was false, as I had never testified to this fact. The New Haven FBI office would have been tasked with the bulk of Bailey's background investigation, as he had lived and worked in Connecticut his entire life, with the exception of his college years.

Bailey's motive was clear no matter how adamantly he denied it. He was being considered for a prestigious position he coveted, which required the involvement and endorsement of the same agency he was bending over backwards to appease.

Bailey's unenforced media policy was a weakness of the defense case. Karen attacked it with a witness that O'Neill did his best to keep out of the courtroom: Frank Garr. A former Greenwich police officer, now an inspector at the Fairfield State's Attorney's Office, Garr doggedly pursued the Martha Moxley murder case his whole career, even when it went cold.

To expose Bailey's double standard in enforcing the rule against talking about ongoing criminal investigations, she showed him articles from the *Hartford Courant* and asked him if he was quoted offering his opinion about evidence and suspects in the ongoing investigation. "It's possible," he said.

The dapper investigator, with his ponytail, tinted glasses, and Italian loafers without socks, admitted in effect to numerous violations of the media policy.

> Q: Did you, sir, also participate in an interview with a reporter named Lynne Tuohy who at that time was a reporter for the *Hartford Courant*?
>
> A: Yes.
>
> Q: And did you, in fact, discuss during the course of that interview the murder of Martha Moxley?
>
> A: Yes.
>
> Q: Did you discuss during that interview the fact of an investigation into the murder of Martha Moxley?

A: Yes.

Q: And isn't it true, sir, that in that interview you actually talked to a reporter about suspects in that case?

A: Yes.

Q: And those suspects were identified in that article, were they not?

A: Yes.

Q: Those people have not been charged, have they?

A: No.

Q: They have not been found guilty of anything, have they?

A: No.

Q: And their names are in that article, correct?

A: Yes.

Q: And you talked about that, didn't you?

A: Yes.

Q: And to your knowledge, sir, did your comments to a reporter get published by the *Hartford Courant* on or about May 21, 1998?

A: Yes.

Karen asked Garr who was the head of the agency he worked for, and Garr answered directly: "Jack Bailey."

As the trial wore on, Bailey had no supporters on his side of the courtroom; now he arrived and left the courthouse every day alone. The FBI agents saw where this was headed and were nowhere to be seen.

Bailey began his defense by calling my direct supervisor, Chief Inspector David J. Best. Dave was my friend, but he owed his position to Bailey. He was Bailey's driver and confidant, but I know he felt the Fugitive Squad should never have been disbanded.

On the issue of whether I had been unfairly passed over for promotion for retaliatory reasons, "Best said he backed Coffey for the supervisory position in the statewide prosecution bureau, which handles white-collar, environmental, and other crimes, because he was hoping to reassemble the fugitive squad and put Dillon back in charge of it," Alex Wood reported in the *Journal Inquirer*. "Best said he didn't remember telling Dillon that he had gone out to lunch and returned to find the selection made."

Morano fell on the sword for his boss by taking credit for the decision to transfer me to Litchfield. Frank Maco, the Litchfield state's attorney, testified how his office was always shorthanded and needed extra help, now feigning ignorance of the fact that assignment to his station was considered a hardship tour. Executive Assistant State's Attorney John "Jack" Cronan spoke to Bailey's budgetary concerns in disbanding the fugitive squad. And then on Tuesday, the man we'd all been waiting for: FBI Special Agent in Charge Merrill Parks Jr.

Parks strode into the courtroom like a whiskerless Yosemite Sam, short, short-tempered, and all business. Finally, someone from the FBI in the courtroom, on the stand, and under oath. Bailey had obviously hoped Parks could save the day by refuting the allegations.

The FBI internal probe was the elephant in the room. Bailey had been stronger in support of the FBI agents than he was of his own men. He disparaged our complaint as mere allegations without proof—"our word against theirs" as he put it—despite the substantial documentary evidence we had provided him to back it up.

After much legal wrangling and bickering between the attorneys, Judge Arterton finally ordered SAC Parks to explain—without identifying anyone by name—how many agents had been disciplined and the details of the punishment. Christian Miller of the *New Haven Register* reported:

> Parks revealed for the first time that four FBI agents were reprimanded for their roles in the preparation of the seven federal warrants, but he testified that he could not disclose their identity because of privacy concerns.
>
> The stiffest penalty meted out was a letter of reprimand and five-day suspension, Parks testified. Court documents have identified Special Agent Ralph A. DiFonzo Jr., who coordinated the task force, as the recipient of administrative discipline, which according to sources was the five-day suspension.[36]

After US District Judge Janet Bond Arterton ordered him to provide specifics on the punishment, Parks said one agent was ordered to submit to "counseling" from him, another was given an oral reprimand, and the third received a letter of reprimand.

Alex Wood of the *Journal-Inquirer* had further analysis:

> This is an example of the slow, strange process by which bits and pieces of information about the FBI's action on the state inspectors' allegations have become public

---

[36] SSA DiFonzo appealed the five-day suspension, arguing he was overburdened with other "job-related responsibilities," that the complaint was made by "disgruntled employees," the distraction of his mother's illness, and he had already "been punished enough by being falsely accused of criminal acts." The following year, his suspension was reversed with "reinstatement of full pay and benefits."

to date. But no information has been made public as to why the FBI imposed the administrative penalties on the agents, why there was no criminal prosecution, or what evidence the FBI's internal investigation uncovered.

All the disclosures about the disciplinary action stem in one way or another from Dillon's lawsuit against Bailey and the state. Court procedures on disclosure of information have overcome the wall of secrecy erected by federal laws and regulations on disciplinary action against federal employees.

Parks did not make a favorable impression upon the jury. He was smug and arrogant, and his efforts at humor fell flat. The demeanor of the jury panel was somber throughout his testimony.

Karen Torre questioned him sharply. Bailey had repeatedly tried to minimize Parks's explosive reaction to the accusations, brushing aside suggestions he himself had been intimidated or overreacted. The blustery Parks was no help in that regard. Asked about his threat to end all joint law enforcement operations with the state over the matter, not only did Parks confirm it, he seemed proud of it: "I was hotter than a two-dollar pistol." He smirked, then scanned the jury for their reaction. Karen and I both caught the flat expressions and stiff body language of the jurors. "They did not care for that—at all," she whispered to me.

After Parks was forced to acknowledge the gentle discipline he was ordered to impose by FBIHQ, Karen had another exchange with the short-fused witness on recross:

Q: You said you took this matter very, very seriously; is that right?

A: Yes, ma'am.

Q: But isn't it true, sir, that while this matter was still pending, meaning the allegations of perjury, you promoted Ralph DiFonzo?

The judge overruled O'Neill's objection, and Parks explained a painfully convoluted system of how the selection process began with a career board in New Haven, but then a different career board at FBIHQ made a final determination, so it was out of his hands.

Q: All right. Now, did you at the time say to anybody in the FBI, gee, while one of our agents is being accused of lying to federal judges, maybe we ought to put this promotion on hold until it's determined whether he did something wrong or not?

A: No, ma'am.

Q: So, while allegations of perjury were pending against Mister DiFonzo, the FBI gave the guy a promotion?

A: Yes, ma'am, they did.

Q: Now, do you believe that that kind of conduct inspires confidence in the public in the operation of the FBI?

A: I don't know.

The jury didn't seem to think that was funny either. His next attempt at levity fell equally flat. The *Journal Inquirer* had inadvertently listed Parks's name under a photograph of his assistant special agent in charge, Gary Rohen, who, although close in height, was quite bald while Parks had a full head of hair.

Q: I have one final question, and that is Mister Bailey made a number of statements, comments if you will, regarding this matter, meaning the OPR investigation to the press, didn't he?

A: To whom?

Q: To the *Herald*, *New Britain Herald*, and the *Journal Inquirer*, the one that had your picture in it, the *Journal Inquirer*?

A: That wasn't me.

Q: Your picture wasn't in the paper?

A: No, ma'am. That was actually my assistant special agent in charge.

Q: That's right. I thought you looked a little different.

A: I thought something horrible happened overnight.

Parks again smirked and scanned, but there was no reaction from the stone-faced jury. Bailey's legal team looked glum as Parks sauntered off the stand. Assistant Attorney O'Neill stood and glumly announced he had no additional witnesses. "We rest at this time."

Although time was running short, Karen called me back to the stand as the final witness:

Q: Finally, Inspector, there was testimony yesterday from I believe Mister Cronan and Chief Inspector Best to the effect that you had no economic damages, meaning no out-of-pocket monetary losses, sir. Do you remember that testimony?

A: I do.

Q: Are those the losses that you are concerned about?

A: No, ma'am.

Q: What are the losses that you are concerned about?

A: My reputation and credibility have been affected probably permanently within the law enforcement community because of what's taken place and the way this has been handled.

Q: And do you believe, sir, that your career options have been affected by anything Mister Bailey did in this case?

A: Yes, ma'am. I'm only forty-two years old. I still have quite a few years left in my career, I believe.

Q: Thank you, sir. I have nothing further.

In her closing argument, Karen tied it all together as she made our case for a violation of my First Amendment rights:

> Think about it. When the Constitution is violated or if you think your constitutional rights have been violated, what do you do? You file a lawsuit. So you see the critical importance of your role here. You are the ones to decide whether and to what extent you're going to breathe life into the First Amendment. Not a politician, not a governor, not a senator, not a congressman, not a rich guy with a lot of power and connections, ordinary folks like yourself get to come into a federal court and decide the meaning of the Constitution in our day-to-day lives.

Karen went through the facts chronologically, recapping the testimony and evidence as it was presented to the jury. She then addressed the demeanor of the key witnesses who had testified:

> I will ask you, ladies and gentlemen, you listened to Mister Bailey for days. Do you believe his testimony? Do you believe he gave a straight answer to a straight question? I am standing here now, and I am dizzy even trying to figure out what Mister Bailey's testimony was because it was contradictory, it was all over the place, and it was ludicrous.
>
> Compare the appearance of Greg Dillon, a man everyone who's taken the stand in this case admits is a man of honor, honesty, and integrity, a man who will not lie for anybody or anything. He gave a straight answer to a straight question. It didn't matter whether I asked it or whether Mister O'Neill asked it. Greg Dillon was as candid and forthright and responsive to the questions posed by Mister O'Neill as he was with me.
>
> Mister Morano, he wasn't as bad as Mister Bailey, but was he forthright? No. Did he try to play games with me? Yes. Did he try to tap dance around the question? Yes. Did he try to appear somewhat cute and glib? Yes. What is his interest in the case? He's Mister Bailey's top deputy. Clearly he is allied with Mister Bailey in this case.
>
> What I found most annoying throughout the cross-examination of these witnesses was the frequency with which "I don't recall that" was employed by these defense witnesses. It was the term of art of the day in this courtroom. "I don't recall." Did you say this? "I don't recall." Did you accuse somebody of this? "I don't recall." Did you threaten this person? "I don't recall."

It's almost as if they all got in some kind of command center and said, "Okay, folks, when they ask you that question, just remember, I don't recall. Don't deny it because that might be lying. Just say I don't recall." There is no other explanation for the fact that that was a term of art used again and again and again, and when I pushed each and every one of those witnesses to say, "Look, did you say this or not?" all we got was "I don't recall." Almost like it was a sound bite.

Karen identified the three issues the jury would decide: Was the Fugitive Squad disbanded as retaliation, was I transferred to the Litchfield office as retaliation, and was I denied the supervisor's position in the Statewide Prosecution Bureau as retaliation? She discussed each of them in detail, then moved on to the issue of damages:

You have also been told the fact that he has suffered no out-of-pocket losses by the way of salary and benefits is immaterial; that you're entitled to compensate for emotional harm, personal indignity, embarrassment and humiliation; and I leave it to your good judgment to determine to what extent to compensate him for that.... Punitive damages have a completely different purpose. They serve to punish and deter, to punish a defendant for acting in reckless disregard of someone's constitutional rights. That's the standard.

I don't mean to be cute when I say that free speech must be free. It is not free speech if you can speak, but must lose the assignment that you love. It is not free speech if you can speak, but must suffer a disbanding of your unit and transfer to the hills of Litchfield. It is not free speech if you can speak, but must suffer the humiliation and public indignity of doing work that is not a supervisor's work in a place where you spent three hours in a car every day. It is not free speech if you can speak, but must lose a promotion that you've earned, that you have a right to have. It is not free speech if you can speak, but must be humiliated by reporting to someone who used to be under you. In short, it is not free speech if you can speak but must fall victim to the whims of a publicity seeking, self-serving, selfish politician.

Karen closed with this:

> When officials violate constitutional rights, the only remedy is a jury. In a sense, you, ladies and gentlemen, serve as the brakes on official misconduct, and I am asking you to operate as a good braking system in this case and issue both a compensatory and a punitive award, number one, because Greg Dillon deserves it and, number two, John Bailey deserves it. Thank you.

Terrence O'Neill in his closing argument had a problem: the notebook of rough drafts and approved UFAP warrants I had submitted to Bailey was now Exhibit #1. The jury could finally see for themselves exactly how and where the FBI agents had lied.[37] There would be no question the documents had been falsified with the added fictional information attributed directly to the inspectors. O'Neill couldn't argue this away, so instead he chose to attack me for the timing of my complaint:

> The plaintiff first learns that there is a possibility that something is misrepresented in an affidavit that he worked on. He doesn't talk to the person who signed that affidavit. He doesn't check to see if the person who signed the affidavit had done further investigation. He

---

37   Copies had been made for each juror to expedite the deliberation process.

doesn't check to see if the person who signed the affidavit had his or her own work files with the materials in it. He doesn't check with that person's supervisor to see if any of those things exist. But it comes to his attention and he's concerned and he's so concerned he's paralyzed. His testimony is he was paralyzed on that. He decided if it ever happened again, he would do something about it.

I have no idea how he thought this would help him. It was clear from my testimony, as well as Kumnick's and Freddo's, that each case was assigned to a single investigator; there was zero chance additional work had been done without the knowledge of the lead investigator to whose name the falsified information had been attributed. O'Neill was overplaying his hand.

O'Neill next tried to minimize my transfer to Litchfield:

The claim here is that he had added commuter time.... How many of us get to commute, as Mister Dillon did, with a state car, state gas, state insurance, and state maintenance? Where is the harm? Other than the time, where is the harm?

O'Neill hewed to Bailey's version of events, discounting any testimony that was at odds with it: Bailey only disbanded the Fugitive Squad because of fiscal constraints; Inspector Coffey was promoted over me because he had more law enforcement experience; Bailey's long-term plan was to resurrect the Fugitive Squad, hoping to reinstate me as the head of it.

O'Neill maintained that because there had been no testimony or evidence as to what my salary was, the jury was not in a position to address the issues of compensatory damages. Because I had never sought therapy or counseling, I continued to exercise regularly, and I performed all the duties my job required, he said, I had therefore not suffered sufficient emotional damages:

Ladies and gentlemen, there isn't even testimony in this
case that Mister Dillon took a sick day or a vacation day
or anytime off from work as a result of any of this.

There I was caught in a bind; if I'd done any of these things, they
would have questioned my fitness for hazardous duty service.

O'Neill said the true source of my torment was the FBI, "what they
put him through by putting his name in these warrants," not Bailey. If
the jury decided to consider punitive damages, they were misguided if
they awarded them at Bailey's expense.

O'Neill concluded with an appeal to the dignity of Connecticut law
enforcement, saying of his witnesses:

> They're law enforcement officers and state's attorneys
> in this state. They're prosecutors. If they answered a
> question in a certain way, I respectfully ask you, do you
> really believe based on the evidence of this case that the
> many law enforcement officials, including the four I just
> named [Maco, Morano, Best, and Cronan], would come
> into court and lie? What evidence has been produced in
> this case to show that the people that have been brought
> into testify in this matter would lie to you?

Karen's rebuttal was short and to the point:

> Mister Bailey's responsibility, as the head of an agency,
> is not to Merrill Parks, it is to the people of the State of
> Connecticut. It is to the interest of the citizens of the
> state of Connecticut, and it is to the interest of the op-
> erations of his own agency, and what Mister Bailey did
> in handling the FBI situation in transferring Greg, in
> shooting people out to different locations, in conduct-
> ing investigations, in denying people promotions was
> to destroy the working relationships in his own agency,
> never mind the relationship between state and federal.

This man went on a spree which destroyed morale and the working relationships of people who had all gotten along and loved their jobs before.

This is not a personal injury case. There are no broken bones here. That's another courtroom up the street.... This is a federal courtroom where I believe more important injuries are addressed, the injury to constitutional rights, the injury to your reputation, to what you are in the community. I just don't think the defense gets it.... You can put a cast on a broken leg, but you can't put a cast on a fractured reputation.

Karen pointed her finger directly at the squirming Bailey, who sat just feet from the jury.

Do you realize what Mister Bailey did here? He has basically chilled every single state employee from speaking out [on] a matter of public concern. Greg Dillon was injured by that, and a lot of other people were too. That's why I've asked for a punitive award.... I wish you could restore the standing Greg Dillon had before this happened. You can't. The only thing you can do is try to compensate him for it, and at this point, as difficult as it is, I give this case up to you.

And that was the last word on the record in the trial of *Dillon v. Bailey*.

The jury retired for what remained of the day. Later, they sent a note to the judge, indicating they would like to return the following morning. They were excused with the standard admonitions: do not discuss the matter and avoid any news coverage of the trial.

The next morning was the day before Thanksgiving, and we were back in the courtroom fully expecting a decision by noontime, due to the fast-approaching holiday. Inspectors Kumnick, Freddo, and Malchik were in the courtroom with me. The head US marshal, John O'Connor, whom I knew when he was a captain on the New Haven Police Department, stopped by our table. He said he was going to make a prediction: the jury would ask that an early lunch be sent in—as it would be a free lunch—then would announce their decision right after. He paused, then added with a wink: "And you're going to win big."

I had always believed we would win. The question was how much? I was not counting on a large payout, perhaps even less than the last settlement offer. But for me it had never been about the money. Settling the case would have let Bailey off the hook, and the public would have never heard the testimony of the last seven days. The trial had been covered by every local TV news station and newspaper, which was exactly what I wanted from the start: my day in court with everyone under oath.

As the morning dragged on, I indulged my sweet tooth and went out for a brownie at a nearby coffee shop. Oddly, I felt comfortable, not as anxious as the rest of the group, just stretching my legs on a sunny day and indulging in my chocolate treat with a cold glass of milk. Partway through my reverie, Steve Kumnick came in, breathless and red-faced, and announced the jury had sent out a note. I asked him to sit down for a minute and join me while I ate my brownie. They weren't going to start without me. Time was moving in slow motion now, as I felt all my senses heightened with the adrenaline rush. I had to force myself to relax, breathe deep, and remain calm.

As we walked back toward the courthouse with Kumnick urging me on, I knew my life was about to change, either for the better or worse, depending upon the decision of eight strangers.

> The Court: The jurors by note have indicated that they have reached a verdict on this phase. We will bring them in.

I had faith in the jurors, who were neither beholden to, nor in fear of, John M. Bailey. The evidence spoke for itself.

Karen had told me not to react, regardless of the outcome. Karen had already told me if the jury decided in our favor, that Bailey had violated my right to free speech, the jury was going to be sent back to deliberate on the issue of constitutional damages.

The jury was seated and the foreman, a Mr. Sarner, was identified and interrogated by the clerk:

> Do you find any of the following employment actions were adverse to the plaintiff: Disbanding the Fugitive Squad?

> Yes.

> Reassignment to Litchfield?

> Yes.

> Denial of supervisory inspector assignment awarded to Inspector Charles Coffey?

> Yes.

> Has plaintiff proven that his protected speech or intended speech related to his making allegations of FBI misconduct was a motivating factor in defendant's decision to take adverse action?

> Yes.

> Has the defendant John M. Bailey proven that he would have taken the same adverse employment action even in the absence of the plaintiff's acts of expression or speech?

No.

We had run the table. Now I was holding my breath.

What compensatory, if any, damages do you award to the plaintiff in violation of his constitutional rights?

$800,000.

There were audible gasps in the courtroom. Karen, whose right hand had been resting on my left forearm, squeezed hard, but her gaze remained focused on the jury.

The Clerk: Do you find that the defendant acted willfully, maliciously, or in reckless disregard of the plaintiff's rights by taking adverse employment action?

Yes.

Punitive damage: $1.5 million.

Karen now squeezed my arm so hard, I winced. I looked at her and saw a tear forming in her right eye, which began to roll down her cheek before she caught it. The $1.5 million award—which now brought the total to $2.3 million—caused a stir within the courtroom; reporters were scribbling furiously and whispers were being exchanged in the gallery. Bailey looked like he'd suffered a concussion. He kept looking at O'Neill, who was sinking deeper into his chair.

The clerk had one more question for the jury:

Has the plaintiff proven by a preponderance of the evidence that the defendant John Bailey orally warned the inspectors at the staff meeting of January 9, 1998, that any inspector who wished to express or share a personal opinion to a reporter would first have to resign from his job with the State of Connecticut?

"Yes," came the answer. Bailey had violated my constitutional right to free speech. That meant there would be a second phase of the trial, constitutional arguments, and a decision by the jury on an additional award.

The judge excused the jury for a moment and invited the attorneys into her chambers. O'Neill begged her not to go forward with the second phase. The compensatory and punitive awards were already large, he argued, and any additional award "will only be seen as excessive." Karen countered that an appellate court would surely determine if the awards were excessive, and for that reason, the second phase should continue. An appellate court could reduce the original award, but the constitutional award—if any—might stand. The judge agreed, saying the jury that had heard all the evidence should also consider the award on the constitutional claim.

The jury was brought back to the courtroom. As word had spread about the size of the award, other attorneys and courthouse personnel now crowded the courtroom to see the final chapter play out.

The judge thanked the jury for its finding of fact on Bailey's "should resign" speech, and explained in legal terms her ruling that his directives had violated my First Amendment rights. The jury's role was to now decide if additional damages applied. The judge cautioned them these damages "must not duplicate what you have already awarded for that same injury if you found the same injury to have resulted from defendant's retaliatory employment action."

In her remarks to the jury, Karen offered a scathing critique of Bailey's public conduct as head of a state agency:

> While allegations of perjury were pending against the FBI agents, Mister Bailey, exempting himself from his own unconstitutional ban, was lauding the FBI, expressing confidence in them, expressing confidence in

his personal friend Merrill Parks, and humiliating and embarrassing his own people.... He sacrificed his own people for his own political ends.

The Division of Criminal Justice had treated me most unfairly, Karen said, and the defense at trial had abused me as well:

> Indeed, didn't it happen again in this room? I personally was offended that my client had to sit in that witness stand and be subjected to questioning about whether he had made baseless accusations.... "Mister Dillon, wasn't it a typo?" "Wasn't it just a mistake?" "How come you didn't talk to Lisa Bull?" "You made these accusations without talking to anybody...." My client was put through the same thing in this courtroom that he was put through in the newspapers, and I think that was a shame, especially in light of the fact that Merrill Parks traipsed in here and admits four agents were disciplined for lying on those applications.

O'Neill continued inexplicably to defend the FBI and gave this extraordinary speech in which he twisted the actual facts of the case the jury had just decided. He had learned nothing from his hour-old mistake:

> I reassert to you that throughout the last two years, the motivation behind Mister Bailey's actions were allegations of misconduct that were being investigated in a criminal investigation by the United States Department of Justice. A resolution of that investigation was favorable on the criminal matters. There was no testimony, as Attorney Torre just said to you, that these FBI agents were found to have lied. In fact, there was a finding by the Department of Justice that there was no crime.

He begged them not to impose any further penalty. "I respectfully submit to you that you have sent a message," O'Neill said. "You've spoken loudly and clearly."

Karen declined the opportunity for a rebuttal and a final closing argument. O'Neill had done himself more damage than she could, and besides it was the day before Thanksgiving, and the clock was ticking. The jury was back in just over an hour.

> The Clerk: For interference and restraint in exercise of First Amendment rights, what compensatory damage, if any, do you award the plaintiff?
>
> $400,000.

The next day's *Hartford Courant* article finished with this:

> After the jury retired to deliberate again, Torre lightly told Dillon, "You've got the cake. Now we'll see what the icing tastes like."
>
> An hour later, the jury awarded Dillon another $400,000 in compensatory damages, bringing the total award to $2.7 million.[38]
>
> Dillon said it tasted sweet.

Bailey was flummoxed, waiting for O'Neill to explain to him what had just happened. O'Neill was crestfallen, supporting himself on the table with both hands as he stood for the exiting jurors. He had the pallor of a marathoner crossing the finish line after carrying Bailey piggyback for the 26.2 mile course—which was essentially what had happened.

---

[38] The 1998 award of $2.7 million would be the equivalent of $4.5 million in 2022, according to www.smartasset.com.

Any time the state is defeated in court on a First Amendment claim and ordered to pay millions, there is bound to be a lot of media coverage. By the last few days, as things went from bad to worse for the defense, there were camera crews and photographers camped out at the entrance of the federal courthouse each afternoon.

As soon as the judge adjourned court we were swarmed with well-wishers congratulating us and reporters trying to land a quick interview. Karen, looking for a quiet place to make a cell phone call, opened up a side room in the corridor just outside the courtroom, then quickly closed the door. She pulled me aside and told me O'Neill was sitting in the room "crying like a baby." I looked at her skeptically, and she shook her head and said no, she was not exaggerating; he had tears streaming down his face as he held his head in his hands. She said as much as she disliked him and his tactics during the trial, she actually felt bad he was taking it so hard. I was not as sympathetic.

I was on live TV with Judy Chong of WTNH News at 5 p.m. and had this to say: "Because of the fact that I truly believed that I had done the right thing, I felt confident that sooner or later I would be completely vindicated and the truth would come out."

We walked to a local bar, Karen and I, along with her associate, Michelle; my wife, Vilma; Mike Malchik; Steve Kumnick; and his wife, Eloise. We ordered champagne and toasted our victory while watching the live coverage on the bar's overhead television.

It was big news, and the follow-up didn't subside for several days. "Jury Says Bailey Violated Rights, Millions Awarded To Officer Who Said He Was Silenced," blared the usually Bailey-friendly *Hartford Courant*:

> Tall and crew-cut, Dillon, 42, of North Haven was portrayed during the trial as a by-the-book law enforcement official who won glowing reviews from his bosses and intense loyalty from the inspectors he supervised. Two men who once worked for him — both ex-homicide officers — wiped tears from their eyes as the verdict was read in court.

Quoted in his own defense, Bailey said, "I'm not happy with the verdict. I think we have a good chance of having it overturned. I was always taught you can't comment on ongoing investigations. You can ruin lives and reputations...."

Again, the irony was lost on Bailey, considering the jury had just financially flogged him for his indifference to ruining *my* life and reputation for the past two and a half years.

Karen was on top of her game still and riding high:

> We are so very proud of this jury. They acted in this case, as juries do, as conscience of the community.... They [agency heads] cannot control and manipulate public knowledge of the affairs of the agencies. I think it is one of the most important First Amendment decisions in the history of Connecticut.[39]

Karen was on a roll:

> Bailey abused his position as Chief State's Attorney in order to coddle a friend who heads up the FBI.... Everyone knew Dillon had unquestioned honesty and integrity. It didn't hurt that the defendants conceded that.[40]

I felt the same way; I told the *Courant* reporter: "This was a group vindication for me and the other officers of the squad who had to suffer the wrath of an employer who would not support his employees...." To the *New Haven Register*: "This was never a money issue. It was an issue of right and wrong."

Bailey would certainly go to the Court of Appeals for the Second Circuit to try and get the jury award reduced, Karen said. We would have to meet him there. The appeal was not covered by our 40/60 split, so I would again be on the hook for her next series of legal bills.

---

[39]   *New Haven Register.*
[40]   *Connecticut Law Tribune.*

CHAPTER 18

I returned to work the following Monday. I had proven my point, but there was no guarantee of any windfall. A successful appeal by the state could gut my award. What had me most worried on an appeal was the fact the jury had awarded me $800,000 in compensatory damages, despite the fact I had never had my salary reduced or frozen. That, plus the fact that Karen would be entitled to 40 percent of any remaining award, at which time I could look forward to providing another 40 percent to Uncle Sam (it was taxable, as there was no physical injury). Plus, I was still counting on a pension, which required ten more years of service.

As before, some offered immediate congratulations in public, some only in private. Bizarrely, others attempted to act as if nothing had happened during the last three weeks. A few still shunned me, as they had before the trial. I made a concerted effort not to gloat and went about my business as I always had, waiting for Bailey to make the next move.

Except for Bob Hughes, the original Fugitive Squad was gone. Kumnick and Freddo stayed at the Hartford State's Attorney Office after their 120-day transfers.[41] Mike Malchik, weary of Statewide cases and Chuck Coffey, chose to retire. Bailey, still smarting after being abused by his beloved FBI, ordered John Healy off the task force and back to Rocky Hill. As John's protective younger brother, Chief Inspector Paul Healy, had since left state service for the private sector, the turncoat—expecting a frosty reception—retired before his transfer took effect.

Within a few days, Bailey stopped by my tiny office and deferentially knocked on the open door. He sat in the one chair that fit inside the cramped room and got right to business: "We need to figure out where you would like to work now. A supervisor's position, of course." Before I could respond, he suggested the newly formed Elder Abuse Bureau. I must have grimaced, because he quickly backtracked and said he could not picture me liking that type of work. He then threw out the Medicaid Fraud Bureau, which sounded even worse to me.

"How about Gangs?" I asked. I wanted more "street" work and less "desk" work. I had noticed while there were several inspectors assigned to the Gang & Continuing Criminal Activity Bureau, there was no supervisory inspector assigned there—just like the Statewide Prosecution Bureau had been before I won my lawsuit. Bailey's face lit up as he warmed to "his" idea. It was a win-win, as no one had to be moved, or removed, to accommodate me. Perhaps because of the barrier of my desk and his eagerness to exit my cramped office, he did not extend his hand, sparing us both the awkwardness of me refusing to shake it.

---

[41]   Both Kumnick and Freddo hired a law firm and, without having to even file a lawsuit, received $190,000 each in a settlement with the state.

★ ★ ★

Senator Richard Blumenthal holding a press conference against the
nomination of Amy Coney Barrett to the U.S. Supreme Court.
(Associated Press)

Bailey, sickened at the outcome of the trial, now asked Attorney General Richard Blumenthal to allow him to hire private counsel to handle the appeal—at taxpayers' expense of course. Bailey hand-picked attorney James Bergenn, a rising star with the prestigious Hartford law firm of Shipman & Goodwin.

Blumenthal had the authority—under unique circumstances— to approve Bailey's unusual request. Ironically, one of the duties of Blumenthal's office was to protect and advocate for whistleblowers like myself, although I was never once contacted by him or his office. The result was that I now had to foot the bill for the appeal while Bailey had the unlimited resources of the state, plus a private law firm, and was financially responsible for none of it.

Although I sensed Bailey wanted to adhere to a truce, his number two, DCSA Morano, was not having it. Morano bristled at the sight of me and soon made it clear he would eventually even the score.

My attention was now split between supervising a very active bureau that covered the entire state and preparing for Judge Arterton's upcoming injunction hearing, which was only weeks away. As expected, Bailey would bring in several "experts." During the trial, Bailey attempted to have Dr. Henry Lee testify on his behalf, but the judge decided Dr. Lee had insufficient involvement to justify his appearance. Bailey was now finally able to include his close friend, who would reluctantly attempt to defend Bailey's tainted media policy and equally flawed application of it. Bailey thought Dr. Lee's "star power" could persuade any arbiter.

Mike Malchik, Steve Kumnick, Steve Freddo, and I met in Karen's office one afternoon to strategize. Time and again, we kept circling back to how we needed a "Serpico-like" witness, someone who could explain why it was necessary to go public with corruption charges if there were reasons to suspect a whitewash. After various names were bantered about, Malchik finally asked, "How about Serpico himself?" We all sat there in stunned silence, contemplating the obvious. "I just saw a TV special about him not that long ago. He's alive and living in seclusion somewhere in upstate New York." Karen asked Mike how he expected to find a cop living under the radar. Malchik's reply? "We are very good at finding people who don't want to be found. Don't forget, we did it for a living." And that's just what Mike did.

Within a week, Karen and I were in her office, waiting to hear from Serpico's attorney on a conference call in which he would patch us into Frank Serpico himself. Once on the line, Frank asked several pointed questions about the issues in the case. Finally, he said he would talk it over with his attorney and get back to us. As Karen and I discussed the latest settlement offer, we were interrupted by a phone call. We were informed Serpico liked the case and was now on board. We were ecstatic, as this was huge.

Meanwhile, Bailey continued to feel the heat. The formerly fawning *Hartford Courant* took a hard swipe at him in its November 30 editorial:

> Testimony in the case revealed a chilling story: a pliant chief state's attorney muzzling his employees at the

insistence of a bullying FBI official who wanted to keep allegations of agency wrongdoing from the public.... Mr. Bailey, who said he will appeal, has some soul searching to do about his future in the job.... The question is whether Connecticut can afford to have a compromised top prosecutor who was found to have violated the constitutional rights of an employee and was severely rebuked by a judge and jury.

One week into the new year, Judge Arterton released her thirty-three-page ruling, which detailed her decision that Bailey's enforcement of his media policy was unconstitutional. In fact, she felt so strongly about the importance of this case, she took the unusual step of submitting it for publication in West's Federal Supplement. Alex Wood of the *Journal Inquirer* quoted passages in his article on her ruling:

> The matter about which the plaintiff reported, spoke, or wished to speak to others and would have answered media questions about was not a minor form of public corruption, but about corruption that goes to the heart of the integrity of the criminal justice system.
>
> Moreover, without disclosures by law-enforcement insiders such as Dillon, willing to report their well-founded beliefs of the existence of wrongdoing by fellow law-enforcement officers, such corruption is most difficult to detect, prove, or prevent.
>
> As such, the court accords this speech extremely high value in conducting the balancing test, the restraint of which is to be justified only by proof that serious, pressing needs of the employer public agency are or will be seriously compromised or threatened.

I was heartened to see the presiding judge agreed my complaint had been based upon *"well founded beliefs of the existence of wrongdoing by fellow law-enforcement officers...."* Mr. Wood, understandably, could not pry a comment out of Bailey. He, of course, had more success with Blumenthal:

> Attorney General Richard Blumenthal, whose office represents Bailey in the case, declined to comment on Arterton's reasoning. Noting that Arterton had previously announced the substance of the decision, Blumenthal said, "We respectfully disagreed with it then and continue to disagree with it."

Blumenthal was an ambitious Democrat politician and was not about to cut his ties with the powerful Bailey/Kennelly clan. His loyalty would later pay dividends. In 2011, after incumbent Sen. Chris Dodd decided not to run for reelection after five consecutive terms, Blumenthal was easily elected to Dodd's seat.

On January 19, 1999, we were back before Judge Arterton. In addition to Bailey's new attorney, Bergenn was now joined by a senior staff attorney from his firm, Sheila Huddleston, in addition to the attorney general's original team of Terrence O'Neill and Matthew Beizer. Bergenn began by explaining how Dr. Lee's schedule was making it difficult to plan his testimony. Bergenn wished to have Dr. Lee's testimony presented as a recorded deposition, allegedly to speed up the proceedings due to the good doctor's overbooked schedule. The judge was not fond of this compromise or having to delay the proceedings any further.

Karen would have none of it; she pointed out there could be no control over what went into the record, plus she wanted the opportunity to cross-examine the forensic scientist.

Attorney Bergenn next called Milton E. Ahlerich to the witness stand. "Milt" Ahlerich was SAC Parks's predecessor at the New Haven Division from 1990 through 1994; he retired to take a position with the National Football League as senior director of security. Ahlerich walked the court through his impressive twenty-five-year FBI career, and as expected, he touted the company line. He opined that anyone in law enforcement who witnessed another officer's misconduct could *only* report the wrongdoing through the chain of command of his or her own agency. It was never permissible—under any circumstances—to go public. Further, he believed this code of confidentiality had no time limit; one was bound to keep the complaint secret in perpetuity. If the complainant felt there was a cover-up, he or she needed to continue to make their complaint through their own chain of command, regardless of which agency was the offender.

Karen and I felt the judge was not swayed by his absolute faith in the integrity of the FBI's self-policing system.

Our next showdown depended upon the availability of Bailey's star witness, Dr. Lee, who was currently in Singapore. While waiting for Lee's schedule to clear, Bailey's attorneys scrambled Robert Werner as their next witness.

The young barrister took the stand and described his background: he testified his experience in the US Attorney's Office began in January 1989 and lasted until January 1991—twenty-four months. He spent the entire day on the witness stand. Christian Miller of the *New Haven Register* filed this report:

> Robert W. Werner, who spent less than three years in the U.S. attorney's office, admitted he was unfamiliar with all the facts of the Bailey case, but talked of "hypothetical" situations between law enforcement agencies in a joint task force.

> "A leak by one of the participating law enforcement agencies can compromise the investigation...and can impact the inter-relationship between those agencies," Werner testified under questioning by attorney James Bergenn.

> In almost all cases, the need for confidentiality in criminal investigations outweighs the right of the whistleblower to

point out corruption, Werner said. In fact, there are some cases when law enforcement officials can foster stronger trust among one another by keeping secret information about public corruption, he testified.

Good for law enforcement officials; not so good for the public. The article concluded:

But Werner also admitted under cross-examination from Dillon's attorney, Karen Lee Torre of New Haven, there are "multiple exceptions" to the confidentiality rule that would allow breaking law enforcement's rigid chain of command.

The Associated Press also filed an article, expounding that point: "But under cross-examination, Werner acknowledged that if Dillon believed Bailey was corrupt, Dillon might have acted appropriately in speaking with the media."

But of course I had never done so *prior* to the retaliation. I was treated and punished as if I had spoken to the media, but that point was somehow lost during the exchange.

"Top FBI agent dies" the *New Haven Register* reported on March 8. Merrill Simpson Parks Jr. cast off his mortal bonds "after a short illness" at Yale-New Haven Hospital. Sources told me he was admitted originally for another severe asthma attack, then contracted a staph infection while recuperating at the hospital.

On March 31, just weeks after the passing of Parks, I checked my voice mail after lunch. One message, recorded at 12:57 p.m., lasted less than a minute. A male caller, trying to sound as menacing as possible, hissed, *"Dillon, you rat fuck! You're a fucking rat!"* several times before hanging up. As a matter of investigative habit, I made a cassette recording of it. Bailey, upon hearing of this, insisted I file a report with the

Connecticut State Police, which I reluctantly did, knowing nothing would come of it. While I never received another call at work or discovered the caller's identity, I would like to thank him now; it would prove to be a tide-turning development in a most unexpected way.

On April 17, DCSA Morano, likely tired of bumping into me in the hallways of the Rocky Hill office, surprised everyone and moved the entire Gang Bureau to the off-site in Newington, ironically the same place the former Fugitive Squad was supposed to inhabit. Most of the Gang Bureau was happy with the relocation. Even though it was a slightly longer commute, we now did not have the micromanaging Morano looking over our collective shoulders.

File photo of renowned forensic scientist Dr. Henry Chang-Yu Lee.
(Associated Press)

On Wednesday, April 21, the elusive Dr. Lee finally appeared in New Haven federal court to lend his reluctant support to the beleaguered chief state's attorney. I have always held the gregarious Dr. Lee in high regard and still do. While we had limited contact over the years since I first had him as my college professor, any time I would see him at a conference or symposium, he always remembered my name and where I had worked.

After being sworn in, he reviewed his impressive credentials, as he had done hundreds of times in courthouses around the world. When asked if he was familiar with the details of my case, he made it a point to acknowledge me, adding that he remembered me as an excellent student and a good police officer. That simple public compliment made his following testimony bearable. I knew he did not care to be here, but out of obligation to his friend Bailey—plus a subpoena—he gave his opinion on the balance of confidentiality within law enforcement environs.

Christian Miller of the *New Haven Register* followed the action:

> Lee has nearly 40 years' experience in law enforcement, working on cases all over the world. He just completed a review of the evidence in the assassination of President John F. Kennedy—a fact he mentioned several times in court.
>
> But Lee wasn't called to U.S. District Court Wednesday for his forensic work. Attorneys for Bailey wanted to ask Lee—who often gives entertaining slide presentations of his work to journalists—to talk about the importance of confidentiality.
>
> So, given a hypothetical situation similar to the real case, Lee testified that he would maintain confidentiality, but also give the matter priority, take administrative action and immediately notify the U.S. Attorney about the tainted warrants.
>
> Nothing like that happened in real life.

Incredibly, Miller learned: "The U.S. Attorney's office found out about the warrants from newspaper accounts, officials said."

During a recess, I ran into Dr. Lee in the hallway, and we shook hands. He explained he did not want to involve himself in this case, but could not avoid it. I told him I understood his predicament and wished him well.

The day ended before Karen had her chance to cross-examine Dr. Lee. Before court adjourned for the day, the judge invited Karen and Bailey's attorneys into chambers to discuss who would testify next, as Dr. Lee was Bailey's last witness. As I was excluded from these meetings, I sat in the empty courtroom and waited.

Karen came out to break the bad news: the judge was on the fence regarding Serpico appearing as our witness. Karen related the judge's concern that my situation was dissimilar, as there had never been any threat of violent reprisal. While I did not see where this actually made any difference, I mentioned that I had received an offensive anonymous telephone call at work only three weeks earlier. Karen's face lit up.

"Why did you never tell me this?"

"I didn't think it was that important."

"Well, it certainly is now."

She asked me what proof I had; I told her I had reported it, recorded it, and still had a copy in my briefcase. She returned to the judge's chambers, cassette tape in hand. When she returned, she was beaming. And Bergenn was fuming. Karen announced: "That did it. He's in."

Karen told me as soon as the judge listened to the recording, she decided there was now an element of physical threat, and Serpico's testimony was therefore relevant to my case.

Rachel Gottlieb of the *Hartford Courant* witnessed Dr. Lee's next appearance the following week, along with a host of other newspaper, radio, and television reporters.

> Lee testified that officers should not break their chain
> of command or talk to reporters about pending inves-
> tigations. Torre sought to show that Lee himself of-
> ten talks with reporters about open investigations. She

questioned him about comments he made to the press about high-profile cases such as the JonBenét Ramsey homicide in Colorado and the slaying of Yale University student Suzanne Jovin in New Haven.

Lee said he didn't talk about evidence that was unknown to the public or that would jeopardize the police investigations.

Torre asked Lee why he spoke with "Greentown" author Timothy Dumas about the unsolved 1975 slaying of 15-year-old Martha Moxley in Greenwich.

"He interviewed me based on my report," Lee answered angrily.

This was out of character for Dr. Lee, as he was always polite to a fault, never flustered. But Karen was starting to rattle him, and Dr. Lee forgot his manners—and the fact that the presiding judge was also a woman.

As Torre pressed, noting that Lee could have declined comment because the case was pending, Lee yelled, "I had no choice, lady. I'm an agency head!"

The judge rebuked him at once. "That's Ms. Torre," Arterton instructed Lee. Chastised, Dr. Lee apologized, citing his sudden poor command of English.

The article also announced our next witness:

Frank Serpico, the irreverent former New York City plainclothes officer who became a hero for exposing widespread police corruption in the late 1960s and 1970s, is scheduled to testify for Dillon next week. He is expected to talk about the need for police to be able to talk with reporters or others outside their chain of command as a measure of protection when they expose police wrongdoing.

By prior arrangement, Karen and I had made the trip to upstate New York to meet with Serpico. As he still wished to keep his address private, we agreed to meet at a local health food restaurant in Columbia County.

When he arrived, I was taken aback. I had made the mistake of imagining him as he was portrayed in the movie by Al Pacino. Foolishly, I expected a younger man, then reminded myself how many years had passed since he had been a police officer. He was wearing black leather pants, sported a gray beard, and looked like the aging New Age hipster he had become.

Serpico was eccentric, garrulous, and charming all at once. We hit it off, and I offered to drive him to New Haven for his upcoming appearance. Before saying our goodbyes, as politely as we could, we asked him how he would be dressing for court. He nodded, winked, and said he would be sure to dig out a jacket and tie.

The negotiations intensified. Karen was fielding calls from Bergenn and relaying them to me. I felt the momentum was still on our side, as Bailey's witnesses did not appear to sway the judge. Karen noted the jury either overlooked or chose to ignore the fact that I had never been demoted, which would have triggered a reduction in pay. Therefore, the compensatory award of $800,000 might be considered "extralegal" on appeal. Karen predicted the appellate court would take "a chainsaw" to the compensation award, which would proportionately reduce the punitive award. Finally, she emphasized the panel of judges would be reading briefs and snippets of testimony from the trial transcripts and would only hear limited oral argument. Without the impact of actual witness testimony, their decision would be cold, calculating, surgical—and final.

If I had a dollar for every time I heard "best and final offer," I could have paid off all my legal fees. Finally, I gave her my unrealistic bottom line: $1.5 million. She huffed (figuratively) and puffed (literally), cursed me out, and said it would never happen; it was more than double the state's last, best offer. Obstinately, I said Bergenn and company could take it or leave it. If the appellate court decided to reduce the award, it was on the them, not me.

I returned to New York State to retrieve our star witness. I was excited to have a few hours of alone time with someone I had idolized since college. And Frank did not disappoint. We each told war stories of our past police experiences: gruesome calls, dangerous calls, hilarious calls, and everything in between. I asked how he had handled being a pariah at the time and told him about the anonymous call in which I was called "a fucking rat." Frank told me how he defined a rat: someone who got caught committing a crime or violation and "rolls over" in an attempt to save his or her skin. Because neither he nor I had been accused of any wrongdoing—and had both come forward voluntarily—he explained we were not rats at all. As an afterthought, he added with a grin, "Besides, you can't rat on a rat."

Karen had graciously agreed to put Frank up at her second home in Stony Creek. I was grateful, as I had already agreed to make a substantial "donation" to the New York City Boy's Club, which was Frank's fee for appearing.

As we pulled into Karen's driveway, she was standing outside her cottage, puffing away. She was oddly distracted and appeared a bit dazed. While Frank walked around the yard, taking in the ocean view and inhaling the sea breeze, Karen pulled me aside and whispered that she had just gotten off the phone with Bergenn. Then she added, "And they agreed to settle." I asked for how much? Sheepishly, she replied, "At your figure." I was stunned. "One point five?" She nodded. "I thought you said they would never, ever pay that amount?" Karen shrugged, then regained her footing. "We're keeping Frank here. And he goes to court with us in the morning, just in case this thing falls apart. I still don't trust them."

Karen was later interviewed by Paul Frisman of the *Connecticut Law Tribune* and had this to say: "The night before Serpico was to take the stand, all of a sudden money started coming out of nowhere," Torre says. Bailey's May 6 settlement offer of $1.5 million, she says, was "hundreds of thousands of dollars" more than she expected, and "enough to close the deal."

All I could think was that Bailey would have done anything to stop the public spectacle and staunch his political bleeding. It was not lost on him just how much attention had been given to his witness, Dr. Lee. Now newspapers were printing articles prepping their audiences for Frank Serpico. Whatever attention had been given to Lee was certain to be topped by the most famous law enforcement whistleblower of all time. Bailey blinked, the deal was done, and the spectacle was over. Except that it wasn't.

Frank Serpico talks with Inspector Steve Freddo and Inspector Steve Kumnick outside the New Haven federal courthouse. My friends Patty and Steve Johnson are in the background.

In their attempt to make the matter disappear, Bailey and company had waited just a little too long to settle. Had they capitulated even a day earlier, the hearing would have been cancelled, and Serpico would have stayed home. Now, almost three years after I notified Bailey that FBI agents had falsified affidavits, Judge Arterton took the bench to officially record the settlement agreement. Frank Serpico was present, dressed up and ready to testify. Except that now instead of taking the witness stand—and having to dither and spar with Bergenn—he had a one-page typewritten statement he was prepared to read as soon as the settlement was locked in.

Reporters filled the courtroom to confirm the settlement for their story. Bailey was conspicuously absent. Attorney Bergenn, in open court, acknowledged the state was prepared to settle the matter, but then added a twist: he wanted a confidentiality agreement in place to keep the amount of the award secret.

Before Karen had the opportunity to oppose, the judge took over. Judge Arterton declared even if the plaintiff agreed to this—and Karen was shaking her head "no" to confirm her disapproval—the court would not allow it. This entire case had been about cover-ups and lack of transparency; it was not going to end in secrecy. Karen concurred, Bergenn acquiesced, and within minutes the settlement was on the record. With that, court adjourned.

As we were gathering our things, Judge Arterton's clerk told Karen that the judge had requested a private audience with Mr. Serpico in chambers. She wanted Frank's thoughts and insight about the case and was curious as to what he had done since his retirement.

The three of us then headed outside, where camera crews were already positioned on the sprawling marble steps of the courthouse. There the celebrated whistleblower, with Karen and me on either side, stood before an array of microphones as he read the following statement:

> Hopefully this judgment will serve to put law enforcement agencies around the country on notice that when officers of integrity like Greg Dillon complain to their supervisors of corrupt practices within law enforcement they will take swift and appropriate action precluding the necessity of going to outside agencies such as the press. But in my experience as well as that of other honest officers unfortunately it is not yet so.

> The community would be better served if law enforcement agencies would end their policies of restricting officers from exercising their basic freedom of speech without fear of reprisal from their department heads and

colleagues. Hopefully this judgment encourages other officers to come forward openly to report wrongdoing without fear of ridicule or reprisal. And it is always an honor for me to stand beside such men and women who stand for justice and the rule of law.[42]

The impromptu press conference continued as Judy Chong, microphone in hand, interviewed Frank Serpico:

"What would you say to all the department heads out there?"

"To get smart and avoid situations such as this they went through at the cost of the taxpayers and do the right thing and listen to their men."

Karen Torre, me, and Frank Serpico minutes after the settlement was recorded at the US Federal Courthouse.

---

[42]   Serpico autographed the original copy of the statement for me, writing, "Greg, the guy who got the ball rolling. Best of luck."

Then we returned to Karen's office, where everyone congratulated each other. Frank was itching to get out of his jacket and tie, and back into his denims. He was gracious as he posed for photographs with me, Karen, Kumnick, Freddo, and Malchik. Later that night, Serpico, Karen, my wife, and I enjoyed a celebratory dinner. The following morning, I picked up Frank for the drive back to Chatham.

Me, Frank Serpico, and Karen Torre after returning to her office.

Now I could actually enjoy my time with my boyhood hero, as I did not have to constantly mull over legal tactics and witness strategy. I soon discovered Frank had a keen sense of humor and a large repertoire of jokes. I had a fair collection myself, and somehow we got into an exchange. It became a "who can top this?"—each one a little raunchier than the last. Every round of laughs grew louder and longer. To anyone passing our car on the highway, we must have looked like two maniacs on nitrous oxide, pounding the dashboard, wiping our eyes, red faces contorted in laughter.

When we finally arrived in Chatham, I retrieved a book from my backpack and asked Frank to sign it. It was the second printing of the hardcover edition of Peter Maas's *Serpico: The Cop Who Defied the System*, which I had kept since college. Frank was surprised I still had such an old copy, as it had been reprinted many times since. He wrote in it and handed it back to me. I thanked him profusely for coming to my assistance. We shook hands, then hugged. He wished me luck and safety on the job before walking off. As soon as I was back in my car, I opened the book. He had written:

> *Greg Dillon,*
> *A fellow officer and friend.*
> *Peace & Justice,*
> *Frank Serpico*

Bailey's procrastination in resolving the matter had only resulted in more bad press:

> With Frank Serpico, perhaps this country's most famous police corruption whistle-blower about to testify against him, Connecticut's top prosecutor on Thursday agreed to a $1.5 million settlement to end a lawsuit brought against him by one of his own inspectors. Connecticut taxpayers must pay the debt of Chief State's Attorney John M. Bailey, who a judge in November said had violated the U.S. Constitution by trying to keep inspector Gregory B. Dillon from talking about corruption in the FBI.[43]

---

[43] Brigitte Greenberg, Associated Press, "Bailey Suit Costs Taxpayers $1.5M," *Record-Journal*, May 7, 1999.

A week later, an editorial in the *New Haven Register* condemned Bailey's behavior:

> Bailey's justification for attempting to silence his investigator — to maintain the confidentiality of criminal investigations — was limp if not specious. The result of his action was to protect agents who instead of enforcing the laws were violating them.

None of this was good for Bailey's health, which rapidly deteriorated. On February 1, 2001, an email was sent from Bailey's secretary: *Mr. Bailey has been out of the office with pneumonia.* The *New Haven Advocate* next reported Bailey's collapse at Bradley Airport while waiting to board a plane for a family vacation, then being taken by ambulance to Hartford Hospital.

After his release, Bailey's appearances at work became spottier, and his time in the office shorter.

CHAPTER 19

I was now assigned to the Gang Bureau with Supervisory Assistant Attorney Rich Palombo, along with four inspectors, three prosecutors, two secretaries, and a paralegal. Another Bailey creation, it was mandated by state statute in 1994 and was officially called The Gang & Continuing Criminal Activity Bureau.[44] We primarily prosecuted criminal activity by gangs, which meant mostly the investigation of drug dealing; its spouse, illegal firearms; and their offspring, shootings.

Connecticut is typically regarded as a tiny, bucolic New England state, but statistics proved otherwise: Business Insider reported in 2013 that Hartford, Bridgeport, and New Haven were among the twenty-five most dangerous cities in the country, primarily due to gang activity.

---

[44] CGS 51-279b required our office to maintain a unit specifically to "investigate and prosecute" the "illegal purchase and sale of controlled substances, criminal activity by gangs, fraud, corruption, illegal gambling, and the recruitment of persons to carry out such illegal activities."

At the time, the Latin Kings had a robust presence, particularly in New Haven, Waterbury, and Meriden, and were often at war with the Los Solidos, who favored Hartford, Bristol, and New Britain. There were a large number of outlaw motorcycle gangs to keep track of, notably the Hell's Angels in New Haven and Bridgeport, the Outlaws in Waterbury and Enfield, the Diablos in Bristol, the James Gang in Wallingford, along with a smattering of Pagans, Faces of Death, Helter Skelter, Dirty White Boys, Hole in the Wall, Red Devils, Forbidden, and others.

Also on our radar were the drug-dealing cliques usually found in poor inner-city neighborhoods and low-income housing projects. While not as organized or structured as traditional gangs such as the prolific Bloods and Crips—which had an active presence in every large Connecticut city—the neighborhoods' cliques were every bit as dangerous, as they would zealously guard their turf from rival drug dealers by shooting at them. Every city in Connecticut had them: in New Haven, they called themselves the Island Brothers, Church Street South, the Jungle Boys, and KSI (Kensington Street International); Bridgeport had the Bloody Fifth, the Green Top Posse, the Stack Boyz, and the Rats. No city was immune or unclaimed.

It was an active squad, always going in several directions at once. We worked hand in hand with the Connecticut State Police and their specialized units—Narcotics Units, Firearms Task Force, Motorcycle Gang Unit, and Statewide Organized Crime Task Force—preparing trial-ready cases for the four bureau prosecutors. It was a welcome distraction which relieved the tedium of bureaucratic infighting and office politics.

Although I sensed Bailey wanted a truce, Deputy Chief State's Attorney Chris Morano—still taking the whole thing personally—was having none of it. While Bailey went out of his way to acknowledge me in public, I continued to get a bad vibe from Morano, who snubbed me at meetings. What I did not expect, however, was a do-over of the Fugitive Squad debacle. Morano had learned—but only a little—from Bailey's mistakes. Now, instead of simply disbanding the offending bureau, Morano began to chip away at the manpower, incrementally downsizing us over time.

Because Bridgeport saw a record-setting sixty-one murders in 1991—a third of all homicides in Connecticut that year—it became a law enforcement priority. As most of the killings were a direct result of the turbulent drug trade, the theory was that reducing narcotics sales would cut the violence. The Connecticut State Police established a Statewide Cooperative Crime Control Task Force to address this issue, and my bureau was part of it.

In 1998, the focus was shifted to an intersection between Stratford Avenue and Fifth Street in Bridgeport, which residents had dubbed "the Bloody Fifth" due to the high number of shootings and assaults. For six months we conducted surveillances and recorded undercover buys. During the early morning hours of Thursday, February 18, 1999, seventy law enforcement officers—divided into thirteen arrest teams from the Bridgeport Police Department, the Connecticut State Police, and my office—simultaneously executed eight search warrants. We seized two pounds (1,600 pieces) of crack cocaine, three hundred blotters of LSD, $25,000 in cash, and seven firearms, charging forty-five defendants with a laundry list of crimes, mostly for drug sales and firearms violations.

Within seven months after my arrival, Morano began making "paper transfers." Instead of publicly posting an opening—so that any employee could apply and interview—he would transfer his choice directly, in violation of the union contract. The union never bothered to grieve it; everyone knew if the transfer was challenged, Morano would simply post the position, waste everyone's time conducting sham interviews, then transfer his original choice. As a result, one inspector, one clerk, and our only paralegal—all Gang Bureau people—became the newly formed Witness Protection Unit. That one maneuver reduced our bureau by almost a third.

The following year, 2000, we were back in Bridgeport, this time honing in on Trumbull Gardens, a high-crime, 339-unit public housing complex. Again, following weeks of surveillance, undercover buys, and interviews of arrestees, we moved in. On March 1, Bobby Hughes and I were assigned to Team #2 and given a dozen arrest warrants to serve. Over the span of two weeks, we made forty-four arrests, seized 374 pieces of crack cocaine, fifty-five grams of powder cocaine, 164 folds of heroin, five handguns, over $4,000 in currency, and a Lexus. This criminal enterprise was so dangerous, one of the defendants—while still locked up—approached another inmate about murdering the female prosecutor assigned to his case. While a criminal case was never brought due to a lack of evidence, there was enough concern that for several weeks, the prosecutor and her family had 24/7 police protection at her home.

In the spring of 2000, Inspector Hughes was assigned to an eight-month-long grand jury investigation. The next year, one of our two remaining inspectors was "temporarily" transferred—for six months—to a courthouse that was "short-handed." In 2002, we would see two more prosecutors, two more inspectors, and one clerk transferred from our bureau (if one could still call me, two prosecutors, one inspector, and a part-time secretary a "bureau"). Morano was intent on getting his personal revenge. Now that he was no longer personally supervising the bureau, it was expendable.

Several times during meetings, I delicately mentioned to Morano our staffing shortage; I did not want to trigger one of his legendary hissy fits. He would shrug it off each time, casually citing other manpower shortages throughout the division. Eventually, I returned to legal mode and began documenting our conversations by way of notes, then later memos.

In the middle of all this, not unexpectedly, Jack Bailey was reappointed to a second five-year term, while Chris Morano was reappointed to a four-year term.

Former governor John G. Rowland, accompanied by his wife Patty,
arrives in New Haven federal court following his second prison sentence.
(Associated Press)

It was no secret Governor Roland was quite fond of "Jack," and for good reason: Rowland knew Bailey would never cause him trouble. It turns out the less-than-Honorable Governor John G. Rowland was running a crooked game—he was a dirty politician. Jack Bailey was indebted to Rowland for his appointed position—and the prestige—he so craved. There was no way Bailey would willingly commit his office to investigate alleged misconduct by the governor; he knew it was political suicide, plus the fact he was beholden to Rowland. Therefore, as long as Bailey could fog a mirror, his job was secure.

On paper, the Connecticut governor does not technically appoint the chief state's attorney. Rather, the governor appoints the members of the Criminal Justice Commission, which in turn appoints the chief state's attorney. Unlike the "six degrees of separation" concept, there was only one degree of separation between the governor and the chief state's attorney: the Criminal Justice Commission.[45]

---

[45]   The "six degrees of separation" concept is the idea that all people are six (or fewer) social connections away from each other.

Rowland and Bailey enjoyed an unusually cozy relationship, atypical of previous and subsequent chief state's attorneys. Bailey was invited to attend various events with the governor that had nothing to do with the scope or duties of his office, e.g., parades welcoming the University of Connecticut women's basketball team after winning a national championship and severe weather events at the emergency command center. As Steve Kumnick used to quip, *"What is Bailey supposed to do there? Prosecute the snow?"* But Rowland knew Bailey craved the excitement and limelight of big, publicity-heavy events like a short-pants, wide-eyed kid at a circus.

Rowland even remarked at one point about Bailey and his car, a black "Crown Vic" he had tricked out to look exactly like a state trooper's vehicle:

> his official car decked out with every manner of lights, sirens, and police radios, and the cellphones and beepers clipped to his belt. "If you were smart you would never stand next to him in an electrical storm," Rowland quipped.[46]

Then Governor John Rowland speaking at Jack Bailey's retirement dinner in 2002.

---

[46] Lynne Tuohy, "A Good and Gentle Man," *Hartford Courant*, September 26, 2003.

Not self-aware enough to hide the symbiotic relationship, Bailey and his wife posed for pictures with Governor Rowland and his wife at an upscale New Haven restaurant, the Union League Café. The January 7, 2001, Sunday edition of the *New Haven Register* published photos, along with this report:

> Chief States [sic] Attorney John Bailey; his wife,...exchange pleasantries at midnight in the Union League. The Baileys were among the 14 guests in the governor's party.

Knowing this, I was not the least bit surprised when Bailey's five-year reappointment went through without a hiccup. The debacle over the handling of the falsified affidavits and the ensuing lawsuit, which cost state taxpayers millions of dollars, meant nothing. Governor Rowland wasn't troubled; the last thing the soon-to-be-convicted felon wanted was an independent, aggressive chief state's attorney closely watching him.

Rowland cleverly resigned on July 1, 2004, to protect his pension—which he still collects. In December 2004, John Rowland pleaded guilty to a single federal corruption charge. The Associated Press reported Rowland admitted that "he sold his influence for more than $100,000 in chartered trips to Las Vegas, vacations in Vermont and Florida, and improvements at his lakeside cottage." On March 18, 2005, he was sentenced to one year in jail and four months of house arrest. The FBI shrewdly made sure to exclude my office from the investigation—or even the fact it was taking place—to prevent any leaks.[47]

Bailey, who had traditionally maintained a busy work schedule, was now a part-time employee. Lynne Tuohy of the *Hartford Courant* reported:

> Lawmakers and colleagues of Bailey, 58, began noticing earlier this year that he seemed to be having difficulty speaking and was short-winded. Bailey in June said he

---

[47] Rowland was arrested again in 2014 on election fraud charges while working as a "political consultant." Following his conviction on all seven counts, he was sentenced to thirty months in prison in 2015 and released in May 2018.

was recovering from several respiratory illnesses and that he believed the medication in the inhalers he had been prescribed was tightening his vocal cords. Bailey took a one-month medical leave in July, but after his return in August his health appeared to deteriorate markedly.

My dwindling bureau was often called on to participate in various sweeps and roundups across the state, assisting federal task forces and the state police. There was a standard protocol: we would be notified to set aside a day, given a time and place for the operational briefing, assigned to a team, given a role (team leader, evidence custodian, entry team, perimeter, and so on), then provided a target location, a wanted person, or both, along with the requisite paperwork (search and/or arrest warrant). Although I didn't make much of it, I noticed my teams never had any federal agents—or even federal task force officers—assigned to them. Others also began to take note.

After bouncing around the state on various raids and sweeps, we ended up in Bridgeport yet again, this time targeting a "topless cafe." In other words, a titty bar. Although in theory it sounded like fun, it wasn't. Older cops used to refer to a dangerous bar as "a bucket of blood." This place fit the bill. It was the scourge of the neighborhood, and when one considered the neighborhood, that was troubling.

An undercover operation was authorized in December 2000, and within a short amount of time, it was obvious Dangerous Curves was Sodom and Gomorrah: rampant prostitution, overt drug use, liquor violations—and an attempted murder outside the front door. By now, I had become friendly with the state police sergeant, Gary Crawford, who had headed up all the previous Bridgeport operations. Whenever we talked, he would bring me up to speed on the investigation of Dangerous Curves. He explained that he himself had to be used as an undercover because all the other undercover officers had been burned during the previous Bridgeport investigations, hearings, and trials.

Gary explained his biggest concern was a compromised Bridgeport police officer. The bar had an extensive surveillance system. Informants confirmed that the manager would ask the off-duty patrolman to review footage of customers, to see if he recognized any "friends." The dirty cop—who would drink "on the house"—would then point out anyone whom he recognized from the station, essentially killing any chance of an undercover police officer successfully posing as a customer.

Gary explained that because he—as a supervisor—had never been utilized as an undercover, and the fact he lived far from Bridgeport, he and another trooper were the only ones going inside. By now, he and his partner, Eddie, had become regulars, known to the girls there as construction contractors who always had plenty of cash to throw around. Because he and Eddie would always get physically approached (felt up) by the dancers, neither could risk being armed. While there were always backup teams parked outside the place, Gary and Eddy were on their own once inside. After the attempted murder outside the front door, the bosses decided it was too risky to have undercovers inside the place without someone—a shooter—protecting them from the inside. As the operation was wrapping up, Gary asked me to also become a customer. An armed customer.

This was a first for me. It is one thing to be plainclothes, another to be undercover. A plainclothes officer is basically trying to fool the public, but an undercover is trying to fool the criminals. My age worked to my advantage, as not many UCs were in their midforties. So I stopped shaving, dug out my dad's old World War II army jacket, put on my house painting pants, old work boots, watch cap, and secured my holster to the small of my back. Just before heading inside, I left my wallet and keys with our backup team, gargled with a nipper bottle of whiskey, splashed some on my coat, and headed in.

I guess due to my age and shabby appearance, the doorman did not bother to pat me down like he did those who weren't regulars. Before any of the "dancers" could approach me, I took a stool at the bar, got my draft beer, and turned around so that I could press my back (and pistol) into the bar. Each girl who propositioned me would run her hands over and around my chest, hips, and thighs, both to try to get me interested and to see if I was wired or armed. I would then lowball her price so much, she would get fed up and walk away. Eventually I was ignored and overlooked as a cheap-ass bum, thankfully.

Gary and Eddie worked their magic, paying for private dances in the "VIP" room, buying drinks for the girls, purchasing grass and coke from the strippers and their pimps, and declining blow jobs. We hit the place on March 29, 2001, and made nine arrests for thirty-one drug transactions and four prostitution cases.

Later that summer, I was eating lunch with a Gary, who nonchalantly asked me if I had noticed the absence of "feds" on my arrest teams over the years. I told him I had. He then asked me if I knew the reason. I didn't. He told me that the supervisors of these operations had been contacted by federal task force members at the direction of Ralph DiFonzo with a request that no federal agents or any officers assigned to a federal task force be assigned to any team I was supervising. Stunned, I asked how he knew. He admitted he had received several of these calls himself, as well as having heard it from other supervisors. The call never came from the crafty DiFonzo himself, he noted, but rather from subordinates who said they were instructed to do so by DiFonzo.

Now I started to steam. DiFonzo had flirted with professional disaster and had not only escaped with a slap on the wrist, but was promoted while being investigated. It was now five years later, and he was *still* grinding his axe. Gary didn't want me to use his name, but I couldn't make a formal complaint based upon an anonymous source. I asked him to put himself in Greg Dillon's position, and a few days later, he reluctantly agreed. That same day, August 8, I wrote a memo to Bailey detailing my conversation with Sergeant Crawford:

> I have brought this to your prompt attention so that this situation may be addressed at once. More than five years have now passed since I left the FBI task force, yet this cowardly retaliation continues to exist. The consensus of our meeting today was this unprofessional and potentially hazardous conduct needs to be brought to the

attention of the FBI and the U.S. Attorney's Office in order that it may be addressed and corrected. I would request that a copy of this letter be sent to the attention of FBI Director Mueller, to insure it is dealt with in a timely and fair manner. I recommend we request a written response from the FBI, setting forth what action they intend to take to correct this behavior.

Again—just like five years earlier when I had filed my falsified affidavit complaint—an indignant Bailey met with me in his office to discuss my concerns. Only this time, he followed through. Perhaps he feared another encounter with Karen Lee Torre or simply recognized an obvious wrong and finally decided to defend one of his own.

"Enclosed is a copy of the complaint filed by Supervisory Inspector Gregory Dillon concerning the activities of Agent DiFonzo," he wrote Parks's replacement, Special Agent in Charge Michael Wolf, on August 15. "Inspector Dillon said that he would be available to be interviewed on this matter. If any action is taken on this complaint, I would ask that you notify me."

Within a week, Bailey received a terse, two-paragraph response. Wolf minimized the legitimacy of the complaint, as he opined it was based on "rumors, [Dillon's] suspicions, as well as hearsay, sometimes twice removed."

In the blandest bureaucratese, Wolf basically said: we don't like Dillon, and we don't have to work with him if we don't want:

> I encourage all FBI agents to overlook differences that may develop with other law enforcement officers, and to work together collectively to serve the public. However, in those instances where law enforcement officers have not fully reconciled personal or professional differences, sound judgment dictates that the assignment of personnel should be made in a manner to avoid controversy or confrontation.

I used to love the Wanted posters at the post office. Now I was number one on the New Haven FBI's Ten Most Hated list.

Wolf thought Bailey was a pushover. Certainly previous evidence supported that conclusion. I must confess I underestimated Bailey almost as badly as Wolf did, because the very next week Bailey fired off a letter to the attorney general of the United States, the Honorable John Ashcroft, with copies to FBI Director Robert Mueller, the Connecticut US attorney and, as a "courtesy," SAC Mike Wolf. This was a new Bailey. He grew a set of cashews and was now doing the right thing for me and his office:

> I wholeheartedly concur with Mr. Wolf's assessment that personal and professional differences between law enforcement officers may affect their activities...however, it was and is my hope that these issues such as those set forth in the attached correspondence, would be fully explored and resolved so that mutual state and federal interests are preserved, not to mention officer safety.
>
> It is with these interests in mind, and with knowledge of the previous litigation referenced in Mr. Wolf's August 22, 2001 letter, that I respectfully ask your office to review this matter. I am completely willing to engage in whatever process that will ensure that our offices and our personnel are able to function at their highest level.

Somebody important in Washington must have read it and sounded the klaxon, because Ralph DiFonzo abruptly retired. Once Bailey's dispatch landed in Washington, DC, it turned out Ralph had two options: bad and worse. He went with bad, locking in his position and pension before the risk of yet another OPR investigation. Ralph had made a career of dodging bullets and mistakenly thought he was bulletproof.

I received a telephone call from a New Haven agent who explained to me how it all went down. On Thursday, it was business as usual in the office, everyone on the squad looking forward to the quarterly firearms qualifications the following day, because this meant a short Friday and a jump on the weekend.

When the agents returned to work on Monday, Ralph's office was empty—all his personal belongings, plaques, pictures, and gewgaws gone. All that remained was Uncle Sam's sad furniture. The office was abuzz with speculation; his farewell email to the staff offered no clue other than the trite adage, "You can't teach an old dog new tricks."

I remember, back in the FBI Fugitive Task Force days, Ralph would boast how New Haven would be his final office, that he loved his job, and how he planned on staying on until he hit his mandatory retirement age, maxing out his pension. "Butch" suddenly called it a career and moved to Sussex County, Delaware, where he is self-employed as an investigator and security consultant.

More information about what goes on at FBIHQ was pried loose by the unceasing efforts of Alex Wood of the *Journal Inquirer*, who doggedly filed a series of Freedom of Information requests with the Department of Justice to determine how the FBI had addressed our complaint. When Wood was able to peel back some of the layers of secrecy, the FBI's strategy was laid bare. Wood wrote on June 13, 2002:

> The FBI's initial response, in February 2000, was to deny access to any of its records, except 24 pages of newspaper articles. But the reporter subsequently obtained privacy waivers from six people involved in the case, including Dillon, Freddo, and Kumnick. After reconsidering the request in light of the waivers, the FBI released the 61 pages of documents last week, with numerous sections blacked out. But it continued to withhold in full more than 210 pages of other documents.[48] The released documents don't come close to answering a number of major questions that were left unanswered during Dillon's lawsuit. Among them are what the FBI did to investigate the

---

[48]   Wood would later receive another small batch of documents in 2005 that FBIHQ mysteriously acknowledged had been *"inadvertently withheld."*

allegations, what its investigation revealed, why no one
was prosecuted, and why four agents were disciplined.

The papers did reveal that a top FBI official in Connecticut had dismissed the allegations of the state Fugitive Squad as "clearly not made in good faith." The overall tone was critical of the state inspectors and made clear that the New Haven office saw our allegations about the falsified affidavits as "*an attack on the FBI*." The finding of New Haven special agent in charge, Merrill S. Parks Jr., found "no cause for any administrative actions to be taken against captioned agents [DiFonzo, Bull, Brophy, and Treadway]." Parks attempted to dismiss our complaint as sour grapes: "The root of the problem appears to be an attempt by disgruntled inspectors of the Chief State's Attorney's Office to embarrass SSA DiFonzo and the FBI for reasons of professional jealousy." Later in the same report: "OPR agrees with SAC, New Haven that these allegations were probably motivated by disgruntled CSAO [Chief State's Attorney's Office] Inspectors." While the FBI tried to invent and attribute various motives to me, they could never conjure up any for Inspectors Kumnick and Freddo, who drafted four of the seven disputed UFAPs.

Even my letter of inquiry to FBI Director Freeh was harshly rebuked by the FBI's Appellate Process Unit: "Inspector Dillon continued to show his personal vindictiveness by addressing a letter to Director Freeh even after he had been interviewed by OPR."

ASAC Gary Rohen also chimed in with his own memo: "Of particular note is that all of the inspectors assigned to the CFTF are retirees from other law enforcement careers and appear to view this as a retirement position. This manifests itself in their observed work ethic and attitude."

We were happy to correct this libel: Freddo, Hughes, and I weren't retired. I provided DiFonzo's own statistics (photocopies of which I presented to Wood) showing the inspectors were responsible for 85 percent of the CFTF arrests when we made up *less* than half the task force.

"Dillon described Rohen's comments as 'an insult,' saying the fugitive work involved working weekends and holidays and 'putting on 25 pounds of protective gear to go in a house after a dangerous felon.'" Rohen's memo provided insight into the FBI's mindset. Instead of objectively analyzing the complaint to determine if it was valid—the way professional investigators are supposed to—they took the word of the accused liars, circled the wagons, and counterattacked. Ready, fire, aim. The FBI spent far more time making counteraccusations rather than taking a hard look at the irrefutable evidence.

Wood also authored an article entitled, "New Black Eye for the FBI" dated June 3, 2003:

Troubling questions about the FBI's handling of the investigation include the following:

- The FBI's internal investigators gave no polygraph, or lie-detector, tests, even though the three inspectors in the Connecticut Chief State's Attorney's Office who made the allegations and all the FBI agents interviewed agreed to such tests. Lie detector tests might have been useful because there were direct contradictions between the claims of the inspectors and the agents on at least two issues.
- The investigators did no review of case files other than the seven about which the inspectors had raised questions. One of the complainants, Supervisory Inspector Gregory B. Dillon, says he explained to the investigators how such an audit could be done.
- The document setting forth the conclusions of the FBI's internal investigation includes no discussion of a policy announced by Louis J. Freeh, then the director of the FBI, which set the ethical bar in internal investigations of falsification charges considerably higher than in criminal cases.
- The FBI officials found no problem with an arrest-warrant affidavit in which FBI agents attributed a belief about the whereabouts of a fugitive to a police officer in a suburb of Albany, N.Y., even though the agent who wrote the affidavit admitted he had never spoken to the officer. Moreover, there was no evidence that any other member of the fugitive task force had contacted the officer.

This was the Joseph James Dolan warrant, which was the most damning proof OPR did not want to know who was lying and who was telling the truth. OPR noted that the sentence *"Garrett has seen Dolan at this address"* was typed in a different font (meaning a different manual typewriter at a different time), but OPR could not attribute this to anyone: SA Bull and SA Teahan both provided sworn statements that neither prepared that affidavit, while SSA DiFonzo admitted in his statement that he prepared the affidavit, but incredibly maintained he did not know who added the sentence, *"Garrett has seen Dolan at this address."*

Any competent investigator would have recognized two immediate and obvious leads: polygraph the most likely suspect (DiFonzo) to see if he was being truthful, and contact Officer Garrett and ask him if anyone had ever contacted him about the Dolan matter. The first was never done, and the second was curiously handled by way of a footnote in the official OPR report:

> **Patrolman Garrett was not interviewed during this inquiry and therefore Inspector Dillon's account of his conversation with Patrolman Garrett could not be corroborated.*

I had confirmed in a five-minute telephone call with Officer Garrett that he did not know Dolan, that he did not know the street address he supposedly provided, that he had never seen Dolan at that address (obviously), that no one had ever contacted him about the Dolan case, and that he was the only Officer Garrett at the Colonie Town Police Department. There is one reason—and one reason only—OPR failed to contact Officer Garrett: OPR knew I was telling the truth.

In the same *Journal Inquirer* article, Wood noted:

> Although FBI officials found inaccuracies in four of the affidavits at issue, they appear to have been largely incurious about whether other untrue affidavits had been filed. Dillon says he told the investigators he was certain additional instances of falsification must exist because he had been able to review only a small number of files. He also says he explained how investigators could identify other likely cases of falsification by comparing certain

> documents in the files of the fugitive task force with the
> filed affidavits…. However, the FBI documents contain
> no indication that investigators reviewed other files.

Surprisingly, DiFonzo shed some light on this in his disciplinary appeal. Because Kumnick, Freddo, and I were able to review only a handful of previously filed UFAPs, we were never certain how many we had drafted while assigned to the CFTF. Ralph volunteered that fact in an attempt to defend himself: "Steve Freddo filed 17, Steve Kumnick filed 35, Greg Dillon 22." OPR never wanted to test my theory that our seven falsified affidavits were the bare minimum; DiFonzo volunteered we had filed a total of seventy-four. What investigator worth his or her salt— when told by a victim where additional evidence could be found—opts to *not* follow up on that lead? The reason was obvious: OPR had no interest in expanding and building a stronger case. Rather, they were content to do the minimum, go through the motions, then get out of town.

Same thing with the polygraph examinations. Kumnick and I heard DiFonzo openly brag about lying on UFAP applications; DiFonzo, of course, denied it. The inspectors and the agents had all agreed to submit to polygraph examinations, yet no tests were ever administered. So why not see who was bluffing? We couldn't all be telling the truth. OPR noted: "While the statements of Inspector Dillon and Inspector Kumnick were considered by OPR, they, absent other corroboration, cannot sustain an action against SSA DiFonzo for encouraging FBI Agents to lie in their affidavits." OPR was not about to polygraph Kumnick and me; they *knew* we were telling the truth. Realizing the polygraph would only confirm that, OPR also recognized DiFonzo would then have a bigger problem: DiFonzo might contradict his February 19, 1997, sworn statement, forcing OPR to have to recommend far harsher punishment, if not actual termination.

If OPR—during the course of an official inquiry—suspects an agent is "lacking in candor," OPR has the authority to *order* the agent to submit to a polygraph examination. The agent may refuse, but then OPR is compelled to make an adverse inference in determining the guilt of the agent. By OPR *not* ordering that agents be polygraphed, they tipped their hand: OPR suspected agents were lying about the falsifications and did not want to put them in a corner, where they would only have two choices: show deception during a polygraph, or refuse the polygraph and have that held against them during the adjudication phase.

Wood also noted DiFonzo's careless approach to the preparing and filing of UFAP affidavits:

> According to documents released in response to a JI reporter's longstanding Freedom of Information Act request, an FBI agent who headed the fugitive task force in the 1990s admitted he presented his *"assumptions,"* *"opinions,"* and *"beliefs"* as facts in arrest-warrant applications. Moreover, the agent, Ralph A. DiFonzo Jr., didn't sign the warrant applications himself but turned them over to other agents for filing.... FBI officials decried *"an almost casual reliance upon assumptions and inferences"* in the affidavits.

In a letter from C. Frank Figliuzzi, chief of the Adjudication Unit, to SSA DiFonzo, dated May 21, 1998, he reviewed the inquiry and upheld the five-day suspension and six months of probation, explaining his position this way:

> With regard to the preparation of a warrant, The Legal Handbook for Special Agents, Section 2-8, states as follows:
>
> '... Agent is authorized to relate his/her personal observations, **plus those facts acquired from other sources; but, Agent is responsible for indicating which items of information are truly his/hers and which are hearsay and merely being transmitted ... Agents should not, by implication or otherwise, claim credit for information as being firsthand when it is actually hearsay....** *[Emphasis is from the original document.]*

THE THIN BLUE LIE

The above referenced FBI policy is set forth to ensure that the validity and integrity of FBI affidavits could never be impugned. As the supervisor of the CFTF, you should have been more cognizant of the rules regarding the proper documentation of hearsay in affidavits you drafted....

I trust that this period of suspension and probation will convey to you the seriousness with which I view your actions and I trust that I will not have to address a matter of this nature with you again.

Partially because of his strong support from SAC Parks, SSA DiFonzo was able to successfully appeal and overturn the wrist slap of a five-day suspension and six months of probation.

The final insult was the fact that OPR trotted out CSA Bailey's series of apologies to SAC Parks as proof our accusations were done solely out of malice and not out of our concern that our names were being used as the sources of false information in federal affidavits:

"It is important to note the position of the Chief State's Attorney for the State of Connecticut, Mr. John Bailey who apologized to SAC New Haven for his subordinates *[sic]* conduct to the point of removing them from fugitive investigations."

Even OPR in Washington, DC, recognized our Fugitive Squad had not been disbanded because of lack of funding. Interestingly, while the FBI agents who prepared the report were quick to point out Jack Bailey's series of apologies as proof of their agents' innocence, they conveniently ignored my winning of the federal lawsuit as proof I was telling the truth, despite SAC Parks testifying in Bailey's defense.

The last thing OPR wished to do was prove our accusations true. Parks, Rohen, and DiFonzo didn't attack us because they thought we were wrong; they attacked us because they knew we were right.

CHAPTER 20

I n February 2002, Bailey unexpectedly assigned me an interesting case: an allegation that two Connecticut bail bondsmen were illegally printing "insurance issued" bail bond certificates, then using these authentic-looking counterfeits to spring criminals. The pair collected their fees from the defendants and their families, forwarding nothing to the unsuspecting insurance company. Defendants were then released at a heavily discounted rate on unsecured bonds; if the defendants opted to default on the bonds and become fugitives, there was no surety in place for the state to collect. It unraveled when a veteran bondsman questioned how these two young, inexperienced, low-level bondsmen were able to guarantee a $1 million bond for a murder suspect. After doing some snooping of his own, the rival bondsman filed a complaint.[49]

---

[49] In 2007, this bondsman, his father, and his brother (all licensed bondsmen I had dealt with when working fugitives) would be arrested by the FBI and plead guilty to conspiracy to commit bribery; all three were later sentenced to prison by federal Judge Janet Bond Arterton.

Working alone, I now had to identify and physically retrieve eighty-eight counterfeit bonds—ranging from $2,500 to $1 million—filed in ten different judicial districts. Next, I had to locate and interview all the defendants (or their family members) to prove the crime of larceny. I was back to working fugitives, as most of the defendants had been bonded out on major felonies: murder, kidnapping, sexual assault, narcotics offenses, or firearms violations. Worse, the defendants who chose these two bondsmen were considered too risky by other bail companies: career criminals, flight risks, out-of-state residents, or foreign nationals. All told, the cash value of the fraudulent bonds was just shy of $5 million.

On July 2, 2002, after a six-month investigation, I finally arrested twenty-six-year-old Christopher "White Boy" Morley and thirty-year-old John Paolella, both of New Haven, doing business as CM Surety. Each arrest warrant, documenting the convoluted history of the statewide counterfeiting scheme, was over thirty pages long.[50]

In October, Bailey took a voluntary leave of absence for reasons of health. Morano would assume his duties. I was wary Morano would now be emboldened and start making big moves, and indeed he did. During Bailey's absence, DCSA Morano returned to his favorite hobby, the settling of scores. I continued to lose small battles—and inspectors—to Morano. He decided to move the Gang Bureau again, this time out of the Newington off-site and *back* to the main office, complaining to me that two prosecutors and one inspector were not putting in full work days. Bizarrely, he then announced he was reassigning *one* prosecutor and *two* inspectors to Statewide Prosecution. This, of course, made no sense, but that was not the point. None of my reasonable arguments about caseload and manpower made any difference by now.

---

50   On January 28, 2005, Morley and Paolella were each sentenced to twelve years in prison, execution suspended after five years, with five years' probation. Each was also ordered to pay $120,000 in restitution while on probation.

Going a step further, he assigned my single remaining inspector, George Nobile, to a tiny, windowless room that the previous week had been a break room, complete with a coffee-stained rug and food-splattered walls where the microwave had recently sat. In that ten-foot by fourteen-foot space, Inspector Nobile was to fit his desk, chair, computer, file cabinets, and bookcase. Only then was I was told that room was also *my* office.

George and I discovered we were both assigned to the same room, and no, it was not a mistake. We crammed the furniture of two offices into a room not big enough for one. Chief Inspector Best stopped by and wisecracked that we should put up a scenic mural so we could pretend to look outside. I actually had to stand up and move my chair every time George entered or left the room. Former coworkers would drop in, just to see for themselves how absurd we looked seated at our desks.

Weeks later, someone passed by my desk and mentioned that Bailey and his wife were packing up his office. I walked over to the second-floor corridor that led to the balcony—the same spot from which I had witnessed Parks and Bailey's "domestic" six years earlier. Now I watched the ailing Bailey and his wife lug out the last of his cherished plaques and celebrity photographs in a cardboard box. It was bittersweet; I was glad to see him go but knew my protected status was leaving with him.

Every supervisor in the building had their own windowed office, as did almost every prosecutor. One day on my lunch hour, I walked the three floors of our building and counted eighty-four private, windowed offices for a staff of 145. The message was loud and clear.

I wrote a memo to Morano reciting these facts and diplomatically observing: "While I do not wish to inconvenience another employee, I trust I will be offered office space commensurate with my title and seniority when such space becomes available...." When I watched new, unpaid interns being assigned private, windowed offices, I wrote again to no avail.

On October 23, my forty-sixth birthday, I had another run-in with Morano. He was "pissed off" about my memo of an earlier meeting where I complained about the gradual dismemberment of my squad. He said he did not appreciate my "going on paper, all it is missing is an exhibit sticker" referring to a courtroom exhibit. From here on, he explained, we were to discuss matters only in person; he did not want to get into a "paper war" with me like I had done with Bailey. I told him I felt he was "trying to set me up for failure" by reducing manpower while increasing our workload. He made vague promises about getting me some more people "in the future."

To paraphrase a nineteenth-century quote, Morano had forgotten nothing and learned nothing. He was working off of his old playbook: reducing manpower and resources to hamper our efforts, thus making it easier to justify disbanding us. And I went back to my playbook, continuing to work hard and produce results. Again, naively, I felt if our work was noteworthy, we could outrun the grim reaper. In retrospect, it is almost comical how we both resorted to the exact same strategy, and—not surprisingly—it produced exactly the same results.

My sole inspector, George Nobile, and I were now also working a murder-for-hire case. A notorious jailhouse snitch, who had once been a key organized crime figure in the Fairfield area, reached out to George, hoping to parlay some info. A young man who had been arrested in February 2002 for the rape of a female acquaintance had been his "cellie" for a brief time before the accused's parents posted his $100,000 bond. Before his release, twenty-four-year-old Anthony Santaniello and his aging cellmate, Thomas Marra Jr., decided to have the victim murdered.[51] Without a victim, Santaniello believed the charges would have to be dropped. After Santaniello's pretrial release on bond, he and "Tommy" stayed in contact, both by telephone and letter. We orchestrated our plan: Tommy Marra would vouch for and introduce Inspector Nobile as

---

[51] The *Connecticut Post*: "Barely a week didn't go by in the 1980s when Marra's name wasn't on the front pages of Connecticut newspapers. He was the gangster of Bridgeport, the stolen car kingpin and finally the crazed killer who stuffed his victims in metal drums, which he dumped in the harbor."; Daniel Tepfer, "Bridgeport Gangster Tommy Marra Wants Out of Prison," *Stamford Advocate*, October 20, 2012.

a "hit man." George rose to the occasion, as usual. Telephone calls were recorded, letters retrieved, and a price agreed upon.

The victim had attempted to protect herself after the assault by selling her home and moving, trading in her car, and changing her license plates. But Santaniello did his homework. First in a coded letter, followed by a cryptic phone call, Santaniello passed on this information to Marra, including the victim's name, description, social habits, current address, and a description of her new car including the new license plate. Thinking himself witty, the gangster wanna-be signed his letter "Joe Black," apparently referring to the 1998 movie in which Brad Pitt played the Angel of Death.

What made this investigation even more disturbing was that the victim was a single mother raising her young daughter. Worse, Santaniello was the stepson of a Connecticut state trooper and living in his home. George—who did a great job portraying himself as a contract killer—arranged to meet Santaniello in "his" luxury vehicle (the Lexus we had seized during "Operation Trumbull Gardens" in 2000), which we had wired for audio and video. Santaniello failed to show for the face-to-face and now did not return George's phone calls.

Concerned Santaniello might decide to save himself the money—or found someone cheaper—George and I worked as quickly as a bureau of two could. We hurriedly collected evidence, took statements, notified the victim, and turned her over to our Witness Protection Bureau for temporary safekeeping. I quickly authored an arrest warrant and drafted search warrants for Santaniello's car and his parents' home, where he was living.

Wednesday, October 25, 2002, was a bright, crisp autumn day. We set up at Santaniello's place of work, swooped in, and arrested him without incident as he walked to his car. While inspectors searched his vehicle, another team executed the second search warrant at his home, recovering letters he had received from inmate Marra. I interviewed Santaniello at the police station, where statements he made to me were used against him during his trial.

He remained incarcerated until his trial began on January 6, 2004. Both George and I testified at length, along with the victim. On January 21, the jury unanimously convicted Santaniello of attempted murder, first-degree sexual assault, first-degree kidnapping, inciting a person to injury, and intimidating a witness.

Assistant State's Attorney Michael Gailor said Santaniello had a history of violence toward women and cited previous convictions for incidents with past girlfriends. Gailor said Santaniello raped the woman and then victimized her a second time by trying to have her killed. "If this act had been completed, the defendant would be facing a capital felony charge—he'd be facing the death penalty," Gailor said.

"There's not been a single thing I've seen, not a single thing, that shows you have any remorse for what happened," sentencing Judge Lavine said.[52] On March 20, 2004, Santaniello was sentenced to forty-two years in state prison.

★ ★ ★

Jack Bailey being feted at his retirement dinner, flanked by his wife Elizabeth Dee Bailey, Acting Chief State's Attorney Chris Morano (standing), and one of Bailey's defense attorneys, James Bergenn.

---

52   Larry Smith, "42-Year Prison Term Ordered," *Hartford Courant*, March 20, 2004.

The week we arrested Santaniello, Jack Bailey officially announced his retirement due to declining health. Whatever protection I had enjoyed under my truce with Bailey was now gone. Morano was appointed to finish out Bailey's existing term as chief state's attorney. As Bailey had only been recently reappointed, this gave Morano a guaranteed two and a half year reign over the Division of Criminal Justice. He went to work quickly.

So far, Morano had whittled the Gang Bureau down to a nub, moved us out, moved us back, and now had George and me basically sharing a one-man tent.

I usually took the stairs to my closet on the third floor, but one day I was carrying file boxes, so I took the elevator. I was joined by a secretary who had been working there practically forever. Just as the doors were about to close, the secretary held the door for Morano. She politely asked, "Should I push your floor?" His response: "They are all my floors." I know my eyes rolled to the top of my head. I wasn't sure who to be more embarrassed for.

In the spring of 2003, rumors began to surface that Morano might create a third chief inspector's position. When I was hired in 1990, there were actually four chief inspectors. Since then it had been reduced to two, one of whom was Dave Best, who called me into his office one day.

Although our relationship during the trial was strained, time had smoothed things out, plus we now had a mutual adversary. Morano had told him to "strongly consider the retirement buyout package currently being offered." Dave said he asked Morano point-blank if he was being asked to leave, and Morano bluntly told him yes, that he felt Dave was "too close to certain inspectors." "Thanks a lot, Greg," Dave said. I offered an apology, but he laughingly brushed it aside and told me he planned to call me at home that night to get Karen Lee Torre's telephone number.

The following day I asked Dave why he never called. He said he ran it by another attorney and, after consideration, decided not to challenge it. He no longer wished to serve in the current administration anyway. Chief Inspector Steve Grasso had gotten the same speech yesterday, only this time Morano had cited "philosophical differences," and for that reason, Grasso should opt for the "golden handshake." Around the office water cooler, people joked Morano was giving Grasso a "golden shower" instead.

My qualifications and experience were at least equal to any other candidate, so I notified Chief State's Attorney Morano via email of my interest in a chief inspector's position, so there would be no failure of recollection at a later date. In less than an hour—probably the amount of time it took him to stop laughing—he wrote back saying, "At this time there are no vacancies for the positions you speak of.... Thank you for your interest and I will keep it in mind."

Eight days later, a memo announced "the appointment of Lawrence Skinner as Chief Inspector." Skinner joined the DCJ in 1984 as a Hartford inspector; he had been a supervisory inspector in New Britain since 1999. I heard later this had been the plan all along, to make Skinner the sole chief inspector. Skinner and Morano had bonded when they worked together in the Hartford courthouse. Skinner had never worked at the Chief State's Attorney's Office, where criminal investigations were routinely initiated and arrests made. He was used to working behind the scenes in courtrooms, preparing cases for trial. But he was a Morano loyalist, and that was qualification enough. And this explained that while Skinner had been "our" union president, he failed to challenge many of Morano's contract-breaking tactics.

My partner, George—never a fan of Morano's to begin with—could see where this was going and decided to call it a career. He retired on May 30. Now I was supervising myself.

Upon returning from the July 4 three-day weekend, my cell phone rang at 12:30 while I was at lunch. It was Chief Inspector Larry Skinner. A man of few words, he asked me to return to the office and see him immediately. At 12:55 I was at his desk, and his greeting was, "Let's go see the boss." We walked into Bailey's old office, which was now Morano's new office. Morano sat behind the oversized desk, looking even smaller than he actually was, talking on the phone. As we sat waiting, Morano's new deputy chief state's attorney—another Hartford State's Attorney's Office transplant—sidled in and took a seat.

I'm sure Skinner was wondering why I hadn't yet asked him what this surprise meeting was about, but I didn't, because I already knew. Someone close to Morano (who was actually closer to me) alerted me of his plans for a reorganization. Morano intended to disband the Gang Bureau and transfer me to the Elder Abuse Bureau. Nearly my whole career I'd been investigating or supervising the investigation of violent crimes, fugitives, or gangs. At least knowing Morano planned to sucker punch me in front of an audience gave me the opportunity to prepare.

The only thing missing was the plastic tarp over the carpeting. Morano unveiled his plan to create a brand-new bureau called Elder Services, which would combine two separate units: Elder Abuse and Medicaid Fraud. He informed me he had decided the work of the Gang Bureau could be absorbed by the preexisting Statewide Prosecution Bureau.[53] He explained I was now the supervisor of Elder Abuse, in part because "I had made it clear in the past that I should be supervising inspectors" so this would be a good fit for me. The other reason was because that unit was "one of Jack's creations," and he wanted it "to shine." He apparently forgot the Gang Unit was also one of "Jack's creations." He then added with an almost-straight face that as there was such a large backlog of cases, "it should be a very active unit."

With a disinterested expression, I looked directly at Morano and flatly asked, "Anything else?" This was not the response he had eagerly anticipated, and so he baited me, asking how I felt about it. I robotically replied that apparently the reorganization had already taken place, so my feelings made no difference. He kept trying: Did I think it was a good fit? Nonchalantly I explained I didn't know why he thought it would be, seeing I had no actual experience in that area, nor any interest in that type of work. Morano, in an attempt to prolong the discomfort, changed gears and suggested that if I wanted to continue to work gang cases, I might be able to, but I would be assigned to Statewide Prosecution and answer to a supervisory inspector. No one had to remind me of the fact it would

---

[53] Ironically, the state statute requiring the Gang & Continuing Criminal Activities Bureau within the Office of the Chief State's Attorney is still on the books today, although no such bureau actually exists.

be Chuck Coffey, the same inspector promoted over me last time, which was one of the winning claims in my lawsuit.

I sat there and simply stared at Morano. He broke first, saying he did not expect me to make a decision with the three of them watching me, that I should go home and talk it over with my wife and let him know the following day, "as a lot of people are waiting for the other shoe to drop." I told him if he did not hear back from me, he could assume I would be working in Elder Abuse. I went to leave, but Morano said he did not want to leave it like that and expected to hear back from me by tomorrow. While he was still talking, I walked out. He caught up with me in the hallway.

"Hold on, I'm not finished with you yet." I turned and faced him. Looking up at me, he smirked and said, "You're in charge of the evidence room now."

That did catch me off guard. "Instead of Elder Abuse, or in addition to?"

Morano grinned. "Both. You're now in charge of Elder Abuse *and* the evidence room."

With all the sarcasm I could muster I asked him if he had any more assignments in mind before I returned to my office. He said the evidence room was a shambles and in serious need of reorganization. Due to my "organizational abilities," he felt I was the best choice "to take on that responsibility."

"Is that all?" I asked. Not waiting for a response, I turned my back and returned to my office.

I closed my door, picked up the phone and brought Karen up to speed. Morano seemed intent on having his revenge in the most obvious of ways. She told me to call her at home that night; we were going to file a lawsuit.

I had been communicating with Karen regularly, and she mentioned how Morano was risking another lawsuit by his heavy-handed tactics. I did not have enough time in yet to retire with my pension and was not prepared to be bullied by Morano until the end of his career or mine, whichever came first. He had enough involvement in the Bailey lawsuit to know better, as he had been a primary witness. I knew he had now overplayed his hand, and I was not willing to remain passive any longer.

The following morning, I typed an email to Morano saying, "Since I do not want either assignment, I reluctantly opt for the Elder Abuse Unit." As for the evidence room, which previously had been a clerical assignment, I added, "I must say I was very surprised at this, given that such clerical duties are inconsistent with my title, skills, and experience, and no doubt would further interfere with the time needed to transition and orient to new duties in the Elder Abuse Unit."

It may be he had considered that I had called my lawyer. He hastened to establish his own record with a two-page memo (ignoring his own advice of "not going on paper"), now recalling a warm conversation in his office, spinning it in the friendliest of ways. But he was not as glib when it came to the evidence room assignment, and his explanation reflected his growing concern:

> It is true that moments after our initial meeting I spoke with you a second time to advise you of the additional assignment with respect to reorganizing and managing the evidence room. My failure to mention that in our initial meeting was an oversight on my part, and it was always part of my reorganization plan. It is my belief and that of my management team that the organization and management of an evidence room is a critical function and one that requires skill and experience not available at the clerical level. I do not consider such an assignment to be one that is inconsistent with your title, skills, or experience, but rather one that is totally consistent with them in keeping with the high expectations that I have for the professional handling of evidence in the Office of the Chief State's Attorney.

I moved into my new assignment in Elder Abuse and attempted to learn as much about the work and cases as I could. I was uncomfortable assuming the role of supervisor over inspectors who clearly had a better grasp of the work, so I called a staff meeting and explained that while I was not there by choice, I would do whatever I could to support the unit. I then asked for their patience and help as I tried to get up to speed with their cases. Everyone was gracious and professional, and my short time there was pleasant.

As it turns out, most of the cases received by our office were not what I was expecting. I thought we would be investigating cases of physical assault and neglect. Those cases were typically addressed by police departments and social services, with rare exception. Rather, most of our referrals were from family members, usually a son or daughter of the alleged victim. The accused (sometimes a family member, sometimes not) often volunteered to move in with the older person, under the guise that it made it easier to provide assistance. The caretaker would then gradually manage the victim's finances, and that is where the trouble started. Incrementally, this individual would find all kinds of creative ways to justify spending the victim's money. When confronted, the accused would attempt to justify the expense by claiming it was actually to the benefit or for the enjoyment of the victim, such as premium cable channels, trips to the casino, flat-screen TVs, car repairs, or new car purchases.

Sadly, even though the victim was being taken advantage of, he or she often did not want to bring charges, either because they did not want to lose their caregiver, or simply because they were not mentally capable of grasping their predicament. It was difficult work at best with no winners.

CHAPTER 21

Bailey died of ALS in September. Lynne Tuohy of the *Hartford Courant* wrote: "Jack Bailey would have loved his funeral. He loved ceremony. He loved the drumbeat and the bagpipe, and, yes, he loved being the center of attention. Thursday, he was."

They put the state flag on his casket. Pallbearers included retired Chief Inspector Dave Best and forensic scientist Dr. Henry Lee, among his closest colleagues. The governor attended and spoke at his service: "He was a true friend and a reliable adviser." Rowland would soon be indicted on federal charges.

His rivals said how much they had always admired him. "Jack Bailey was a giant — a prosecutor's prosecutor whose outstanding contributions will long outlast his life," gushed Attorney General Richard Blumenthal.[54] Hypocrisy and hyperbole are standard at funerals.

---

54 Diane Scarponi, "Jack Bailey, Former Chief State's Attorney, Dead at 59," *Middletown Press*, September 23, 2003.

Morano now realized I had him over a barrel. Days, weeks, then months went by, and no one mentioned the evidence room to me again; I was never even provided a key. Karen asked me about it several times, and I told her I had heard nothing. Would I now be accused of being derelict in my assignment? Karen said to wait it out.

On October 4, 2003, Chief Inspector Skinner issued a memo to his five supervisory inspectors, announcing: "I have been tasked by Chief State's Attorney Morano with auditing, organizing and running the evidence rooms."

This was a minor victory; it showed Morano was backpedaling. Morano hoped to now make the assignment appear to be quite important by assigning his sole chief inspector to it. He knew he had crossed a line and was worried I would take action. And he was right. Karen notified the Attorney General's Office of her intent to file a federal civil action against Chief State's Attorney Morano. Morano promptly asked Attorney General Blumenthal he be allowed to retain Albert Zakarian as outside counsel to represent him. "In seeking outside legal counsel I mean no disrespect to your office. It is my opinion, however, that this is the best course in light of the unique history of this plaintiff and his allegations."

On February 11, 2004, the *Hartford Courant* learned of the lawsuit, and Lynne Tuohy reported:

> Supervisory Inspector Gregory Dillon contends Morano has violated his civil rights by using his authority to demean, humiliate and punish Dillon for filing suit against Bailey in 1998. Dillon, in his new federal lawsuit, alleges that Morano:
>
> - Told Dillon — who expressed an interest in applying for the chief inspector job — that he was not going to fill it, then a week later filled the position with a Hartford inspector.
> - Failed to invite him to regularly scheduled meetings Morano held with other supervisory inspectors in the state Division of Criminal Justice.

- Put him in charge of reorganizing the evidence room and keeping its records.
- Downsized Dillon's staff in the Gang and Continuing Activities Bureau, usurped Dillon's jurisdiction by creating a new public integrity unit to investigate public corruption, then transferred him to the elder crimes unit of the division.

Dillon contends that Morano's actions were designed "to send a message to staff that [Dillon] was disfavored by him and the agency, and thus should be shunned.

While the lawsuit was pending, I requested a transfer to an open supervisor's position in the Worker's Compensation Fraud Bureau. After I had spent less than a year in Elder Abuse, it was marginally better, and nice to leave an assignment Morano had specifically given me. As it was considered a lateral transfer, it went through without a hitch. Morano then sent me a memo inviting me to check out two different offices on the third floor (both windowed) and then to let his secretary know "which room you would prefer to occupy."

On the other hand, when I got a letter from US Congressperson Nancy L. Johnson congratulating me for my work on the murder-for-hire case and praising me for my "commitment to public service and excellence in your field," my boss was not present at the banquet to present the award. Nor did any of his staff attend.

I saw him at lawsuit-related events, though. His new attorney—the polar opposite of Morano—was no slouch. Albert Zakarian was tall, trim, and distinguished looking. He had served in Vietnam with the Air Force and won a bronze star, earned a Columbia law degree, and had tried lots of labor and employment cases.

I attended a deposition at Zakarian's law office, and he surprised me by first asking was I aware of Morano's home address. I told him I believed he lived in Essex but was not positive. Ignoring my response, he asked if I had ever conducted surveillance on Morano's home. I told him no, reminding him I was not even sure of the town. Had I ever followed

Morano in my car? No-o. Morano was apparently seeing shadows, but they weren't mine.

Zakarian brought up Larry Skinner. I had never been a fan of Larry Skinner. When asked to describe my perceived weaknesses of him as an inspector, I replied that I "found him at times to be sarcastic, abrasive, rude." I questioned his loyalty to the union while serving as president. While he was less than zealous in his role as union president during the witch hunts, I have to admit he did stand up to Cornelius Shea and Chief Inspector Grasso during Bailey's sham investigation.

> Q: During the period that you and Mister Skinner were both inspectors in the Department of Criminal Justice, did you ever have any disputes or significant clashes with him?
>
> A: No.
>
> Q: From what you could observe, based on the interactions you have had with Mister Skinner, what are his greatest strengths?
>
> A: He dresses nicely.
>
> Q: Other than that, any other strengths?
>
> A: None that come to mind.

In retrospect, it was not my most gracious moment. But, in my defense, I was under oath.

I got in another zinger when Zakarian asked me if there was anything I did not like in the way Morano handled his position as chief state's attorney, which was not covered specifically in the lawsuit. I was happy to respond:

A: I dislike the fact that while he publicly claims the Division of Criminal Justice is suffering from a severe budget deficit, he has opted to retain you and your firm to represent him in a lawsuit, when the Attorney General's Office has a budget of $26 million a year and 344 full-time employees, and their primary function is to litigate civil actions brought against the state. I feel that is a frivolous waste of taxpayer money, and I resent the fact that because of his actions, I have been forced to hire my own private attorney, and now the state pays for his own private attorney of his choosing.

A: Anything else?

Q: Not at this moment.

I petitioned the State Attorney General's Office repeatedly for the correspondence between Morano and Blumenthal, the agreements and contracts for his new attorneys, and all the billing records. The details were heavily redacted, but the billing amounts could not be. Zakarian's office provided a lesson in bill padding: organization of documents, study documents, analyze documents, study exhibits, fact investigation, preliminary review, review, draft letter, finalize letter, conference calls, telephone calls, preparation of outline, outline, revise memorandum, finalize memorandum, prepare for meeting, have meeting, obtain copies. And everyone in the office took part: partners, associates, paralegals, library, and courier. They were reimbursed for postage, parking meters, travel, photocopies, even lunch. These guys weren't content to just milk the cow; they were going to drain it, screw it, skin it, butcher it, and then wear the hide as coats. They made vultures look like picky eaters.

I shared my results with Alex Wood, and he did an exposé on how much money AG Blumenthal was doling out to various Connecticut law firms for "special expertise."

Karen urged me to take an out-of-court settlement. In my myopic view of the case, it was a hands-down winner, but Karen pointed out that the first case—as it centered around falsified federal affidavits—was an embarrassment to several agencies, both state and federal. This lawsuit was not as compelling and unlikely to draw as much attention.

"In a worst-case scenario, we could try the case and lose, a possibility that should not be discounted. Morano could be appointed to the state court bench, move on to other things, or die prematurely...and if that happens, your case dies along with him." Additionally, Karen pointed out the worst-case scenario: "Of course, what escapes my clients all the time is the reality that they could try the case and lose. While you do not think this would happen, it can happen, it has happened, and the reasons are myriad...."

Again, we were at an impasse.

My demand was too high ($1 million) and Zakarian's offer too low ($150,000). I was considering my options, knowing there would not be any true negotiation until we started jury selection. But all that went out the window when federal Judge Alfred V. Covello dismissed my lawsuit in April 2006, finding we had not presented sufficient physical evidence to show retaliation on the part of Morano.

I was floored and Karen flabbergasted. We had documented numerous instances great and small of obvious retaliation in the months after the first settlement: depositions, emails, memos, and photographs of my office and the other supervisory inspectors' offices. Judge Covello—without seeing an exhibit or listening to a word of testimony—acted upon Zakarian's motion to dismiss and threw it out.

Karen thought we had a good case for an appeal. We both felt Judge Covello was factually and legally wrong in his decision, and had overstepped his bounds in his ruling—basing his decision on disputed evidence—which legally is the role of a jury, not a judge. While she felt strongly that we would prevail if we appealed, she acknowledged there was no guarantee. Also, any appeal would now come out of my own pocket, of course. This would be an expensive proposition, with no guarantee of a successful outcome.

Now, some would say I was playing with "house money" at this point, but no one had thought it through. My original $2.7 million was settled to $1.5 million, of which Karen received 40 percent ($600,000). Additional legal work outside our contingency agreement and costs for fees, forms, subpoena service, depositions, and transcripts were thousands more. Then, there was the $5,000 "donation" to Serpico's charity, and the surprise $5,000 bill from his nephew attorney. The remainder was taxable income, and the government took a heavy bite, at another 40 percent. So while I was grateful to have what I had—which was now just over $500,000—I was not the multimillionaire people thought I was.

People would ask me why I didn't just resign and live off my award or simply find another job. And my answer was always the same: I went into this line of work as a career choice, not a "job." It's what I had chosen to do; I felt I was good at it, and I enjoyed it—although I admittedly had not enjoyed it for some time. I did not get into law enforcement for the money, obviously. The private sector offered far more lucrative opportunities than government service ever would.

The other thing was, I felt as entitled to be an employee at my office as anyone else there, *including* the chief state's attorney. I had always maintained that hiring and promotions within a government agency should be based upon merit, not cronyism or nepotism. The reason I was fighting this—especially the denial of an opportunity to become chief inspector—was I believed it was fundamentally flawed to advance someone strictly based upon friendship or connections. This was not some private company Bailey or Morano had started from scratch. They were merely temporary stewards of a government agency.

What I was most concerned about was the fact that even if we won the appeal, the case would be returned to Judge Covello for trial. I knew how a judge has tremendous influence over the outcome of a case, and I could not imagine getting a fair shake from Covello if he were reversed and had the case shoved back in his face.

Despite this, I decided to stay the course. My alternative was to drop the matter. I knew if I did that, I might as well return to work and put a sign on my own back reading "Kick Me."

Karen began the appellate process, and I began writing checks. My continued FOI requests showed the Attorney General's Office was writing even bigger checks. By the time we filed our appeal, Zakarian's bill to the state was just shy of $300,000.

Zakarian took the train into the city and stayed at a hotel so he'd be fresh for our hearing before the Second Circuit Court of Appeals, clipping the state another $500 for his trip. Karen took an early train with me in a charitable effort to keep my growing costs down. The courtroom at Thurgood Marshall United States Courthouse on Foley Square was massive; the bench where the three-judge panel sat was like the pulpit within a cathedral.

Zakarian and Karen had filed their written briefs in advance so that the judges were already familiar with the facts of the case. Both attorneys made their oral arguments, sometimes interrupted by one of the judges posing a question or asking for a clarification. Their questions led me to think the panel was leaning toward a ruling in our favor, but we would have to wait another month to find out.

During the month-long wait, there was a mutiny; Morano was forced out as chief state's attorney. While it took some chief state's attorneys their full five-year term to alienate a few state's attorneys, Morano said hold my beer and proceeded to piss off twelve of the thirteen in less than three years.

Eleven out of thirteen state's attorneys wrote a letter to the Criminal Justice Commission asking that he not be reappointed. "It is because of his severe lack of leadership that we have come to this position," they said. Since Bailey's death, their relationship with Rocky Hill had soured. "We have chosen to make this public statement because we do not wish to see the administration of justice suffer as the agency declines under Mr. Morano's leadership...characterized by side deals and a sense of 'divide and conquer' rather than open and purposeful efforts to bring about consensus…Mr. Morano is more interested in advancing his own career than in advancing the interests of the Division of Criminal Justice…."

The only two who did not sign were a young, newly appointed state's attorney and New London State's Attorney Kevin Kane, who the other eleven endorsed for Morano's job.

The press seized upon this unprecedented rebellion, first reporting that Morano mysteriously submitted his application at the last possible moment, then withdrew it just before the selection process began. Morano realized the game was over; rather than risk the embarrassment of not being reappointed, he chose to quit.

Rumor had it he was hoping to be thrown a judgeship from the governor's office, but no bone was forthcoming. As he explained to the Norwalk newspaper *The Hour*: "Morano said he did not have an immediate career plan. 'I don't have a job,' he said. 'I guess I've got to go look for a job.'"

Morano was forced to hang up his shingle in his posh town of Essex and hustle traffic ticket cases and DUIs at various courthouses across the state.

On August 16, 2007, the Second Circuit overturned Judge Covello and cleared the way for my lawsuit against Morano.

I was buoyed by the idea of Morano testifying again before a jury. His performance before the last jury—coupled with his testy exchanges with Karen during his most recent deposition that were sure to come back to bite him in court—made me optimistic. I believed that fact, combined with Skinner's lackluster résumé and Morano's dishonest emails, would give us a strong edge in a trial. I continued to pass along to Alex Wood the updates on Morano's mounting legal costs, which put additional pressure on the soon-to-be ex-chief state's attorney. Karen said in a published email to a reporter, "Mr. Morano spent a bundle of taxpayer money needlessly in a prolonged and failed effort to avoid a trial. I look forward to putting this case before a jury."

Actually, she thought it in our best interest to settle.

We went back to meet with the ever patient US Magistrate Judge William I. Garfinkel yet again, and under his calming influence and empathy we arrived at a fair settlement that brought an end to the protracted litigation against Christopher Morano. That, and my gut telling me Judge Covello was going to make us push a flat rock up a steep hill in revenge for successfully appealing his decision to dismiss and putting him through a civil jury trial. It looked iffy, so I reluctantly agreed to accept a settlement of $400,000.

"Despite having twice clashed with his supervisors in federal lawsuits, Dillon said he plans to keep his job," Alex Wood wrote in the *Journal Inquirer*. Karen added: "I would hope the state, rather than continuing to engage him in disputes, would make use of his skills."

Obstinately perhaps, I still hoped I could resurrect my stalled career and start anew. I was still a few years away from pension eligibility and had no desire to walk away from a job I once loved. Naively, I believed I could advance myself, now that Bailey and Morano were both history. My personnel file was filled with superior evaluation ratings, various letters of recognition from a number of organizations and agencies, and not a single disciplinary action. On paper, by all standards, I should have been regarded as a model employee. But, as I mentioned at the beginning of this book, one's reputation follows and precedes you.

The incoming chief state's attorney was well regarded; few people had a bad thing to say about Kevin Kane. He had the look of a country lawyer and was known to be self-deprecating and humble, not one to put on airs. While I had met him at various events, we had never worked together.

However, I had concerns. Mike Malchik had worked for Kane before transferring to the Fugitive Squad; Mike had been eager to transfer out of Kane's office, and it appeared Kane was happy to see him go. To date, Mike's insight and instincts had proven spot on. Long since retired, Mike warned me that there was a strong possibility that our well-known friendship would be held against me. The fact Kane would be wary of me because of my litigious history with his predecessors didn't help. I remained optimistic though, hoping my achievements would speak louder than my lawsuits. The optimism of the Boy Scout.

Kane, as was his style, quietly moved in with little fanfare and soon issued a memorandum announcing Jack Edwards—previously retired—would be his new chief inspector. I was disappointed but not surprised. Kane was doing what new bosses often do—bringing in his friends and former associates as a kind of praetorian guard. The only upside was Jack Edwards enjoyed a reputation as a consummate gentleman with many years of supervisory experience, a marked improvement over Skinner. We had worked together on a few cases, so I felt comfortable with him and was hopeful this would put me in good stead with the new chief state's attorney.

I was bored by the slow pace of supervising workers' compensation fraud investigations. While the work itself could be interesting at times, it was typically dull and administrative. Someone would claim an injury at work, go to a doctor, and stay out of work for as long as the doctor would allow. As with any type of insurance claim, there are some people who cannot resist scamming the system. Oftentimes, while the malingerer was supposed to be recuperating, they would either work at another job or be physically active beyond their medical restrictions. For example, someone would claim temporary full disability, then be filmed by insurance investigators shingling their roof, parasailing, building a deck, or racing motocross (all actual cases). The insurance claim investigators would then submit their reports and surveillance videos along with the medical files to us for review. I would assign the case to an inspector, the inspector would give the claimant an opportunity to be interviewed, then typically submit an arrest warrant to the prosecutor if the case merited adjudication. It was necessary work, but my heart was never in it. I bided my time.

Our office had gradually begun to get involved in old, unsolved homicide investigations, commonly referred to as "cold" cases. I knew I would enjoy this type of work because in a sense, they were similar to fugitive cases. Most of the fugitive cases were referred to us "after the fact"; the wanted person had a good head start, and no one could find them. In cold cases, the perp had literally gotten away with murder, and the trail had gone cold. The challenge now was to try to find the clue that other investigators had overlooked that would point to a suspect, then ideally put together a prosecutable case. This was the type of challenge elite investigators live for. So when rumor had it that "Cold Case" would soon become a stand-alone unit, I submitted a letter of intent.

Word in the office was Jim Rovella, who was hired in 2004, was going to be promoted to supervise the unit that was about to be formalized and moved to the—yet again—vacant house in Newington. But the interviews would not be held until Rovella had enough time in as an inspector (by union contract, four years) to qualify for a promotion to supervisory inspector.

When I requested a lateral transfer to the position—citing my prior lateral transfer from Elder Abuse to Workers' Compensation Fraud—I was told this wasn't possible. This time, I needed to apply just like any other inspector. When the position was finally posted, I prepared my request, mentioning all my bona fides. Of course I was wasting my time. Rovella was already a lock, a done deal. Still, a pretense was made that the position was open. So I decided to play it out, continuing with the interview process even though the outcome was predestined.

I took my seat at the head of the conference table before the interview panel: Chief State's Attorney Kane, Chief Inspectors Skinner and Edwards, Deputy Chief State's Attorney Paul Murray, and the affirmative action officer.

It was a sham. Every question asked was specifically about my experience with homicide cases, cold case investigations, the medical examiner's office, DNA, the state forensic lab, and VICAP.[55] Finally, after everyone there—except the affirmative action officer—had asked their questions, I was asked if I had any.

As politely as I could, I asked if I was being interviewed for an inspector's position, or a *supervisory* inspector's. I pointed out that the job description specified supervisory and organizational skills, yet at no time

---

[55] Violent Criminal Apprehension Program, an FBI database designed to collect and analyze information about homicides, sexual assault, and missing persons.

was I asked *anything* about my twelve years of supervisory experience in four very different bureaus within the office. There were now the nervous glances, the clearing of throats, the shuffling of papers, and the checking of wristwatches.

I further explained that there was a strong parallel between fugitive cases and cold cases, how in both instances an investigator reviewed what had been done and went back to see if anything had been overlooked. My experience in that arena, along with the fact that the position required the organizational skills of an experienced supervisor, should weigh heavily in the selection process. Kane acknowledged the panel was wrestling with the issue of that balance, thanked me for my time, and said there would be a decision the following week.

It was actually a full two weeks before the fait accompli was released. Kane wasn't wrestling with his decision; he was trying to make sure it wasn't vulnerable to a union grievance or a legal challenge. He wrote me a gracious letter thanking me for applying and explaining his decision.

It had now been four years since the Gang Bureau had closed shop, and I had become something I never wanted to be: a desk jockey. My fascination with law enforcement had always been the excitement of doing dangerous work, targeting society's underworld and the people that everyday citizens did their best to avoid. I had thought I would get a second chance with an outsider like Kane taking over, but it was now apparent this was not to be.

Chief State's Attorney Kane stopped by my office to make sure I had received his letter. I told him I had. He asked me if I had something to say, and I told him I did, but he likely did not want to hear it. To his credit, he closed my door and sat down.

I told him flat out that the interview process was a charade, that Rovella had the position locked up before it went up on the bulletin board. Kane tried to dispute it, but I continued: the entire interview process completely ignored the skills—my skills—specifically listed in the posting's job description.

I told him the charade had fooled no one; I knew Rovella had the job beforehand, Rovella knew he had the job beforehand, and so did every other candidate. Everyone in the entire office knew he'd selected someone who had never worked as a supervisor over several candidates who had been supervisors for most of their careers.

Doing his best to be gracious, Kane said he knew how I was feeling. He claimed he had gone into the interview process with an open mind. I told him, with all due respect, that I had been lied to by Chief State's Attorney Bailey, I had been lied to by Chief State's Attorney Morano, and I wasn't buying his spin either. He kept his cool, calmly explaining when he took over the office, his intent was to start everyone off with a clean slate. He assured me he thought well of me and was always happy to see me in the building.

I told him his two predecessors had done everything they could to force me to retire, and I had no intention of leaving. He assured me that he did not want to see me go. He recognized that there was a lot of underutilized talent in the building and there were still changes he wanted to make.

After saying his piece, he slapped his palms on his knees, stood up, and shook my hand. With that, he walked out the door, along with any chance I might have had to thaw my frozen career.

About this time a law enforcement colleague introduced me to a trending fitness regimen called CrossFit. I thought the concept was genius—a huge advancement from the traditional bodybuilding workouts most people tried to emulate. It was demanding and different, while being time efficient and effective. I began taking CrossFit certification courses, joined a CrossFit gym, and began considering life after law enforcement.

Because fitness was a core component of my lifestyle, and I had always been intrigued by the idea of owning a business, I began to explore opening a CrossFit gym. There were fewer than ten in the state, and if I got into the market early, I felt I would have an advantage.

In the spring of 2008, the rumor mill brought word of the impending retirement of Chief Inspector Skinner. There was talk that the state would offer another incentive plan to encourage eligible employees to make their exit, saving the state money. I still hoped that I would be given the opportunity to reestablish myself within the hierarchy of the office. If not, I'd open a CrossFit box and be my own boss.

Hoping Chief State's Attorney Kane would be true to his word about everyone starting with a clean slate and wanting to make use of the underutilized office talent, I began to prepare myself for the interview process for the expected chief inspector's vacancy. The rumor mill said Jim Rovella was the flavor-of-the-month; I was seen as a long shot despite my experience, seniority, and spotless record as far as actual police work went. The rumor mill was seldom wrong. Kane was approaching select candidates in private, asking certain inspectors if they were interested, without posting the position publicly, just like Morano had done. There were several interviews, I was never invited, and Jim Rovella was promoted once again.

With that, I knew it was time to move on. Once the state announced they were offering a "one-time only" buyout, where anyone eligible would essentially be given three years' service (6 percent of one's annual salary), it was a no-brainer.

"I do this with mixed feelings," I wrote in my resignation letter to Chief State's Attorney Kane, "because while I still enjoy the challenges of law enforcement, I have been unable to advance my position here since 1995. There have been two Chief Inspector vacancies filled since your appointment, and I have never once been interviewed for this position, despite my well-documented intention of seeking advancement. This fact, plus the denial of a lateral transfer when I was the only supervisor to apply for the Cold Case Bureau opening, has made it clear to me that my realistic chances for promotion are non-existent within the Division."

Kane, as expected, never acknowledged my letter. However, Chief Inspector Jim Rovella tried to convince me to reconsider. Since his appointment, he had put me in charge of an ad hoc task force to address complaints that some Connecticut pawn shops were doing a brisk business in stolen merchandise. Although several local police departments, along with security experts from Home Depot and Target were involved, no progress had been made, and the investigation had stalled; not a single arrest had been made. I was assigned to jump-start it. I invited the state police organized crime section—which had a talented, smooth-talking, Spanish-speaking undercover in the unit—to join our group. With Home Depot providing "stolen" merchandise, we video/audiotaped illicit sales at various pawn shops. After paying the undercover pennies on the dollar, these state-licensed "fences" offered the merchandise on their online eBay stores, advertised as "NIB" (new-in-box). We bought the items back, confirmed the serial numbers, and prepared our cases.

After several months of recorded undercover sales, we set up our sting operation: several pawnshops agreed to buy a shrink-wrapped pallet of several thousand dollars' worth of Home Depot power tools. Once the pallet was delivered—with the Home Depot bill of lading attached—the undercover officer accepted a large cash payment. As soon as our UC left the store, we descended upon the pawnshop, arrested the employees, executed the search warrant, confiscated all the NIB merchandise in the store, then rushed the pallet to the next target location. On June 3, 2009, we hit four pawnshops in four different cities, arrested nine employees, and seized so much merchandise, we had to rent a warehouse the next day to store the evidence.

I penned a congratulatory letter to the members of our hodgepodge group two days after our raids concluded:

> I just wanted to express my thanks to everyone who participated. This was a great example of just how effective a law enforcement task force can be. In a relatively short amount of time, with limited resources, we were able to expose criminal enterprises that had operated under the radar for far too long....
>
> As all of you know at this point, I will be retiring at the end of the month. I had fully expected that my last

several months would merely be wrapping up loose ends and house cleaning—I certainly did not expect the pleasant surprise of being involved in good, old-fashioned police work with a bunch of great cops. Thanks for making that happen. It was a nice way to go out.

Chief Inspector Rovella tried one more time to persuade me to rescind my letter of retirement. He told me he planned on getting the office to commit to more proactive, traditional criminal work, and he did not expect I would spend much more time supervising workers' compensation fraud.

I was tempted. Friends of mine in the office pointed out that Kane was already sixty-three. If he stayed for his full five-year term, he would be sixty-eight, giving him just under forty years of state service. Colleagues suggested I should wait him out, like I had Bailey and Morano. But I wasn't convinced Kane would retire. While not a glory hound like his predecessors, he certainly enjoyed the prestige of the position. I went with my gut.

Regrettably, Kane and I had not gotten off to a good start. He had headed the New London State's Attorney's Office for ten years and was used to getting his way, while during that same time I was having to document and challenge every process to avoid being trampled by the system. It was not a great dynamic, and I was skeptical it would ever improve.

Once again, I trusted my instincts and was glad I did. In July 2011, Kane was reappointed to a second five-year term; in 2016, a third. He finally retired in 2019.[56]

I thanked Rovella for his flattering proposal but explained that I had already committed to buying a business and intended to follow through. By that time, I had begun renovations at my gym. My last official day of work was July 1, 2009. Thirteen long years had passed since my July 12, 1996, memo to Jack Bailey, alerting him to the falsified FBI affidavits. It had been a long climb to the bottom.

---

[56] The seventy-six-year-old Kane retired after forty-seven years of state service, becoming the longest-serving chief state's attorney in the history of the division, holding the top position for thirteen years.

*Reunited at Quantico, VA, with several former co-workers at the 2004
retirement dinner of Al Malinchak. (from left to right) SA Marc Ukleja,
Unit Chief Al Malinchak, me, and my old partner SA Dennis Condon, Jr.*

EPILOGUE

I originally began writing *The Thin Blue Lie* upon my retirement when I realized that many people I knew—even some close friends and family members—did not know what actually happened to force me to file two federal lawsuits. My hope is that anyone reading this account is inspired to stay true to their ethics and moral code, while being cautioned about the risks involved. To the person considering a career in law enforcement, search your soul first. Steel yourself for the tribulations of performing difficult and oftentimes dangerous work while being second-guessed by the public and supervised by careerists—bureaucrats who weigh decisions based upon the political climate and their own aspirations. My hope is that those reading this book are savvier for having read it. I can only share with you what I experienced; you need to weigh it and apply the lessons accordingly.

While writing this book, I began to realize how the FBI has been able to operate outside legal scrutiny for decades, how this has created an environment that lends itself to "coloring outside the lines" at times. The Bureau is called on to investigate all manner of alleged misconduct by other agencies—police departments, sheriffs' offices, correctional facilities, and district attorneys' offices—but then is trusted to police itself.

While the Office of the Inspector General has the legal authority to do so in extreme cases, it ultimately can only author an investigative report and submit the findings to Congress. This is a toothless bite.

The Office of the Inspector General, Evaluation and Inspections Division published *A Review of the Federal Bureau of Investigation's Disciplinary System* in 2009. This report was in response to growing complaints from FBI rank-and-file that OPR investigations were inconsistent and that discipline was lenient when the targets were management. Surprisingly (or maybe not surprisingly), one of the findings concluded: *However, thirty percent of survey respondents who had observed misconduct said they either never reported misconduct they observed or reported less than half the misconduct they observed.*

More troubling were the reasons the respondents listed for their unwillingness to report coworkers' misconduct: 16 percent said, *"I feared retaliation for reporting misconduct,"*; 14 percent said, *"I believed that the employee would not be disciplined even if I reported the misconduct,"*; 13 percent said, *"I believe that management would not be supportive of my decision to report misconduct,"*; 5 percent said, *"I did not want to get a co-worker in trouble,"*; and 4 percent said, *"I did not want to get involved."*

In my case, several examples of ethical shortcomings were exposed: FBI agents falsified federal warrants, the head of the New Haven office predetermined his investigation cleared "his" agents; OPR eventually arrived several months later and conducted a limited-scope investigation; guilty agents were mildly admonished; the most culpable agent was promoted during the OPR investigation; and the SAC legally refused in open court to identify any agents who were found at fault. Certainly criminal defense attorneys would have liked to have known which agents were fudging federal affidavits. None of this generates public trust in a federal agency that has such tremendous investigative authority as the FBI.

OPR investigators even sought the input of John H. Durham, *"First Assistant United States Attorney, New Haven, Connecticut."*[57] I had first

---

[57] In May 2019, US Attorney General William Barr appointed John Durham to conduct a special investigation into the FBI regarding FISA warrants used to

met John Durham when he was a young state prosecutor working in the New Haven State's Attorney's Office; I was in college at the time working as a courtroom sheriff in the same courthouse. Durham transferred to the Connecticut US Attorney's office in 1982. He was asked by OPR to review and opine on the Dolan and Rodriquez UFAP warrants, both filed by SA Lisa Bull. OPR quoted AUSA Durham as follows:

> ...[he] advised that if information is hearsay, the fact that the information is hearsay should be made clear in the affidavit for the UFAP warrant so that the information does not appear to be first hand information. He added that the information contained in the affidavit must always be truthful, and if in fact Bull never spoke to Inspector Dillon about the facts in the Michael Thomas Rodriquez matter and/or the Joseph James Dolan matter, then it should not have been stated that Inspector Dillon advised SA Bull of the facts in the matter, as is presented in the affidavits in the Rodriquez and Dolan matters.

Upon review of the seven falsified affidavits, I counted at least twenty-one "untruths" that OPR attributed to assumptions, miscommunications, and sentences added by unknown authors. If these were, in fact, honest mistakes and unintentional, then common sense dictates roughly half would have increased probable cause, while the other half would have lessened it. But twenty-one out of twenty-one times the probable cause was enhanced, guaranteeing a federal prosecutor and judge would authorize the warrant.

Upon OPR concluding their inquiry, documents showed a tentative decision was made to suspend SSA DiFonzo for only three days. Some fifteen months later, two days were added to the suspension, bringing DiFonzo's punishment to a five-day suspension and six months of probation. Ultimately, after another two years of legal wrangling and appeals, DiFonzo's suspension was nullified and his pay loss restored.

---

spy on Carter Page and the Trump presidential campaign.

The manner in which the New Haven FBI agents conducted themselves, and the subsequent sham OPR investigation, is likely the reason the FBI has regularly had to deal with ethical lapses, misconduct, and criminal behavior. FBI management has been content to "paint over rust" and move on. I get it: no one is infallible, we are all human, and everyone can make a mistake. No agency or organization will ever be perfect. But the failure to adequately address bad behavior—or to make excuses for misconduct—only encourages more of the same. Any agent in the FBI who witnessed, or later became aware of, what happened in my situation learned this lesson: lie your ass off, hang tough, appeal, and wait it out. The involved agents were given cash incentive awards, Quality Step Increases, and one a promotion, and in turn received mild or no sanctions for gaming the system. There is no disincentive when the rewards outweigh the punishments.

Which brings me to this conclusion: perhaps the FBI is incapable of policing its own and there needs to be a separate entity to investigate allegations of misconduct and impose sanctions, for the same reason accounting firms do not audit themselves. For a long time OPR has had a reputation of being notoriously lax when it comes to rooting out misconduct and meting out punishment for agents held in good stead. Veteran agents realize—as a last resort—if they are caught "dead to rights," that they only have to resign, thereby locking in their rank and guaranteeing their pension. Not only does this create mistrust in the public, it also confirms to honest agents that it is a rigged system that protects its own—as long as you are on the "A" team. If not, you may be dealt with harshly.

Looking back over my career, I fondly recall it as eventful and exciting—the beginning, a roller coaster ride; the middle, the hall of mirrors; the end, a kiddie's merry-go-round. Overall, it was still a helluva ride. I met villains and heroes, sinners and saints, with a random mix of eclectic characters that fell somewhere in between. During my thirty-year career, I was able to experience many different facets of law enforcement, criminal justice, and the court system—people, places, and events that most people will only experience through their television sets or at the movies.

As one veteran officer told me early in my career: "Welcome to the greatest show on earth, where we always have the best seats in the house."

I am proud to have been an FBI agent, which I still believe to be the premiere law enforcement agency in the world. But to be the best and stay the best requires vigilance and steadfast improvement. Whitewashing and cover-ups erode trust, both from within and without. I pray the Bureau will maintain the high ethical standards they espouse if they are to retain the respect and confidence of the citizens of the United States. Fidelity, Bravery, and Integrity.

CHARACTER UPDATE

John M. "Jack" Bailey. Died at the age of fifty-nine. The Office of the Chief State's Attorney building in Rocky Hill is named after him, as well as a high school scholarship. Ironically, the annual mandatory law enforcement seminar on new legal updates is also named in his honor.

David J. Best. Retired from the Division of Criminal Justice in 2003.

Richard Blumenthal. Elected to the US Senate in 2011. Still serving as of this writing.

Gregory B. Dillon. Opened CrossFit Cheshire in Connecticut in 2009 (sold in 2011). Co-owns 13 Stars Community Fitness in Morristown, New Jersey, which opened in 2013.

Ralph A. DiFonzo Jr. Retired from the FBI in 2001. He opened RAD Consultants LLC in 2012 in Delaware, where he contracts privately as an investigator, as well as being a FEMA contractor with the Department of Homeland Security.

John "Jack" Edwards. Retired as an inspector in the New London State's Attorney's Office and was rehired in 2007 as a chief inspector by Kevin Kane. He re-retired in 2015.

Steven C. Freddo. Upon the disbanding of the Fugitive Squad, Steve was transferred to the Hartford State's Attorney's Office as an inspector;

he remained there as an inspector until his retirement in 2015. He succumbed to cancer the following year at the age of sixty-four.

Robert J. Hughes. Remained at the Chief State's Attorney's Office. In
2011, Bob was promoted to supervisory inspector. Upon Chief Inspector
James Rovella's retirement, Bob was promoted to fill his position. Bob
retired as a chief inspector on April 1, 2015.

Kevin T. Kane. Replaced Chris Morano as chief state's attorney in
2006 and remained until his retirement in December of 2019, after being
reappointed in 2011 and again in 2016.

Stephen A. Kumnick. Upon the disbanding of the Fugitive Squad,
Steve was transferred to the Hartford State's Attorney's Office as an inspector. He was later promoted to the position of supervisory inspector
in 2011 and retired from state service in 2017.

Henry C. Lee. Currently is the chief emeritus for scientific services
for the State of Connecticut. He lectures occasionally at the University
of New Haven, where he helped establish the Henry C. Lee Institute of
Forensic Science.

Michael W. Malchik. Retired from the DCJ in 1998 and worked "Of
Counsel" at the law office of Steven Reck, LLC, in New London County,
Connecticut, until his death from heart disease in May 2016.

Chris L. Morano. Opened the law office of Christopher L. Morano
on Main Street in Essex in 2008 and was an owner of a liquor store located next door to his law practice.

Merrill S. Parks Jr. Died at the age of fifty-five. The New Haven FBI
building, built in in 1999, is named in honor of him.

James C. Rovella. Retired from the OCSA as a chief inspector in
2012 to accept the position of chief of the Hartford Police Department,
from which he retired in 2018. He became the commissioner of the
Connecticut Department of Emergency Services and Public Protection
in 2019.

John G. Rowland. Resigned during a federal corruption investigation
in 2004; he later pleaded guilty to several corruption charges and was
released from federal prison in February 2006 after having served ten
months in custody. In April 2014, Rowland was found guilty following

a jury trial and convicted of two counts of causing illegal campaign con-tributions, and one count of conspiracy for his role in an election fraud case. He was sentenced by Judge Janet Bond Arterton to thirty months in prison, a $35,000 fine, and three years of probation following his release.

Francesco "Frank" Serpico. He retired from the NYPD in 1972 after receiving the department's highest award, the Medal of Honor. After living overseas for several years, he returned to the States in 1980 and lives in semi-seclusion in upstate New York.

Richard Teahan. Joined the FBI in 1991. He spent a decade on the fugitive task force in Connecticut, followed by a stint at FBIHQ. A Massachusetts native, he transferred to the FBI's Boston office in 2008 and retired as a supervisor in 2017.

For additional information, video, photographs, links to the full court decisions, as well as author contact information, please visit: www.thinbluefliebook.com

ACKNOWLEDGMENTS

Any list I attempt to compile in an effort to thank those for helping me along the way would either be incomplete or too long to include. If your name is not listed, it is not because you were overlooked or forgotten; the fault lies with me and my limitation of space.

First, I must thank God. I asked for the courage to persevere and the wisdom to make the right decisions, and was never let down; my ex-wife, Vilma, for her steadfast support through a very trying time; my mother Evelyn (deceased), my father Bernard (deceased), and my aunt Lucille (deceased), for instilling in me the core values that brought me through the ordeal; Karen Lee Torre, Esq. and her then assistant and now practicing attorney Michelle Holmes for their legal acumen; Frank Serpico for riding in like the cavalry just in the nick of time; Paul Vagnini, Tim Sugrue, Raymond Wiederhold, Mike Malchik (deceased), Steve Kumnick, Steve Freddo (deceased), and Cecilia Bratten for their wise counsel and unwavering support; Gary L. Crawford Jr., Thomas R. Murray, and Edward J. Lynch of the Connecticut State Police for their encouraging words during my darkest hours; Steve and Patty Johnson, Eloise Kumnick, John and Lisa Gibson, and Terry Johnson for their bravery in attending the trial; Alex Wood for his interest in covering this story and his tireless inquiries and efforts in his search for the truth; Magistrate Bill Garfinkel, retired FBI agents Dick Harrington, Jack Whitney, Ray Mey and Al Malinchak for their sage advice; Dion Baia (author of *Blood in the Streets* and *Morris PI*) for introducing me to the publishing world; the Bellow brothers, Adam and Daniel, for their editing prowess; Holly Layman for her keen eye and copy editing skills; Tori Dauria for her cover design concept art; Filomena Giannico for her insight and support; and finally family members, colleagues, and friends who provided emotional sustenance throughout my ordeal and to this day.

GLOSSARY OF TERMS

ASA Assistant States Attorney: in the DCJ: an entry-level state prosecutor

ASAC Assistant Special Agent in Charge: in an FBI field office, the second in command, supervises SSAs

AUSA Assistant United States Attorney: in the DOJ, a federal prosecutor

CFTF Connecticut Fugitive Task Force: the New Haven FBI's task force

CI Chief Inspector: in the DCJ, supervises the SIs in the

CSAO (not to be confused with Confidential Informant)

CSA Chief State's Attorney: in the DCJ, the top prosecutor

CSAO Chief State's Attorney's Office: sometime referred to as OCSA

DCJ Division of Criminal Justice: responsible for the investigation and prosecution of all criminal matters in the state of Connecticut

DCSA Deputy Chief State's Attorney: in the CSAO, the second in command, the person directly under the CSA

DOJ Department of Justice: the federal executive agency responsible for the enforcement of all federal laws and the supervision of all federal LE agencies, including the FBI

EASA Executive Assistant State's Attorney: in the CSAO, the third in command, the person directly under a DCSA

FBI Federal Bureau of Investigation: in the DOJ, responsible for the investigation of specific federal crimes, national security, and domestic intelligence

LE Law enforcement

LEO Law enforcement officer

OCSA Office of the Chief State's Attorney: sometimes referred to as the CSAO

OPR Office of Professional Responsibility: in the DOJ, responsible for the investigation and discipline of employees accused of crimes or misconduct

RA Resident Agency: a satellite office of an FBI field office headed by an SSA

SA Special Agent: in the DOJ, the title of entry-level federal LE agents

SAC Special Agent in Charge: in the FBI, head of a field office

SASA Supervisory Assistant States Attorney: in the DCJ, supervises ASAs

SI Supervisory Inspector: in the DCJ, supervises inspectors

SSA Supervisory Special Agent: in the FBI, supervises SAs

UC Under Cover: a police officer posing as a civilian

Unsub Unknown Subject: FBI term when a person's identity is unknown

USA United States' Attorney: in the DOJ, the top federal prosecutor of a federal district

88 FBI File designation prefix code for a fugitive case

91 FBI File designation prefix code for a bank robbery